Knowledge Making

Paper has been the material of bureaucracy, and paperwork performs functions of order, control, and surveillance. *Knowledge Making: Historians, Archives and Bureaucracy* explores how those functions transform over time, allowing private challenges to the public narratives created by institutions and governments.

Paperwork and bureaucratic systems have determined what we know about the past. It seems that now, as the digital is overtaking paper (though mirroring its forms), historians are able to see the significance of the materiality of paper and its role in knowledge making – because it is no longer taken for granted.

The contributors to this volume discuss the ways in which public and private institutions – asylums, hospitals, and armies – developed bureaucratic systems which have determined the parameters of our access to the past. The authors present case studies of paperwork in different national contexts, which engage with themes of privacy and public accountability, the beginning of record-keeping practices, and their 'ends', both in the sense of their purposes and in what happens to paper after the work has finished, including preservation and curation in repositories of various kinds, through to the place of paper and paperwork in a 'paperless' world.

The chapters in this book were originally published in a special issue of *Rethinking History: The Journal of Theory and Practice*.

Barbara Brookes is Professor of History at the University of Otago, Dunedin, New Zealand. Her research interests lie in medical and gender history. Her award-winning *A History of New Zealand Women*, Bridget Williams Books, was published in 2016. She is currently working on a biography of Anna Longshore Potts MD.

James Dunk is a historian of medicine and science at the University of Sydney, Australia, and is working on psychological and public health responses to global environmental change. His history of madness in colonial Australia, *Bedlam at Botany Bay*, was published by NewSouth in 2019 and shortlisted for the Ernest Scott Prize.

Knowledge Making
Historians, Archives and Bureaucracy

Edited by
Barbara Brookes and James Dunk

LONDON AND NEW YORK

First published 2020
by Routledge
2 Park Square, Milton Park, Abingdon, Oxon, OX14 4RN

and by Routledge
52 Vanderbilt Avenue, New York, NY 10017

Routledge is an imprint of the Taylor & Francis Group, an informa business

© 2020 Taylor & Francis

All rights reserved. No part of this book may be reprinted or reproduced or utilised in any form or by any electronic, mechanical, or other means, now known or hereafter invented, including photocopying and recording, or in any information storage or retrieval system, without permission in writing from the publishers.

Trademark notice: Product or corporate names may be trademarks or registered trademarks, and are used only for identification and explanation without intent to infringe.

British Library Cataloguing-in-Publication Data
A catalogue record for this book is available from the British Library

ISBN13: 978-0-367-48186-5

Typeset in Minion Pro
by codeMantra

Publisher's Note
The publisher accepts responsibility for any inconsistencies that may have arisen during the conversion of this book from journal articles to book chapters, namely the inclusion of journal terminology.

Disclaimer
Every effort has been made to contact copyright holders for their permission to reprint material in this book. The publishers would be grateful to hear from any copyright holder who is not here acknowledged and will undertake to rectify any errors or omissions in future editions of this book.

Contents

	Citation Information	vi
	Notes on Contributors	viii
	Introduction: Bureaucracy, archive files, and the making of knowledge Barbara Brookes and James Dunk	1
1	Asylum case records: fact and fiction Sally Swartz	9
2	Bookkeeping madness. Archives and filing between court and ward Volker Hess	22
3	Work, paperwork and the imaginary Tarban Creek Lunatic Asylum, 1846 James Dunk	46
4	Papering over madness: accountability and resistance in colonial asylum files: a New Zealand case study Barbara Brookes	76
5	Paper Soldiers: the life, death and reincarnation of nineteenth-century military files across the British Empire Charlotte Macdonald and Rebecca Lenihan	95
6	Red ink, blue ink, blood and tears? War records and nation-making in Australia and New Zealand Kathryn Hunter	123
7	A tale of two bureaucracies: asylum and lunacy law paperwork James Moran	139
	Index	157

Citation Information

The chapters in this book were originally published in *Rethinking History*, volume 22, issue 3 (September 2018). When citing this material, please use the original page numbering for each article, as follows:

Introduction
Bureaucracy, archive files, and the making of knowledge
Barbara Brookes and James Dunk
Rethinking History, volume 22, issue 3 (September 2018) pp. 281–288

Chapter 1
Asylum case records: fact and fiction
Sally Swartz
Rethinking History, volume 22, issue 3 (September 2018) pp. 289–301

Chapter 2
Bookkeeping madness. Archives and filing between court and ward
Volker Hess
Rethinking History, volume 22, issue 3 (September 2018) pp. 302–325

Chapter 3
Work, paperwork and the imaginary Tarban Creek Lunatic Asylum, 1846
James Dunk
Rethinking History, volume 22, issue 3 (September 2018) pp. 326–355

Chapter 4
Papering over madness: accountability and resistance in colonial asylum files: a New Zealand case study
Barbara Brookes
Rethinking History, volume 22, issue 3 (September 2018) pp. 356–374

Chapter 5
Paper Soldiers: the life, death and reincarnation of nineteenth-century military files across the British Empire
Charlotte Macdonald and Rebecca Lenihan
Rethinking History, volume 22, issue 3 (September 2018) pp. 375–402

Chapter 6
Red ink, blue ink, blood and tears? War records and nation-making in Australia and New Zealand
Kathryn Hunter
Rethinking History, volume 22, issue 3 (September 2018) pp. 403–418

Chapter 7
A tale of two bureaucracies: asylum and lunacy law paperwork
James Moran
Rethinking History, volume 22, issue 3 (September 2018) pp. 419–436

For any permission-related enquiries please visit:
http://www.tandfonline.com/page/help/permissions

Contributors

Barbara Brookes, History and Art History, University of Otago, Dunedin, New Zealand.

James Dunk, Department of History, University of Sydney, Australia.

Volker Hess, Institute for the History of Medicine and Ethics in Medicine, Charité University Medicine, Berlin, Germany.

Kathryn Hunter, History, Victoria University of Wellington, New Zealand.

Rebecca Lenihan, History, Victoria University of Wellington, New Zealand.

Charlotte Macdonald, History, Victoria University of Wellington, New Zealand.

James Moran, History Department, University of Prince Edward Island, Charlottetown, Canada.

Sally Swartz, Department of Psychology, University of Cape Town, South Africa.

INTRODUCTION

Bureaucracy, archive files, and the making of knowledge

Barbara Brookes and James Dunk

Introduction: bureaucracy, archive files, and the making of knowledge

In the 2017 Reith Lectures, the historical novelist Hilary Mantel reminded us that writing history is an 'interpretative act'. Evidence is 'always partial' and 'facts are not the truth but the record of what's left on the record'.[1] But writing is never simply 'left'. Every record is also an interpretive work which sifts and selects from a vast array of experiential data and wraps this data in language, fitting it into linguistic categories which give it form and protect it from oblivion. Many 'records' have been gathered into archives, repositories which house not what is left but what has been *kept*, and organise these calcified writings into hierarchical families which limit and shape the range of possible interpretations. A workshop at the University of Otago in May 2017, sponsored by the Centre for Research on Colonial Culture, interrogated the ways that bureaucracy has governed these siftings and keepings. The scholars whose work is presented here discussed the ways in which public and private institutions – asylums, hospitals, and armies – developed bureaucratic systems which have determined the parameters of our access to the past. The workshop delved deeper, however, than the parameters and systems, to consider how the very materiality of the paper has influenced the records which it accommodates. At a time when digital data teems around us, paper becomes rare and its qualities come into focus. As bureaucracy abandons paper, we pause to ask how paper itself has shaped our knowledge.

The articles which follow are case studies of paperwork in different national and transnational contexts which engage with themes of privacy and public accountability, the beginning of record-keeping practices and their 'ends', both in the sense of their purposes and in what happens to paper after the work has finished – from preservation and curation in repositories through to the place of paper and paperwork in a 'paperless' world. Each article engages in some way with the way paperwork has been used to create order and control, but also the ways that it allows private challenges to government and institutional realities.

'Bureaucracy', wrote the French dramatist and social critic Louis-Sebastien Mercier: 'a word coined to indicate, in a clear and concise manner, the overgrown power possessed by simple clerks' (Mercier 1999, 172). Ben Kafka (2012) whose work was one stimulus for our workshop, suggests that Mercier helped to revive the word, a superb French pun evoking government by a piece of furniture, the bureau. Our aim in this special issue is to interrogate the ways in which this power, overgrown in eighteenth-century France and still more distended since then, shapes our historical knowledge. We are interested in the ways that the clerks, having risen to power and helped create bureaucratic structures, continue to exert influence through the study of their accumulated paperwork. The clerks 'are all the more powerful with their pens', Kafka quotes Mercier, 'because their actions are never visible' (80). The essays collected here help to reveal the pens of clerks in a range of institutional settings, and the configurations of their power.

Sally Swartz leads our special issue with a reflection on the writing and reading of records. It is 'dwelling in the archive' of paper, as others have discussed, that makes historical work possible (Burton 2005; Steedman 1998; Stoler 2009; Kafka 2012; Hull 2012; Farge 2013). These paper archives were produced historically: records were made, many by clerks, but also kept and organised, or in certain cases, left in the narrative disarray which produced them. This too is a form of arrangement. The work of protecting, arranging, and sometimes destroying records represents investment in certain pasts, by present governments and private organisations. Paperwork, the pride of generations of multitudinous clerks, becomes, in Swartz' formulation, sanctionable knowledge, set apart for historians to render into narratives. Those narratives, in turn, are necessary to make the past comprehensible to readers.

To take archives as they present themselves, however, is to submit to that 'overgrown power' unthinkingly. The articles in this special issue pull us back from the archive to the institutions in which they were created. They are chiefly essays on the complex praxis that surrounds writing, and produces paperwork, within the political, professional, and emotional interstices which inhabited the institutions of the nineteenth and early twentieth centuries. Some are physical institutions, with walls which delineate or even enforce the division between internal and external populations. Others, like courts, were tollgates in the flow of people between institutions, or, like armies, aggregations of that global flow. In each, however, abstracted 'identities' were superimposed upon persons. These were 'documentary identities', a concept that has been explored by historians (Caplan and Torpey 2001) and by a strand of anthropology interested in problematizing the 'document' (Hull 2012; Ong and Collier 2005).

Origins

These identities were also, of course, paperwork: abstractions, to be sure, but set down in ink on paper in history, like the other genres of record created by these institutions. Ben Kafka encourages readers to look closely – historically – at these individual and seriate records. One means of doing this is to pay attention to origins – to study the purpose and function of records from their genealogy. Volker Hess, working with German sources, writes against the assumption that psychiatric practice evolved in a vacuum of pure scientific thought. At the Charité Hospital in Berlin the patient file, so prized by the psychiatrist, in fact had its origin in the 'kitchen economy', as efficiency demanded close accounting of the number of meals prepared each day. 'The epistemological precondition for psychiatric narration' came, therefore, from the kitchen. This resembles other alternative genealogies for medical records (Anderson 2013).

There are other means of studying origins. James Dunk focuses closely upon the narratives of medical record-keeping which a parliamentary inquiry revealed as being in competition in a lunatic asylum near Sydney in the colony of New South Wales. Here the beginning of bureaucratic forms of record-keeping was not the kitchen economy, although parsimony played a part, but the internecine politics of a colonial medical community. Public accountability had special significance in a colony with a strong executive government, argues Dunk, which had been established for convict discipline. Bureaucratic record-keeping was instituted, at least in part, for its claims to transparency and 'responsibility' in a colony alarmed by the effects of 'irresponsible' governance, and making a bid for 'responsible' government, in which the local population elected representatives and held them accountable in a way they never could hold imperial governors to account.

Colonial societies held out the promise of being freed from oppressive traditions of the old world yet they looked to that world for bureaucratic models when inventing their own. Examining the development of lunacy legislation in New Zealand, Barbara Brookes argues that the very blurred boundary between reason and unreason occasioned an avalanche of paper to assure settlers that the newly-founded state would not deny the liberty of the subject. Using asylum archives she argues that asylum paperwork had unexpected outcomes, where the Weberian triumph of rationality came up against the disorder of madness. The paperwork multiplied in response to the demand for greater accountability that even put paper into patients' hands and, occasionally, led to their release.

Ends

The generative power of accounting in creating material records is at the heart of Charlotte Macdonald and Rebecca Lenihan's examination of nineteenth century British imperial military files. 'Lives in the Lines' proceeds from the utilitarian imperial origins of military 'identities' to their material presence in the pockets of their 'redcoats', to the way in which the modern digitalization of these files changes their role in shaping knowledge. The army evolved bureaucratic processes early, in order to ensure an 'effective strength' for combat: tracking the legitimate movement of men, money and supplies, but also allowing the assessment of individuals. Macdonald and Lenihan focus upon paybooks and discharge certificates, which were made from durable paper stock and linen. They were documents intended to last, and often outlasted service. Though many soldiers were illiterate, they recognised the value of their paperwork, and carried it closely. Pension claims were dependent upon these documents, which were able to meet changing demands upon them in the lifetimes of the soldiers, and still more demands as they were archived, and became records of a different nature.

One private archival collection of a different nature lies in the files of the St Andrew's Colonial Homes, a residential school in Kalimpong, North East India, which were the means of tearing families asunder. Jane McCabe, who participated in the Otago workshop and whose contributions influenced this collection, speaks to this history of enforced separations in her 2017 monograph *Race, Tea and Colonial Resettlement: Imperial Families, Interrupted* (McCabe, 2017) – a history which the school's files, for all their bureaucratic detachment, struggle to contain. Having survived the national rupture of partition and the migration of its children, the small, private archive on site at the Children's Homes now enables families to restore the rifts captured on the paper which created them. The peculiar quality of the Children's Homes as a still-functioning institution which guards a private colonial archive in a postcolonial setting points to the special tensions of colonial institutions. In such institutions paperwork may, in fact, offer more than the hope of decolonial subversion – they may offer the hope of restoration.

Birth and rebirth

Kathryn Hunter traces the frustration of the families of defence force personnel as they tried to obtain information and seek compensation in the wake of the Great War, the first to be labelled a 'world' war. Hunter shows the way bureaucracies interacted during and after this global conflict, and the legacy of their arrangement. The files of the Australian and New Zealand defense forces worked, argues Hunter, to shape the war as a Dominion and national moment rather than an Imperial one. It was the prosaic growth of bureaucracy, she argues, rather more than the distinctive heroics of the ANZACs, that came to define the national parameters of New Zealand and Australia in the early twentieth century.

Working on nineteenth century New Jersey, James Moran compares the bureaucratic legacy of the asylum and that of the civil law in knowledge production about madness. Whereas asylums and their bureaucratic legacy are familiar to those working in the field of madness studies, lunacy investigation law has received little historical attention, despite the pioneering work of Akihito Suzuki (2006) and treatments which approach the investigation from different perspectives (Stebbings 2012; Dunk 2018). Moran's 'Tale of Two Bureaucracies' incorporates his own research narrative – a chance discovery of a rich seam of legal files which offered insight into the workings of madness outside the institutions designed to contain it. Such institutions developed powerful conceptual frameworks, as asylum historians have become more aware, so that reading the two bureaucracies together, legal and psychiatric, is instructive. More than this, however, Moran encourages us to take a broader view of the way that histories of madness have been guided by the ready archives left by asylums, their records protected and arranged by the medical and archival apparatus of states. Not only the paperwork itself but the politics of preservation and organisation has had profound influence on the histories we have written.

Digitization leads to a new kind of rebirth, or as Macdonald and Lenihan put it, to reincarnation. They note how the 'digital collapses space and time' in a way 'perplexing to creators of historical knowledge trained to consider context, provenance, selection, silence and position in the "sources" they consult to "make" history'. Much greater accessibility comes at the cost of the clues that lie in the very material of the archive. Brookes also notes that the curating of psychiatric files for online exhibition gives them an order and neatness masking the hierarchy and disorder apparent in the original documents.

Historians are, in a sense, hostages to the archive. Footnotes, which are integral to our practice, pin us firmly to it. References give the impression of mastery over archival material, but archives have an anterior influence over the arguments and narratives we discover in them. But what determines this narratival field? Traversing kitchen accounts and structures of institutional accountability, the making of nations and the restitution of histories long buried and forgotten, the essays in this collection draw attention to the generative role of institutional bureaucracies in the creation of the archive, and of its power to shape knowledge. The pasts that present themselves in archives are those which clerks, superintendents and responsible ministers created when they demanded and set down certain information. Paperwork is therefore far from transparent or natural. And it is powerful.

It is for this reason that in this collection we follow Swartz' call to pay attention to the work of writing, navigating between the private writing of doctors for the purposes of their diagnoses, through the demands of institutional knowledge and government oversight that records be public, visible, and legible by clerks and ministers everywhere. To look again at the afterlives of these records and the ways they can be made comprehensible in different places and times, and for different purposes (recalling Stoler 2009 reading 'along the archival grain' of the paper legacies of empires), demonstrates the extent to which institutions authored their narratives, and historians in archives can disassemble and reassemble them. Close reading may reveal the mixture of fact and fiction and demands of institutional narrativisation lying under the authoritative gloss of the medical register, personnel file, and requisition form.

The work of Verne Harris (2012, 2015) and Wolfgang Ernst (2015) reminds us of the deep politics of archival work, and by extension, our narratives written in and from them. Several essays in this volume demonstrate the ways in which paperwork itself carries the potential for resistance and subversion; official narratives may be undone by recourse to the scribbles and scratches, for instance, in a paybook carried by a soldier on long marches, in humid postings and desperate battles.

While it may elide such scribblings and other marginalia, digital access to written records promises perhaps to liberate us from archival politics, and from the more mundane calculus of research funding and travel expenses. But universal access (pointed to in the already-passing technical language of the URL, or 'universal resource locator') is a euphemism, since resources are not universally made locatable. Digitisation has its own politics which surfaces in digital curation (replicating earlier politics) but also in access to funding. Political decisions are made about what to make accessible and we are faced with the paradoxical outcome that military records from the First World War for example, which contain detailed medical information, are freely available online, whereas psychiatric records from the same period may be closely guarded. Even when psychiatric records date from years preceding whatever embargo period is legislated, names may be removed. Clearly in serving one's country, rights to privacy get lost whereas in the psychiatric archive, the stigma of mental illness is imagined to continue after death.

The vast digital accretion of sources by companies such an Ancestry.com present the past as densely populated, and knowable, but this is a fiction with which we have to reach some kind of accommodation. Such corporations promise an ever-growing harvest of 'facts', and lead the researcher down apparently seamless paths, click by click, tap by tap. We know, however, that those paths are full of fissures and deceptions: paper has been lost or never made; people doctor forms; everything is more intricate than it seems. By dreaming the archive we restore imagination to what is supposed to be a bureaucratic dullness, and leave space for the unknown and unfinished in our project of writing the past.

Note

1. Michael Durrant. 2017. '"Facts are not Truth": Hilary Mantel Goes on the Record About Historical Fiction'. *The Conversation*. Accessed 17 December 2017. http://theconversation.com/facts-are-not-truth-hilary-mantel-goes-on-the-record-about-historical-fiction-79359. To listen to the lecture series go to http://www.bbc.co.uk/programmes/p04rkn39.

Disclosure statement

No potential conflict of interest was reported by the authors.

References

Anderson, W. 2013. "The Case of the Archive." *Critical Inquiry* 39 (3): 532–547. doi:10.1086/670044.
Burton, A., ed. 2005. *Archive Stories: Facts, Fictions, and the Writing of History*. Durham and London: Duke University Press.
Caplan, J., and J. Torpey, eds. 2001. *Documenting Individual Identity: The Development of State Practices in the Modern World*. Princeton and Oxford: Princeton University Press.
Dunk, J. 2018. "The Liability of Madness and the Commission of Lunacy in New South Wales, 1805–12." *History Australia* 15 (1): 130–150. doi:10.1080/14490854.2017.1413942.
Ernst, W. 2015. *Stirrings in the Archives: Order from Disorder*. Translated by Adam Siegel. London: Rowman & Littlefield.
Farge, A. 2013. *The Allure of the Archives*. Translated by Thomas Scott-Railton. New Haven: Yale University Press.
Harris, V. 2012. "Genres of the Trace: Memory, Archives and Trouble." *Archives and Manuscripts* 40 (3): 147–157. doi:10.1080/01576895.2012.735825.
Harris, V. 2015. "Hauntology, Archivy and Banditry: An Engagement with Derrida and Zapiro." *Critical Arts* 29 (Suppl. 1): 13–27. doi:10.1080/02560046.2015.1102239.
Hull, M. S. M. 2012. "Documents and Bureaucracy." *The Annual Review of Anthropology* 41: 251–267. doi:10.1146/annurev.anthro.012809.104953.
Kafka, B. 2012. *The Demon of Writing*. New York: Zone Books.

McCabe, J. 2017. *Race, Tea and Colonial Resettlement: Imperial Families, Interrupted*. London and Oxford: Bloomsbury.

Mercier, Louis-Sébastien. 1999. *Panorama Of Paris: Selections from "Tableau De Paris"*. Edited by, Jeremy D. Popkin. University Park, PA: Penn State University Press.

Ong, A., and S. J. Collier. 2005. *Global Assemblages: Technology, Politics and Ethics as Anthropological Problems*. Malden, MA: Blackwell Publishing.

Stebbings, C. 2012. "Protecting the Property of the Mentally Ill: The Judicial Solution in Nineteenth Century Lunacy Law." *The Cambridge Law Journal* 71 (2): 384–411. doi:10.1017/S0008197312000530.

Steedman, C. 1998. "The Space of Memory: In an Archive." *History of the Human Sciences* 11 (4): 65–83. doi:10.1177/095269519801100405.

Stoler, A. L. 2009. *Along the Archival Grain: Epistemic Anxieties and Colonial Common Sense*. Princeton and Oxford: Princeton University Press.

Suzuki, A. 2006. *Madness at Home: The Psychiatrist, the Patient, and the Family in England, 1820-1860*. Berkeley: University of California Press.

Asylum case records: fact and fiction

Sally Swartz

ABSTRACT
This paper raises a series of historiographical issues about the nature of lunatic asylum archives. It addresses one central thread, namely the relationship between the phenomenology of mental illness, and the many kinds of records in which it is reflected. It suggests that there is a fundamental paradox involved in the rational, orderly and coherent representation of mental illness generated by lunatic asylum bureaucracy, and the chaotic multiplicity of the lived experience of patients, many suffering from illnesses that involved irrational, disordered and incoherent states of mind.

The paper begins by raising as background the relationship between thought, language and experience, and ways in which this defies straightforward representation in clinical case histories. It goes on to examine aspects of lunatic asylum archives, including statistics, correspondence and case records, and ways in which these might either mislead, or fictionalize histories of these institutions. It suggests that archival work, particularly with respect to capturing the complexity and emotional violence of these institutions might require historians to 'dream the archive'. This is the work of disciplined imagination that might act as a guide in traversing deeply irrational territory.

The paper ends by highlighting several issues that historians of lunatic asylums might address.

This paper is a brief review of one idea that has been central in much of my work on colonial lunatic asylums, and my clinical work as well. I have wrestled with this idea through early work on Virginia Woolf, the study of the incoherent and yet rich speech of manic patients, in and out of historical records and therapeutic encounters with patients, and more recently, surfing the chaos of institutions in transition, student protests and university bureaucracies under fire. I have mulled over the difference between a misspelled angry tweetstorm and a grammatical press release. A flood of profound love in a session, sitting oddly next to my round and cryptic black-inked notes, connected certainly, but the one quite unlike the other. Do words get anywhere near to reflecting experience? Do words in fact capture, coerce and constrain the way we experience, and additionally, allow only bits and pieces¹ to be recorded? How does writing affect memory? Do we experience only that which can be put into words? Why do we rely so much on words (and numbers) to sanctify and make official, to make our experience sanctionable? Who is allowed to write, and for whom? Who reads? How do historians sift through sanctionable, institutionally legitimized knowledge, to reach from the pure gold of an institution's grumbling, potent unwritten life? And what is there to be done in institutions that produce two or three sanctionable narratives, each of which contradicts the other?

These are questions that have been elegantly tackled across different literatures.² I would like to begin my own map of the terrain by sketching ways in which this unifying puzzle has recurred across a range of my scholarship and professional domains.

Virginia Woolf (subject of my first Masters), in *Between the Acts* has a character, Bart Oliver musing: 'Thought without words, can that be?' Woolf's own thoughts raced unbearably and incoherently at times, but words were her anchor, a route to herself and others. Also in *Between the Acts*, Miss la Trobe is producing the village's pageant, a tour through the ages. For the present day, she has an empty stage, reflecting the audience and actors back at themselves; it collapses, the audience is restless, dismayed. From behind a tree, she says to herself, 'Reality too strong'.³ In her novels, Virginia Woolf tracks back and forth across ways in which words on a page protect from too much reality, inserting both irony and the prosaic, but also speak of our aloneness, our inability to share mindedness.

Then as a psychologist in training, I sit with a bipolar patient in a manic phase of her illness. She is experiencing herself as profoundly incoherent, and to try to pin down her thoughts she writes as she murmurs to herself, the names of Lawrence Durrell's novels, the name of her gynaecologist, her birthdate and her father's birthdate. Soon the page is full, all higglepiggledy. She turns her attention to me. 'Who *are* you,' she says. 'Groot ore,' she says. (Yes I am indeed listening, as hard as I can, but in this swift-moving jumping babbling I am in fact just tumbling over and over, grasping at islands of whole sentences when they appear.) In the file, the psychiatrist notes: 'Flight of ideas. Racing thought. Manic.'⁴

I am teaching students to write 'histories' of their first cases. Eight students watch an intake interview from behind a one-way mirror. Their task is to produce a history, with each piece of information recorded under the correct heading. Followed by a formulation, this history is intended to distil a knotty, bumpy, noisy and contradictory interview, in which doors have been slammed, a mother has cried, a child has pulled off the head of a doll, into a central problem statement, a diagnosis, and a plan of intervention. Days later I sit with the eight student transcripts: and yes, there are eight totally different families described, right down to the kinship ties between attending members. The beheaded doll, probably the most significant event of the session, remains unseen by the trainees, and is not mentioned. She in effect then stands in for a subaltern, along with the erasure of children's purposeful and pointed play.[5]

I wander through the local mental hospital's registry, looking for samples of files from current patients to samples from previous decades. I want to know how history-taking has changed with shifts in psychiatric training and diagnosis, the spike in the presence of psychologists, the beginning of short admissions following the introduction of psychotropic drugs. As I scratch, I find a dog-eared folder from 1892, rubbing shoulders with one from 1992. A photograph of a bearded man in a hat glares back at me from the first page. Twenty years in the asylum. 'Incoherent. Dirty habits. Died.' Where I stand was where there was once a workshop or a stable. Had he stood here too? With a pig or a horse? Did he babble like my manic patient? There was absolutely no way to know.[6]

I watch two truncated Youtube clips, both of my university's library entrance. In one a student hurls a dustbin in a high arc towards the glass door, his whole body magnificently committed to this act, feet off the ground, hair curling behind. The police move in. Second clip. Same door. This time the clip begins when the dustbin has fallen. The police moved in. Now they grab a woman by her arms, her hair. A braid falls to the ground. And from this two 'official' narratives are born. Violent students. Violent police. From the minutes of an executive committee on that day, an hour later: Item 1, Library closures; Item 2, Deferred exams. It would take a deft historian to match these minutes with what we had been called on to witness on campus that day.[7]

Of course a century from now, our deft historians will be sifting through records very different from ours. So then, the question becomes, where right now, as we watch, as we react and talk, record in minutes, letters, emails, is our subaltern? How would we define her? Where are our thoughts without words?

Statistics

In this landscape of narrative, the matching of word to feeling, event to its official afterlife, inside voice to the stubborn crudity of fact, statistics have a privileged position. It is a brave historian who resists the lure of a number, that last bastion of something that can be nailed down. This number died that day. £4 per month to feed a patient, eggs additional. 20 admitted. 10 discharged 'recovered'. It is precisely this fiction of accuracy that gives statistics their authority over us. The countability of things.[8]

One of my early experiences of archival work involved a wrestle with numbers. No matter how many times I added up columns of official asylum statistics, I could not get them to reconcile. The deeper I dug, the worse it became. I found the hand-written tables sent through to the colonial office. Squinting hard, I could imagine them to have been translated into the 'official' printed table. But what did 'recovered' mean? 'Improved'? In my worst moments, even 'died' danced before my eyes like a phantom – had she not died the year before? Had she died twice? No this cannot be.

One of the dramatic effects of statistics is to translate peaches + pears into 'fruit', and then all sorts of things can happen. We can compare rates of fruit incarceration in several colonies. And more significantly, we can instruct fruiterers to spend £4 on each peach, each pear. One can scold Colony X for having too much fruit, or Colony Y for bruising their most vulnerable fruit.

Statistics allow prediction, budgeting; they influence behaviour, change perception, they measure catastrophe and disaster, popularity and the 'normal'. They create a level of surveillance unimaginable without them, and in my work on colonial office regulation of lunatic asylums, I argued that statistics played a pivotal role in allowing the Colonial Office to watch their colonial lunatic asylums from afar, through a peep-hole as it were, counting and comparing, ordering and budgeting, measuring room size and numbers of bathrooms and pieces of bread. And it was also a performance of something, a rhetorical device, language, a metaphor, bearing a relationship to that which it described. Standing in place of it. Not the thing in itself.[9]

As historians working with institutions, how do we read their statistics, and more importantly, our own? In relation to those in the public record, we accept that something has been counted. We cannot possibly vouch for the count itself, but we cross-hatch where we can, triangulating reports with census data and newspaper accounts and diaries. Less than 100. More than 50. But what next? Then we begin making counts of counts, turning tables into percentages, running T-tests, and correlations. So the institution's statistics, which can be read as one kind of a text, gets translated into a version of itself in our treatment of it, and sometimes the apparently 'obvious' conclusions of each set of numbers, embedded in their own pieces of writing, war with each other over versions of the count.[10]

It is clear that when we move into the statistics-narrative intersection, peering beyond the numbery web, the one that privileges countability, we are in a shadowland, where there is everything that cannot be counted. Many of us reject the fiction that only the countable is real. We accept the significance of outliers, the unique case. And rely on our good judgement to distinguish between banality posturing as uniqueness and uniqueness presenting itself as everyday run-of-the mill.

To illustrate, I would like to give an example.

In my earliest forays into asylum case records, I was struck by the number of times lunatic patients were described as having 'dirty' or 'faulty' habits. Equally, there were patients noted to have 'clean' habits. This was a countable phenomenon, and count it I did, along with a number of other behavioural 'countables'.[11] Let us begin with the purpose that might be served by such a statistic. Firstly, having clean or dirty habits predicts a number of things: severity of disorder, degree of chronicity, size of the presence or absence of dementia or psychosis; degree to which particular patients needed intensive nursing care; likelihood of outbreaks of sewerage-borne illnesses; numbers of cleaning staff needed to clean bathrooms; and so on. One could even take all these variables, and run a correlation statistic between them.

With an immediate snag. With an archive like those surviving from many lunatic asylums, we have no reliably standard form of data collection (beyond a few demographics like age and gender, place of birth, and possibly religious affiliation). We cannot know numbers of patients per ward with 'faulty' habits, although with very well kept casebooks, estimates might be made. Nonetheless, the very fact that the term 'faulty' habits crops up frequently as a phrase in casebooks does seem to warrant enumeration.

Now to turn to the other side, the shadowland into which the numbers cannot reach. First, some definitions. 'Habit' might be defined as 'custom', 'manner', 'inclination', all fairly neutral in their line of associations, but there are other associations less benign: 'proclivity', 'bent', 'proneness', 'obsession', even 'weakness'.[12] Now we put this semantic web with 'dirty' and 'faulty', often used synonymously, but each with its own line of meaning. 'Dirty' means not clean and evokes grime, smut perhaps, whereas 'faulty' implies corruption, a broken machine. And at the heart of the meanings generated by this term, used so often it slips past the eye, hardly worthy of being caught and pondered over, each time in its own nest of sentences, there is an essential ambiguity: what was *not* being named here? Are those with 'faulty' habits broken machines with respect to toileting? Are the 'dirty' patients caught in the smut of lewd thoughts and sexual acting-out? Not so countable.

There is a further layer to this, the one that perhaps leads most fruitfully from the numbers to meanings to a very rich landscape indeed. In making sense of case records, of what was recorded, whether seldom or frequently, of how words were chosen, and what they meant to the writer, the audiences those words addressed, included and excluded purveyors of information, we are very far indeed from counting. The words chosen, and repeated, are like day residue, are triggers. But we must 'dream' the text. It is to this that I will turn in the next section.

Dreaming the archive

I would like to begin this section by introducing a proposition and a position from which to argue. Histories of lunatic asylums, like psychoanalysis, involve dreamwork.

Psychoanalysis is many things: a discipline, a thought-regime, a system of surveillance, a method of treatment, a radical intervention in the social construction of identity. But at its most prosaic end, it is deeply involved in history, the telling of histories, the construction of the 'facts' of a life. It often seems to buy into a determinist universe that insists on the sequentiality of all things: in short, on consequences. The unfolding is various – for some branches of psychoanalysis consequences are predicated on biology, instinct and its vicissitudes. For others trauma is a cause of a future unravelling.[13] But what is the relationship between the psychoanalytic narrative we construct with our patients, the historical narrative, and what actually happened?

Psychoanalytic histories are a kind of history, one with a particular focus on meaning. It is a version – and just as gender histories, or economic histories have a field, psychoanalysis takes subjectivity as its field. Like history, it works closely with texts. These texts are often spoken, and are generated between interlocutors. There is an important sense in which the 'history' so located, with its meaning, and its possibilities for discovery and rediscovery, are *imagined*, and insofar as they remain uncountable, unverifiable in the sense that they *cannot be lived again*, they *stand for* a version of a life. Moreover, they are a version saturated with personal meaning, idiosyncratic associations, unique ways of linking one thing with another. This is the sense in which they are dreams, and as Thomas Ogden argues, as much a way of consciously intervening in the unconscious, as raising the unconscious to consciousness. As Ogden explains: 'When I speak of "dreaming up" a text, I am referring to the conscious and unconscious psychological work of making something of one's own with the text one is reading'.[14] The imagined history of a patient has a relationship to truth for the analytic couple, its rightness resonant, congruent, and recognizable as a set of meanings paradoxically akin to statistics, in that they control, predict, carve a way forward. The 'history' is not fake news, does not misdirect even when it offers a variety of disguises, riddles, gaps.[15] I am arguing that just as we dream up our patients, we dream up our archive, as we interact with it in order to create a narrative.

But what does dreaming an archive mean? Those immersed in an archive know, but do not often write into the final report, the delight, disappointments, obsessions, boredom and moments of exhilaration involved. It is akin to a thrilling treasure hunt at times, and at others is doggedly mechanical: there are surges of adrenalin and periods of longing for the next coffee break. Staring out the window, we dream up the letter, the cache of documents, the photograph that will make us queen for the day. And in that dreaming is the creative work that is essential to what we find, fuelling the search to look at this, overlook that. It is a state of unintegration, a relaxation into what initially lands on us as overwhelming, meaningless, chaotic or even empty; the dreaming is the work that gathers the bits and pieces.

Just like the unconscious, an archive can never be fully known – it allures and tantalizes, beckons and frightens and draws us in; and consciously we pick up pieces of it, and drift towards a coherent narrative. The narrative we are captured by, the one that drives us to write, is the product of the dream, the bits and pieces, flotsam and jetsam, offered up by the archive-sea, our desire, the treasure we conjured up for ourselves and created by hunting. All that needs to follow is the accounting. Just like the unconscious, the archive itself does not produce fake news. The 'lie', when it happens (and we can talk about how often), is something produced by the reader, who is perhaps driven by a wish to mistake the part for the whole.

I would like to mention two ideas in support of my proposition. One of the analytic giants of twentieth-century psychoanalysis, Donald Winnicott, was clear that a successful analysis depends on capacity to play – in other words, the capacity to step into an imagined world and use it to test and try out, to control and be controlled, to find the limits (or imagine new ones). Those who cannot play must be taught to play, and then analysis can begin, dependent as it is on the creative work of dreaming oneself up, and then living oneself into the dream, piece by piece.[16] In a similar vein, Odgen talks about patients who are unable to dream – unable to do the conscious and unconscious work of formulating experience, with all its attendant terrors, to associate and create, transform and look complexity and contradiction in the eye.[17]

There are times when I have encountered myself and others unable to play with or to dream up the archive. In this situation, the dusty boxes seem to hold no gifts or clues. They seem to have been rendered useless, meaningless, random, unattached to lives lived. The inner despair of the archival reader, and the collapse into apathy, protest or depression is not unlike the picture of the small child who – for reasons of complicated attachment – is unable to organize him or herself into play. Similar is the patient unable to dream, locked into a world that has no meaning beyond its surfaces, a world of objects, and mired in bewilderment, boredom and repetitive complaint.[18]

I have two examples here. Over the years, I have worked with many young researchers, drawn to my projects perhaps by a fascination with lunatic asylums and mental illness, or simply the need for a project that does not involve interviewing live people. One was locked in a struggle with her own mental difficulties, money worries, and single-parenting. Over the course of a long nine months, she railed against me and the archive I had pointed to, telling me over and over again that it was empty, nothing could be said about it; that I had offered her a project that was a mirage; that no matter how she tabulated and counted there was no story to be told. She was also unable to read the literature – papers accumulated and were dismissed as irrelevant, became dog-eared and coffee-stained in heaps on her desk.

Together we drew together the bits and pieces into a shabby project, an impoverished mimicry of a study, but it had no intellectual aliveness. It was a storeroom, not a lived-in, loved-in room. In the course of our time together, I encountered over and over her bits and pieces, a painful disintegration in which the task of imagining lunatic histories as representative of lives lived was simply impossible for her.

Different was a researcher who organized a defence against disintegration, not the disintegration itself. She was a coolly intellectual young woman, who read widely, and loved the world of ideas, but had some difficulty translating them into her archival research. The reading was a psychic retreat[19] in which there was little intersection with her unlived, practical, undreaming, unplaying being. A point came in her project during which she became absorbed with patients' photographs. She took more and more photographs of photographs, circling around them, puzzling about their purpose, ruminating on a particular face. She and I would stare together at the faces, and I would be aware of immense sadness and the dislocation between these mugshots, and the lives they so poignantly failed to represent. I was not sure what she felt, only that she was stirred up, angry, provoked.

Eventually, my young researcher produced a project in which she returned to the haven of her ideas-world, creating a highly sophisticated argument about transfers of patients between asylums in the Cape. The photographs became nothing more than a footnote, although they had absorbed most of her time. I read her absorption with them as a traumatic, pre-play, pre-dream search for something to attach to, a repetitive journey across a surface that teased but offered little sustenance. Like flashbacks, repetitions of trauma are not transformative; they simply rescore scars.

The narrative, fiction and the subaltern voice

Dream-work in the archive leads to the narratives we create from the fertile chaos of dream and paper-scraps: we gather together the terrifying 'bits and pieces' and we plot and plan a fiction that represents a thing-in-itself. A story is told, with twists and turns, major and minor characters, dialogues, tables and maps and diagrams. It is not the whole truth, because it is partisan and incomplete, a version, a metaphor. It uses facts like children use toys, to make up a story, with a beginning, a middle and an end. It is always a fiction in two ways: firstly, it substitutes story for bits and pieces, condenses and substitutes, symbolizes, takes a part for the whole; and secondly, it persistently privileges representation over the experience itself.

So I return here to the place from which I began. What relation do histories have to the events and people they describe? What reads like 'a good history' of a lunatic asylum, or a patient, or an asylum doctor? I think this is an important point of discussion for projects finding a way towards writing about institutional writing. We will dream up the relationship between asylum paperwork and asylum life, and in our dreaming we will associate to other bits of institutional paperwork, and to letters home and to colonial offices and magistrates and nurses and doctors. As the perspective broadens and deepens we will become more and more sure-footed in our version, the meaning of our dream.

In doing this we might also avoid the pitfall of taking the case-notes for the truth of a patient, or the doctor's writing as addressed to us, his avid reader. Also the pitfall of dreaming up a subaltern voice that the 'record' never recorded, or discarded.

One of the paradoxes of this branch of historical work is that much of what is written about the insane is saturated in rationality, and so we become complicit in erasing the very phenomenon with which we are preoccupied. But in archival reading, particularly its dreamwork, there is a way of conjuring up our subaltern: there are traces everywhere of the underworld of the asylum, its shadowy or forgotten pieces, its madnesses. We have many subalterns in this project – but this seems to be at its heart. What is it like to be psychotic, falling to pieces, locked up and discarded, with filthy habits, beaten and bruised by hallucinations and attendants, frantic or undreaming, busy or silent, or in a long sleep?[20] It is to this final issue that I now turn.

Concluding thoughts

I would like now to draw together the argument, and to do this by posing a series of questions that I believe arise from it. I have confined myself specifically to questions about lunatic asylum archive, but the issues raised do have broader significance in considering institutional histories.

I will begin with the question that seems the most fundamental. In histories of madness, where is the madness represented? Constructions of coherent narratives so central to recorded histories obviates against representing madness, which by definition departs from rationality. If madness is to be represented, does this entail description of disordered behaviour? Is the voice of the patient, speaking of inner demons, essential? To write histories of lunatic asylums that do not describe patients' experiences seems deeply problematic. On the other hand, trying to reconstruct patients' experiences from the shreds of evidence in casebooks and files runs the risk of inaccuracy or superficiality. As with all endeavours historical, in writing histories of madness, parts will stand in for wholes: we will never know the full extent of patients' internal worlds, just as we will inevitably be tempted to overlook the extent to which patient populations were richly variable both socially and psychiatrically. There are issues with respect to protecting the privacy of patients and their families. Added to this are the forms of distortion imported into descriptions of patients' experience through doctors' knowledge about, and approach to the stories they were hearing, and the behaviour they were seeing. Further, what questions, as historians, would we want to entertain about patients' representation of their own states of mind, and experience of incarceration? The challenge seems to be to accept the necessity and the challenge of respectful representation of mental turmoil; to resist reductive accounts by prizing individual's journeys through insanity as unique; and to try to find multiple perspectives on patients' experience (for example case-notes, letters, court records – none of which are reliable as a single source) so that a potential solidity might emerge. There are more prosaic questions woven into this too. In the asylum and lunacy archive, what has been preserved, through which lines of authority? Who has access to voice? Where are potential archives located, what varieties of rules governed their collections of documents, and how do they intersect with each other? How might statistics be sensibly used in accounting for mad states of mind? Underlying this is a plea once again for awareness of intertextuality in crafting institutional histories of lunatic asylums.

Directly from this emerges the second question. Is there a place in the project of writing about asylum histories to understand writing itself? Although this will seldom be the main thrust of the research, it seems to me that especially in the representation of mad states of mind, we have an obligation to reflection on the complexities of language as representations of thought, the relationship of thought to emotion, and ways in which the act of writing folds itself in and out of conscious and unconscious processes.[21]

In thinking about representations of madness, whether through histories of lunatic asylums, fiction, biography or genealogies of psychiatric thought, there are questions to be asked about both its distinctiveness, and its capacity to attract an appalled, enthralled audience. Here, histories of physical illness, medical hospitals, and genealogies of disease seem an essential counterpoint, and the ways in which treatments of bodies and minds in families, hospitals, courts and governments diverge is a potentially rich focus. Specific questions would include exploring how psychiatric histories have changed over time, and under what kinds of institutional or bureaucratic influence, and how the languaging of lunacy records might be different to that of physically ill patients.[22]

Finally, there are questions about space and time – the trajectory of bodies struggling with the terror and tyranny of madness, travelling across locations, in and out of their bouts of illness? Mostly particularly, how do bodies get organized in institutional space, and what shapes are taken by the daily collisions and collusions between people inside and outside of asylums?[23] This question focuses on all the ways that paperwork in an asylum network addresses, beckons, interrogates, demands answers from multiple surrounding sites, and circles back to the question of audience.

These questions are perhaps best addressed through a generous archive-dwelling, to toleration of bits and pieces and chaos, and dreaming, preoccupation, and trust that a narrative will grow at its own pace.

Notes

1. Donald Winnicott, psychoanalyst uses this homely term to describe the gathering in needed in order for the infant to achieve cohesiveness. He makes an important distinction between unintegration, which is the state before 'unit status' is achieved, and disintegration, which involves a painful 'mad' state of 'going to pieces'. Archival work involves states of both unintegration and disintegration. See Winnicott, "Primitive emotional development," 137.
2. See Barrett, *The psychiatric team and the social definition of schizophrenia*; and Ogden, *Rediscovering psychoanalysis*; and Stoler, *Along the archival grain*.
3. Woolf & Hussey, *Between the acts*; and Eisenberg, "Virginia Woolf's Last Words on Words," 253–266.
4. Swartz, & Swartz, "Talk about talk," 395–416; and Swartz, "Issues in the analysis of psychotic speech," 29–44.
5. Swartz, "Using psychodynamic formulations in South African clinical settings," 42–48; and Swartz, "Shrinking," 150–156.
6. Swartz, *Homeless wanderers*.
7. Swartz, "Rome Falling," ; and Swartz, The Missing Middle.
8. Asad, "Ethnographic representation, statistics and modern power," 55–88; and MacDonagh, "The Nineteenth-Century Revolution in Government," 52–67.
9. Swartz, "The regulation of British colonial lunatic asylums and the origins of colonial psychiatry," 160.
10. Swartz, "Changing diagnoses in Valkenberg Asylum,", 431–451.
11. Swartz, "The black insane in the Cape," 399–415.
12. I am assuming here that we can leave aside habit as a form of apparel, although there is no doubt that some inmates at times did wear the results of their proclivities about their person.
13. Mitchell, & Black, *Freud and beyond*.
14. Ogden, *Rediscovering psychoanalysis*, 9.
15. The unconscious is not transparent, but is also unable to produce untruths (as in Gerard Manley Hopkins' poem 'As kingfishers catch fire': 'myself it speaks and spells'). Where patients produce fake narratives consciously, these very often reveal an unconscious purpose, consciously unknown to the narrator.
16. Winnicott, *Playing and reality*.
17. Ogden, "On not being able to dream," 17–30.
18. Fonagy,The mentalization-focused approach to social development. *Handbook of mentalization-based treatment*, 53–100.
19. Steiner, *Psychic retreats*.
20. I know I am side-stepping here fierce debates about what makes for 'good' history, whether owning up to multiple perspectives, and conflicting points-of-view challenges our arrangement around the facts of a case. I do know that the histories I find least coherent, that I can least hold in mind, string facts together without dreaming life into them. They are a resource, not a spark, a source.
21. In both of these first two questions, Catharine Coleborne's use of letters in relation to representation of family and emotion comes to mind as a way of complicating the received, bureaucratic archive, although their performativity needs underscoring. Coleborne, *Madness in the family: insanity and institutions in the Australasian colonial world*.

22. See Hess, & Mendelsohn, "Case and series,"287–314; and Pols, "The development of psychiatry in Indonesia, "363–370.
23. David Wright's direction in this regard remains critical; Wright, "Getting out of the asylum", 137–155.

Disclosure statement

No potential conflict of interest was reported by the author.

References

Allen, J. G., and P. Fonagy, eds. 2006. *The Handbook of Mentalization-Based Ttreatment*. New Jersey: John Wiley & Sons.
Asad, T. 1994. "Ethnographic Representation, Statistics and Modern Power." *Social Research* 61 (1): 55–88.
Barrett, R. J. 1996. *The Psychiatric Team and the Social Definition of Schizophrenia: An Anthropological Study of Person and Illness*. Cambridge: Cambridge University Press.
Coleborne, C. 2009. *Madness in the Family: Insanity and Institutions in the Australasian Colonial World, 1860–1914*. New York: Springer.
Eisenberg, N. 1981. "Virginia Woolf's Last Words on Words: Between the Acts and 'Anon'." In *New Feminist Essays on Virginia Woolf*, Eisenberg, Nora and Marcus, Jane eds., 253–266. London: Palgrave Macmillan.
Hess, V., and J. Andrew Mendelsohn. 2010. "Case and Series: Medical Knowledge and Paper Technology, 1600–1900." *History of Science* 48 (3–4): 287–314. doi:10.1177/007327531004800302.
MacDonagh, O. 1958. "IV. The Nineteenth-Century Revolution in Government: A Reappraisal." *The Historical Journal* 1 (1): 52–67. doi:10.1017/S0018246X58000018.
Mitchell, S. A., and M. J. Black. 2016. *Freud and Beyond: A History of Modern Psychoanalytic Thought*. London: Hachette UK.
Ogden, T. H. 2003. "On Not Being Able to Dream." *The International Journal of Psychoanalysis* 84 (1): 17–30.
Ogden, T. H. 2014. *Rediscovering Psychoanalysis: Thinking and Dreaming, Learning and Forgetting*. London: Routledge.
Pols, H. 2006. "The Development of Psychiatry in Indonesia: From Colonial to Modern Times." *International Review of Psychiatry* 18 (4): 363–370. doi:10.1080/09540260600775421.

Steiner, J. 2003. *Psychic Retreats: Pathological Organizations in Psychotic, Neurotic and Borderline Patients.* London: Routledge.
Stoler, A. L. 2010. *Along the Archival Grain: Epistemic Anxieties and Colonial Common Sense.* Princeton: Princeton University Press.
Swartz, S. (2016). "Rhodes Falling." Paper presented to the International Association of Relational Psychoanalysis (IARPP), Rome, June.
Swartz, S. (2017). "The Missing Middle." Paper presented to the International Association of Relational Psychoanalysis (IARPP), Sydney, May.
Swartz, S. 1994. "Issues in the Analysis of Psychotic Speech." *Journal of Psycholinguistic Research* 23 (1): 29–44.
Swartz, S. 1995. "Changing Diagnoses in Valkenberg Asylum, Cape Colony, 1891–1920: A Longitudinal View." *History of Psychiatry* 6 (24): 431–451. doi:10.1177/0957154X9500602402.
Swartz, S. 1995. "The Black Insane in the Cape, 1891–1920."." *Journal of Southern African Studies* 21 (3): 399–415. doi:10.1080/03057079508708454.
Swartz, S. 1996. "Shrinking: A Postmodern Perspective on Psychiatric Case Histories." *South African Journal of Psychology* 26 (3): 150–156. doi:10.1177/008124639602600304.
Swartz, S. 1999. "Using Psychodynamic Formulations in South African Clinical Settings." *South African Journal of Psychology* 29 (1): 42–48. doi:10.1177/008124639902900107.
Swartz, S. 2010. "The Regulation of British Colonial Lunatic Asylums and the Origins of Colonial Psychiatry, 1860–1864." *History of Psychology* 13 (2): 160–177.
Swartz, S. 2015. *Homeless Wanderers: Movement and Mental Illness in the Cape Colony in the Nineteenth Century.* Cape Town: University of Cape Town Press.
Swartz, S., and L. Swartz. 1987. "Talk about Talk: Metacommentary and Context in the Analysis of Psychotic Discourse." *Culture, Medicine and Psychiatry* 11 (4): 395–416.
Winnicott, D. W. 1945. "Primitive Emotional Development." *The International Journal of Psycho-Analysis* 26 (3/4): 137–143.
Winnicott, D. W. 1971. *Playing and Reality.* Hove: Psychology Press.
Woolf, V., and M. Hussey. 2008. *Between the Acts.* Boston: Houghton Mifflin Harcourt.
Wright, D. 1997. "Getting Out of the Asylum: Understanding the Confinement of the Insane in the Nineteenth Century." *Social History of Medicine* 10 (1): 137–155.

Bookkeeping madness. Archives and filing between court and ward

Volker Hess

ABSTRACT
The paper reconstructs the invention of the loose file system in German psychiatry in the early nineteenth century as a special case of medical and juridical relationship. The loose file allows the gathering of all information of the treatment of the respective patient in one folder, which enables it to be reordered for the different ways of reimbursing care, providing cure, and to store the patient's file for re-use in the case of re-admission. Psychiatry was the first discipline to introduce the new filing system. The reason for this was not, I argue, a medical one. Legislation and juridical debates about the status of the mentally ill person prompted a new admission procedure. The new Prussian General Law Code required a formal 'declaration of lunacy' which was negotiated in a regular trial. 'Lunatics and raving mad persons' came under the 'special supervision and preventative care of the state'. The legal procedure produced questionnaires, reports and protocols which drove the patient-related record keeping in the psychiatric departments.

The relationship between German psychiatrists and their files can really only be described as libidinous. The patient's medical history is documented devotedly. Such files not infrequently run to several volumes, particularly in state hospitals. In addition to the standard documents, all reports[1] with any kind of potential relation to the patient's condition are tirelessly gathered: the patient's postcards, letters from relatives, handwritten résumés, shopping lists, sketches, drafts and pictures of the patient, even the person's handicrafts merit inclusion (see Röske 1995; Ankele 2009). To this day, such collections are carefully tended and cared for in psychiatric institutions. Many departments refuse keep their patient files in a central archive and preserve them well beyond the legally prescribed storage times.[2] It is not uncommon for comprehensive file holdings to stretch back well into the nineteenth century (see Klöppel 2009).[3] Although the existence of wartime or pre-war patient files from surgical departments is rare, extensive collections are almost to be expected in the basements or attics of psychiatric institutions, still under the supervision of long-serving resident doctors or senior physicians. Older clinicians, in particular, love to talk about 'our archive' as if the carefully ordered records in the filing registry were their personal possessions. It is only recently that these historic treasures have become endangered owing to the rigid space management and virtual room rents which have accompanied the economisation of university hospitals (see Hess 2011b).

It is remarkable that, of all people, psychiatrists should have such a close relationship to patient-related documents. However, the reason for this special affinity has never been properly investigated. Among the theories are that the special status of the psychiatric archive is due to the characteristically lengthy nature of psychiatric illnesses and to the biographical focus of psychiatric knowledge (see Engstrom 2005). The lack of other diagnostic techniques (laboratory or necropsy findings, imaging methods, pathogen detection or histology) is one reason for the enduring documentation of clinical observations.[4] In short, the shortage of hard data explains why psychiatrists accord records from clinical practice more importance than clinicians in other fields. Some even claim that the special status of psychiatric knowledge, the narrative structure and the poetic construction of clinical disease patterns prompted this particular professional group's special attachment to their files. The argument goes that it is because psychiatric knowledge is formed and organised by narrative that the media involved in this process – progress reports, patient files and archives – have acquired such a central importance in psychiatry.

This argument is elegant, but perhaps a little too elegant. Perhaps the reverse may be true: psychiatrists love collecting patient files not because of the narrative order of psychiatric knowledge,[5] but rather they base their knowledge on case histories because they have always had to keep files. Because they have always been involved with files, psychiatric knowledge developed on the basis of the ordering of the file and the registry. I would like to apply the standard terms for archiving and administering files to characterise clinical bookkeeping in institutional business operations – as opposed to the historical archive. At the very beginning of psychiatry, this article will argue, were the file and the registry. This explains why psychiatric knowledge was articulated and consolidated in these media. The file and its registry are thus not the means and instrument of a prior poetelogical purpose but instead formed, in a way which became peculiar to psychiatry thereafter, both the occasion and reason for a narrative organisation of knowledge. So the file is not the consequence but the epistemological precondition of psychiatric narration.

This thesis will be outlined in three stages. First, the origins of the psychiatric patient file will traced. Second, the practice of file-keeping will be described in a little more detail to distinguish this institutional bureaucracy from the organisation of the archive on the one hand and from a natural history collection on the other. Third, this article will argue that this apparatus of institutional bookkeeping played a crucial formative role in the development of psychiatric knowledge.

As a preliminary, however, it is necessary to briefly examine the medium: patient case histories are not medical histories. In reality, they represent a system of collection of diverse documents related to the patient by different authors. This system of recording (*Aufschreibesystem*), as was argued in my research on Berlin's Charité hospital, can be traced back to an early modern kitchen economy – both literally and figuratively.[6] In this institution for the poor funded by the Prussian state, the daily food bill was the biggest cost driver – and thriftiness was a Prussian virtue. So, surgeons sent for further training at the largest hospital in the Prussian empire were required to keep a daily record of the patient's diet and give the kitchen sufficient notice of it. The meticulous listing of consumption and replenishments was necessary to maintain provisions for some 500 patients and invalids (see Hanke 1981, 60). The list also formed the basis for a balance sheet of the institution's expenditure and revenues. As a result, not only the acquisition and preparation but also the prescription and consumption of daily portions came under surveillance and were controlled by the senior authorities (see further Thoms 2005).[7] As the patient's diet related to their physical condition, this recording practice developed epistemological effects, which should not be underestimated. As part of this kitchen economy, patients were examined daily, their condition was written down, perpetuated in the form of a daily notation, formalised in patterns and schemata and finally aggregated in monthly and quarterly accounts (see Hess 2008). That trainee military surgeons and future *physici* were thereby simultaneously learning and practising Prussian administrative techniques was a welcome added bonus.

In the Charité, as a contemporary noted when making a comparison with other European countries, there was an insistence on a particularly 'strict system of reporting', which was 'a little overdone' (Oppert 1883, 187). However, the kitchen economy was a model for the emergence of a recording practice oriented towards the patient in other institutions as well.[8] This supports the basic argument, which is further buttressed by a second development in psychiatry, lending patient-oriented documentation a significance far beyond hospital administration. It leads us from the kitchen to the courtroom – and from the early eighteenth century into the Prussian reform era.

I Land law and psychiatric reform

The opening of the first provincial lunatic asylum in the Mark of Brandenburg at the beginning of March 1801 ushered in a new era of 'lunatic treatment'. The Neuruppin institution received a 'very special assignment': The mentally disturbed were not only to be held 'in safekeeping for their own security and that of the public', but also 'as far as is possible restored from their illness'.[9] This dual purpose provided the blueprint for a reform of the customary Prussian confinement practice. More asylums quickly opened in Marsberg (1814/1835) and Siegburg (1825) as well as three in Silesia, at Leubus, Brieg and Plagwitz (1830). These new institutions were explicitly following a treatment mandate whether singly as a sanatorium and nursing home only or combining both functions under one roof (see Damerow 1840). Doctors at the Berlin Lunatic Asylum, which was transferred to the Charité in 1799, also saw themselves as running a model establishment in this vein. This vision was manifested in elaborate apparatuses, complex methods of treatment and a therapeutic optimism which is hard for us to understand today (see Hess 2010a).

Accompanying this expansion was the development of an institutional bureaucracy. In Neuruppin, patients were already required on admission under 'instructions from the General Provincial State Poor Relief and the Invalid Lodging Directorate' to provide an original, properly filled out transportation form as well as a medical history from the doctor who had previously treated them, which, together with an interview with the patient's escort, were all recorded, preserved and presented at the monthly review (Augustin 1818, 10–12). This flood of papers was triggered not by the treatment mandate but rather by legal regulations. To prevent any abuses, just one year after opening of the lunatic reform asylum, the Prussian king insisted that an application for admission to the reformed lunatic asylum be based on the presentation of a 'findings report (*Erkenntnis*)' in a court order.[10] Just one year later, a Prussian State Council rescript repeated the regulation's universal validity: No-one was to be admitted to a lunatic asylum, before 'the findings report had declared the person to be lunatic and idiotic'.[11] Admission to the Siegburg sanatorium required a 'duly certified verification' that 'the judicial authority concerned had placed the patient, being unable to use their mind, under a guardianship order.'[12] This provision was also used in Silesian institutions.[13] Even private madhouses were not excluded and were only permitted to take patients in accordance with 'the necessary legal formalities'.[14]

The 'declaration of lunacy' (*Blödsinnigkeitserklärung*) was by no means a new legal instrument. Wardship due to feeble-mindedness or mental illness (*cura furiosi*) was, however, traditionally assigned to the family (Roman law), the clan (German law) or – in some statutes of separate German legal entities (*Partikulargesetzgebungen*) – to voluntary jurisdiction (*jurisdictio voluntaria mixta*). That also meant that 'it was up to the guardianship authority to determine whether there was sufficient evidence that wardship on the grounds of mental disorder was necessary' (Daude 1882, 10). Contemporaries, however, considered the legal incapacitation of those with mental disorders increasingly problematic since both 'the holiest right, human freedom' and 'the dictates of humanity' had to be preserved to 'protect the poor, mentally ill people from the greed of bad characters' (Gageur 1852, 231). Therefore, Prussia took a different approach (as did Württemberg and France with the Code civil). The Prussian General Land Law (1794, *Allgemeines Landrecht* shortened here to ALR) placed all those people who 'due to a lack of mental forces were unable to properly deal with their affairs' (ALR I, Title 1, § 32), which under §27 also included 'lunatics and raving mad persons' under the 'special supervision and preventative care of the state'.

Around 1800, the protection of personal freedom had become the business of the Prussian state (see Arnold 1861, §1, §27). State care for civil liberties (ALR II, Title 8) was enshrined in the *Allgemeinen Gerichtsordnung* (General Law Code), which came into force at the same time as the ALR. So, the official judiciary alone acted as a guarantor of the 'preventative state care' being demanded (Arnold 1861, §26f.). Moreover, official proceedings required a proper legal process: Under the Law Code, a trustee had to be appointed, but 'under no circumstances [...] was he to have the slightest connection to matter, because he had to protect the interests of the patient.' Reports on the patient were collected, one from an expert named by the family and one from the trustee's nominee. Then, the patient was investigated in the presence of a representative of the court, examined and the findings were documented according to a template stipulated by the legislature:

> What signs of lunacy has the mad person in question exhibited until now, since when and what phase of life, has it been continuous or in [...] alternating intervals, could serious or less violent outbursts be recognised, what forcible means, either severe or less so, have had to be employed so far to combat the harmfulness of such outbursts; [...] have cures already been tried on the said person, if so which ones and with what effect, finally how has the person been cared for.[15]

If the two experts were not able to agree, either a third was called in or the 'written reports, including supporting reasons', were submitted together with the rest of the files to the relevant *Collegium medicum* which was asked for the 'disclosure of an informed opinion'. This resulted in, at the very least, an official 'findings report', that meant an assessment of the mental state certified and issued by the court (Friedrich Wilhelm [II.] 1795, Part 38, § 4–8).

In Prussia, therefore, the concept of personal freedom became part of the institutionalisation of modern clinical psychiatry. Financial considerations certainly played a role in this, as the complaint of the Prussian monarch shows 'deliberate abuse' was making the new institutions overcrowded. Whoever 'for their own benefit or with some other dishonest intention' was delivering 'to the lunatic asylum, under the pretext that they were mad, persons whose maintenance and handling [...] was a burden to them' would face fully 'the punishment due for such a deprivation of freedom laid down in the General Land Law'.[16] However, this cannot entirely explain the use of the proper legal form. The common practice of getting rid of people in this way[17] could also have been prevented – presumably more efficiently – through administrative measures. Therefore, the insistence on the new legal instrument[18] underlines the growing significance of bourgeois civil rights and liberties.

This very use of the rule of law had a drawback, however, as the legal process was not suited to emergencies. The bureaucratic organisation was unwieldy and slow. Although exceptions were tolerated, they were not desired, as can be seen repeatedly in the decrees. On the other hand, psychiatrists were trying to get the asylums' new clientele, those with treatable mental disorders, excluded from the legal provisions. They pointed to the discriminatory nature of the proceedings – particularly their public character – as well as to the levels of effort and costs for the lifting of the findings of lunacy and idiocy (*Blödsinnigkeits-Erkenntnis*)[19] upon discharge from the institution. As a result, in 1839, patients thought to be curable were did not face the 'opening of lunacy proceedings'. However, even in these cases, the courts had to receive 'immediate notification of the admission of a person with a mental disorder to a public lunatic asylum'.[20] In other words, the institutionalisation of psychiatry was accompanied by the development of a legal, bureaucratically organised procedure.

Two points should be noted here: At the beginning of modern institutionalised psychiatry was not the word, but the file, more precisely, the judicial file. The admission of a patient into a new institution was connected to the creation of official written submissions. These were the application, the appointment of a trustee, the initial assessment (*Erstgutachten*), second assessment (*Zweitgutachten*), the questioning of one or more witnesses, the transcript of the interview and examination, the sending of the file and the drawing up of a lunacy findings report. These documents were, as is fitting for an administrative body, authenticated, copied, inventoried and systematically filed. Even provincial governments received the 'court findings report' together with copies of the assessments and transcript.

Second, the determination of lunacy was not a medical diagnosis but rather a legal judgement. The decision on the need for admission and treatment was not a medical matter but, instead, the result of a legal process. Obviously, the judge's verdict was based on the opinion of the 'expert doctors', although the wording used suggests that this attribution was certainly not taken as read. From a procedural perspective, these assessments were one element of the collection of evidence and examination of witnesses. They certainly did not constitute a forgone conclusion. As part of the due process of law, lunacy declarations were, on the contrary, a procedure involving two parties conducted under the watchful eye of a justice system which did not 'claim for itself the rights of the person to be stripped, but instead aimed to uphold those rights' (Arnold 1861, §36).[21] This distinction between medical assessment and legal judgement is important. Even if the grounds for the verdict followed the doctors' opinion, the weighting and evaluation of the arguments was based not on a medical decision-making process but on the legal consideration of legal interests.

II Filing and the registry

The bureaucratic organisation of the legal procedure, therefore, supplied the template for the new institutions' documentation. The General Law Code produced more than just paperwork. It also shaped the communicative action between the patient, physicians and relatives. Although the official papers were normally 'kept in the relevant files in the official record office',[22] in the case of provisional admissions, the medical institution replaced the court. If a declaration of lunacy could not be obtained in time, then the admission was carried out according to the directives of the legal code. In this case, the 'questioning' of the patient and their escort was to take place in the way described above, as two-party proceedings under the direction of a judicial officer involving the consultation of the administrative director and the resident physician. Then, a written record was made of whether the 'disease of the mind' of the potential patient was 'to be considered incurable or curable with careful treatment', whether or not precautionary measures to ensure the 'safety (of the patient) or the public were necessary' and whether the subject really could be treated 'nowhere else sufficiently well other than in a lunatic asylum'.[23]

The judicial proceedings which would later follow justified comprehensive observation, the documentation of this and the preservation of these records. The resident physician had to report to the inspector of the facility all observations which could relate to the 'retention' of the admitted patient. The pair would then notify or, in accordance with their duty, submit an application to the Institute Director who then, in turn, addressed the poor relief administrators in a 'submission with supporting reasons'.[24] The higher authority, did after all, require that such observations be properly recorded, the transcripts kept safe and the assessments filed in such a way that they could be retrieved. This was important for the monthly cash audit when the house inspector, together with the resident physician, presented 'the admission orders for patients who have been brought in in the intervening period' along with the related transcripts of the questioning upon entry.

In this way, legal procedures created the need for medical documentation. This connection was also emphasised by Ernst Horn, who boasted, upon official recognition of his work at the Charité, that he had ordered 'a special journal' be made for every patient with a mental disorder. The careful recording 'of all speech, acts and conspicuous behaviour', he believed, would help to 'uncover and put on paper those facts which' characterised the disease state in a justiciable way (Horn 1818, 212): 'Such a collection of journals [...] cannot be preserved and complemented carefully enough. They acquire legal value and facilitate judgements in the future on dubious states of mind since the past life of such patients can shed light on and clarify the true nature of present acts.' (Horn 1818, 214) The introduction of a patient (-oriented) journal was not motivated by scientific considerations. The medical records served instead, as Horn explained through one example, to convince sceptical judicial authorities 'that the apparently healthy person is still very seriously mentally ill' (Horn 1818, 211f., Note). In order to permanently preserve this evidence in the asylum, its first head even established his own personal registry 'in which all journals of the healed and those discharged unhealed as well as deceased mentally ill patients were stored in alphabetical order' (Horn 1818, 214). An alphabetical index made it easier to find former patients – and for the supervising authorities to carry out their annual inspection. During this check, officials wanted to know 'whether the admission of the mentally disordered presently in the institute satisfied the current legal regulations'.[25]

The intertwining of legal file-keeping and medical documentation is highlighted particularly well by the example of another paper technology. To obtain reliable information upon admission, Horn had the already well-known list of questions, now in a slightly modified form (Figure 1), sent to relatives. The clear differentiation of the legal template was doubtless based on medical beliefs concerning the cause and origins of illnesses, yet the legal rules of procedure remained the reason for the writing down. In this entanglement, the legal formalisation structured the patient history and diagnosis. According to Horn, the written 'answering of certain questions' gave greater clarity concerning the condition of the patient than the 'random and often irrelevant remarks and essays which patients' relatives generally send in answer to a doctor's request'. Furthermore, the legal form caused the patient themselves to write. If the relatives were not known, the patient received a form to record details of their life, career, desires and inclinations – leading to a result that surprised psychiatrists:

*) 1) Von welchem Temperamente, welchen Neigungen ist der Kranke? Unter welchen Verhältnissen hat derselbe sonst, und unter welchen kurz vor seiner Aufnahme gelebt? Womit hat er sich beschäftigt?

2) Findet eine erbliche Anlage zu diesem Uebel statt? Litt der Vater, die Mutter, die Großältern, die Seitenverwandten vielleicht an demselben, oder an einem ähnlichen Uebel?

3) Wie fing das Uebel an? Wann und unter welchen Umständen, mit welchen Zufällen und Erscheinungen? Welche Art des Benehmens, der Reden, der Handlungen des Kranken wurden bisher bemerkt, nach denen man ihn für geisteskrank gehalten? Welche Veränderungen bot der bisherige Gang der Krankheit dar?

4) Fand früher, und wann schon, dieselbe oder eine ähnliche Krankheit statt? Oder ist dieses Uebel jetzt zum ersten Male eingetreten? Wie befand sich der Kranke vor demselben? Gingen andere Krankheiten vorher, und welche? Litt der Kranke vielleicht schon an Epilepsie, und wie lange und wie oft traten die Anfälle derselben ein?

5) Welche Veranlassungen zur Entstehung der Geisteskrankheit gingen voraus? Körperliche? und welche? Etwa andere Krankheiten? Oder geistige? und etwa heftige und angreifende Gemüthsaffekte, und welche, und unter welchen Umständen? Wirkten auf den Kranken ein heftiger Zorn, Kummer, Nahrungssorgen? Oder fand eine Kränkung seiner Ehre statt, oder ein Verlust des Vermögens oder geliebter Verwandten, oder eine verfehlte Hoffnung?

Figure 1. Questionnaire at patient admission (from: Horn 1818, 208).

'These answers often were [...] so good that I gained insights which I would have had difficulty in obtaining even from continuous observation.' The self-disclosure served on the one hand as a document and was given to the judge as proof in the case of a 'questionably sick person in an apparently good state', so that it left no doubt 'concerning the true state' (Horn 1818,

210). On the other hand, the ego-document provided the doctor with a means of making a nosological diagnosis of the illness. Seldom was the term 'writing illness' (Wübben and Zelle 2013a) so apt as in the legally inspired narrative laying down of madness prior to its medical documentation.

This is not to suggest that the Prussian legal regulations dictated the content of the psychiatric anamnesis. However, the bureaucratic procedure of those regulations provided a formal structure, through which a psychiatric knowledge interest could develop. This is demonstrated by the aforementioned questionnaire. The template sent to doctors or relatives seeking confinement in the mid-nineteenth century included all the key elements of a psychiatric anamnesis. However, the form could not hide its origins – neither could the 'Actum' (Figure 2), which was created from 1860 onwards in the Charité's so-called questioning room each time a patient was admitted (Esse 1850, here 534–537; p. 539: Questioning).

As the example of the Charité shows, upon the patient's committal, more was acquired than simply the transportation form, the declaration of lunacy, assessments and transcripts. Together with these official documents, the whole accompanying administrative apparatus found its way into the hospital. Until then, in addition to the courts, only Prussian medical officers and forensic doctors had kept a proper registry.[26] Now, the lunatic asylum was expected to do so as well. The annual audit explicitly included the registry, involving special checks on the proper filing and administration of official documents.[27]

The legal use and purpose demanded careful treatment of such papers. There were numerous complaints about the unsatisfactory nature of the file-keeping. The laxity of military interns was bemoaned (the 'journals are, however, often kept irresponsibly badly'). The lack of supervision by senior doctors concerning 'the keeping of journals, particularly on the lunatics' ward' was censured and reminders given to present them 'on that Sunday morning' (because of their importance 'in police or judicial investigations'). There was also a need to regularly provide receipts for proper checks (UAHU, Akten der Charitédirektion 1725–1945, No. 1237).[28] The concern over proper file-keeping did not follow the standard pattern of 'hospital versus administration'. Instead, it pervaded the whole institution and became part of its housekeeping.

This form of institutional file-keeping can be characterised in different ways. The bookkeeping is not secret, just invisible. It only shows itself when something malfunctions. In the files themselves, there is no reference to file-keeping, as long as it works. It is only when a file cannot be found, when no information is available, when claims for the reimbursement of costs for treatment and hospital stays cannot be verified that the paperwork leaves self-referential tracks.[29] These tracks show an active and comprehensive use of files. Enquiries posed by the authorities responsible for maintaining public order

Actum Charité-Kranken-Haus, den ᵗᵉⁿ 183 94

Dato wurde vorschriftsmäßig vernommen.

Namen.	
Stand und Gewerbe.	
Geburtsort, Vaterland und wie lange daraus entfernt.	
Alter	
Religion.	
Krankheit.	
Tag der Aufnahme.	
Wer d Kranke zur Charité gesandt hat?	
Wie lange in Berlin?	
Ob d Kranke einen Hausstand bildet und eine eigene Wohnung hat?	
oder	
Ob in Schlafstelle liegt oder als Geselle oder Dienstbote bei einer Herrschaft ist?	
Namen der Herrschaft und Wohnung.	

Figure 2. Form of the questionnaire at patient admission ('Vernehmungsbogen') List of questions for admission of patient to Charité in 1830s (University Archive of the Humboldt University, CD, No. 41, Bl. 94 (with kind permission of the Humboldt University archive).

and by the courts required the consulting of files, the copying of individual papers or the sending of fascicles ('the attached files, 1 Vol of 88 pages, are expected back together with your report') (UAHU, Akten der Charité-Direction, no. 41, p. 19). Institutional files were, therefore, certainly not simply stored or even locked away. On the contrary, the whole organisation of the registry was designed to aid the rapid identification and supplying of the files. Berlin's police headquarters instructed Charité administrators in the summer of 1825 that when an enquiry was made, the file had to be sent the next day. Delays of more than three days would 'be subject to a penalty'.[30] The guiding principle of the institutional file-keeping was not storage but mobilisation.

A complex apparatus was created for the use of the registry. Files were started to unite, label and identify written documents, to pull them out and put into different trays and pigeonholes and pass on, so that costs could be calculated, collected, home municipalities written to and authorities informed. Files were logged, arranged in alphabetical order, sorted and put back, and they were registered, indexed and inventoried. The development of a group of workers made available for this at the Charité can be traced. In the early 1830s, the 'invalided Sergeant Bartholome' was appointed registry assistant as part of the department's reorganisation. He was the senior military physician responsible for the reports and registers of the dead. He also had to keep an account of the patient journals, returning them to the registry in good time after compiling weekly, monthly and annual reports. This senior military physician was also charged with 'the bookkeeping concerning the dead who were sent to the anatomy department'. Besides that, there was one clerk dedicated to the correspondence with and questioning of patients, another in charge of the store of writing materials and forms as well as registry clerk Lesser. The latter's job was to enter all patient arrivals in the admission books, calculate the number of days in hospital as well as 'keep a record of the arrival and departure of patients' and (for good measure) prepare extracts from newspaper reports affecting the Charité. Although this group did not appear itself in the institution's staffing plan, the registry already had at least five workers around 1830 – from former Sergeant Bartholome and his unnamed clerk, to registry clerk Lesser and senior military physician Luge and cashier's office administrator Westphal (Esse 1850, 43–45).

III Bookkeeping

Thus, a 'bookkeeping of madness' emerged in the nineteenth century, which can be differentiated from other material forms of knowledge storage.[31] In light of the often metaphorical use of the term 'archive', it is important to highlight the role and function of the psychiatric medical record archive as a registry in contrast to either a historical archive (Prototype '*Geheimes Staatsarchiv*' [Secret State Archive]) or a collection

(Prototype 'Natural History Cabinet').[32] Six differences can be determined with regards to purpose, status, ordering and object in these three material forms of organising knowledge:

- When it is functioning well, psychiatric bookkeeping activity is not done in secret. It is simply, as mentioned above, invisible. This distinguishes bookkeeping both from the historical archive (Litschel 2010) and from the collection, which is always designed for the public te Heesen and Michels (2007).
- The registry's tasks are, in contrast to those of the archive and collection, not storage, conservation and representation, but rather the supplying and use of files – without consideration of wear and tear.
- A registry (like the medical records archive) is, again in contrast to the historical archive or collection, not meant for the long-term. Today, legal limits regulate the keeping of such documents: 3 years for receipts for the tax authorities, 10 years in financial bookkeeping, 20 years for patient files and finally 30 years for all records covered by the Radiology and Radiation Protection Ordinance. Thereafter, the files are generally destroyed.
- Within these time limits, however, the guiding principle is completeness. Every file is kept, every procedure regulated, in contrast to the archive, which arises through the application of cassation, that is, through the selective setting apart and destruction of files, which creates great gaps in the original registry. Such gaps are inexcusable in both bookkeeping and collections, though for totally different reasons. Although completeness represents the goal to which every collection aspires but fails to reach, it is the essential pre-requisite of all bookkeeping.
- Documents contained in files are generally unique; at least, the medical records of patients are. What is gone is gone and cannot be replaced. A collection piece, on the other hand, can generally be replaced. The replacement might not be as beautiful or as typical, but the gap caused by a loss can be filled.
- The ordering of a collection might be a key driver for collecting, but it is ultimately arbitrary. For a specific space, one arrangement might be better, more instructive, more representative, etc. than another, but this ordering of objects in the collection is not pre-existent. In contrast, the ordering of the registry is constitutive for each file. Only the registry number turns the cover into a file and the written document into a file document. According to Cornelia Vismann, the ordering of the registry is the product of a self-documenting action which remains self-referential for as long as it performs its function (see Vismann 2000, 24f.). This also applies, with some exceptions, to every archive

which uses provenance as its guiding criteria and reflects the activity structure of the agency in its document filing.

The registry thus forms the material foundation for a bookkeeping of madness. It is an expression of communicative action which sediments itself in the form of forms, letters, written or even ego-documents. The clinic's registry took the formal lunacy findings report from the legal code of the day as its starting point, whereby the legal use and purpose formed an important motor for the establishment and differentiation of institutional paperwork. Therefore, it was the legal state of lunacy which demanded an 'orderly maintaining of journals, namely, in the psychiatric department' and the timely delivery of the files. This legal state also made necessary the separate storage of psychiatric patient files upon admission. However, it could also earn hospital managers a reprimand for the negligent care of these files where this had prevented the swift admission of the mentally ill. The legally-motivated paperwork preceded the scientific evaluation both in time and in institutional terms and was simultaneously the model for clinical usage. *Looping effects* between the court and hospital bureaucracy stabilised the psychiatric documentation system. Following Horn's questionnaire outline, lawmakers required that, as once in court, now upon admission to a psychiatric institution, 'a full history' of the illness and 'life circumstances' of the person involved had to be submitted.[33] The aforementioned instances of malfunctioning, which help trace the formation of a 'business routine' in the Charité registry, triggered *looping effects* between the legal requirements and institutional practice. Therefore, it is no coincidence that the patient, whose delayed admission provoked the ire of the ministry in this case, was mentally ill.[34] As the Charité registry was not able to provide the file in time, the infuriated minister sent the administrative director 'a copy of the regulations issued by the late Prime Minster His Excellency Freiherr von Altenstein on business routine in the ministry'. The education ministry did admit that the regulations issued in 1839 were not applicable 'in their full extent' to a hospital but that the ministerial rules of procedure would provide the Charité with 'a solid base' for 'institutions through which an orderly and supervised business routine could be ensured' (UAHU Charité-Direktion no. 41, p. 164).[35]

Therefore, in the mid-nineteenth century, Prussia's biggest hospital had at its command an administrative apparatus whose arrangement in several respects, including its business routine and registry, was patterned on a government authority. Such administrative stipulations provided the model for the development of a recording praxis oriented to the clinic. In the case of the psychiatric patient file, this was the General Law Code. Only when the Code of Civil Procedure was introduced after the founding of the

German Empire was the connection between the legal and psychiatric recording system lost.

The clinic's bookkeeping of madness is consequently born out of the legal context. This does not, however, prove that this system of recording also served scientific purposes or that the legal models had epistemological effects. Today doctors still spend a lot of time (at least in their view) filling out administrative forms without this paperwork bringing any recognisable scientific benefit. One proof that the system did produce such benefits comes from the stream of publications psychiatrists produced at that time. This was clearly based on the paperwork of the registry clerks and senior military doctors which was regulated in detail by official instructions. Karl Ideler, for example, who managed the hospital's fortunes between 1830 and 1860, chose to publish case histories. From his surviving casuistic compilations, it is clear that they served to develop his Kantian theory on the origins of mental disorders. This collection of detailed word painting is just as impressive as the graphics with which Ideler illustrated his patient histories.

Furthermore, Ideler had a new requirement of his patient histories which went beyond the bounds of clinical observation. His demand that 'the individual threads of the fabric of pathological affectations and utterings of the soul' be traced back to the person's earliest years (Ideler 1847, XIII) [36] corresponded to legal documentation praxis in two respects. First, the lengthening of the clinical gaze beyond its own walls established a biographical perspective which put the clinically impressive phenomena into their social and biographical contexts. Second, it supported a psychodynamic approach which traced the development of 'the course of individual mental disorders genetically', that is from social and societal circumstances (Ideler 1847, XVI). Thus, Ideler believed his biographically-oriented patient histories proved that certain ideas, either religious or political, exercised a crucial influence on the emergence and form of a mental disorder. In this way, the filing of records relevant to courts not only acquired, by producing a biological perspective, scientific epistemological value, but also gave the legal structure a medical purpose.

There is no space here to delve into the individual stages of this transformation from an administrative to a psychiatric-scientific system (see Ledebur 2011; Hess and Ledebur 2012). This especially applies to the role of clinical teaching, which through its narrativisation made a key contribution to turning the administrative registry into a register of psychopathology (see Hess 2011a). An argument over administrative forms illustrates this connection:

In the mid-1870s, recordings in the form of files became so important for research and teaching that hospital doctors were convinced that they could not do without them. As Ole Dohrmann showed in 2009, psychiatrists built up their own medical records archive at the Charité through the expenditure of much time and effort (see Dohrmann 2015). In doing so, they took patient documentation almost completely out of the hands of the hospital administration's bookkeepers. The central registry henceforth only received the so-called 'office journal', which consisted of a selective copy of clinical recordings. Some entries were streamlined, questionable passages deleted and drawings, letters and other ego-documents withheld in order to eliminate all possible ambiguity. The original patient journals, including all inserts, however, remained in the clinic – which, since it had the originals, thus retained all paper traces of its work. Owing to a reconstruction of this archive, over the last few years, it has been possible to demonstrate how this originally administrative written product developed a scientific productivity (see Ledebur 2011; Friedland and Herrn 2012; Ledebur 2013; Hess 2017; [submitted]). Central to this scientific work on and with medical files were not only the data and information entered into the pre-printed columns and tables, but also, to an even greater extent, the work on the paper itself – markings, comments, crossings out or overwritings, which represent the fundamental techniques of scientific 'data processing'. The importance of these simple writing techniques should not be underestimated (see Hess and Andrew Mendelsohn 2013). The material media, the design of the entries, the form and not the information as such, that is, the information content stored on the medium carrying the writing, were fundamental to the research process. This is also the reason why clinicians gave the laboriously produced clean copy of a patient journal to the administration while keeping for themselves the messy original with all the scrawlings and disparaging remarks as well as all the additional inserted materials.

Epilogue

Even before the outbreak of World War One, individual members of the German Medical Association had insisted that patient journals could not be archived in the general administration. They should be viewed as the 'private secret' of their doctors (see Fischer 1914, 2274–2276). This matter became a burning topic at the Charité in the post-war period. As part of the demilitarisation, the training of military doctors was halted. That triggered the collapse of the cumbersome system of double file-keeping. There were no more military interns available for the time-consuming copying. At that time, however, it was unthinkable for psychiatrists to surrender their patient journals to a central registry. So instead, it was the administrators who had to forgo their 'office journals'. Thus, clinicians had finally appropriated this central instrument of state bureaucracy. In the space of 60 years, the unbeloved process of writing and copying had become crucial to clinical work. This appropriation did not, however, eradicate the original purpose of the patient file. Now that the central registry was no longer involved, doctors had to deal with inquiries previously handled by the administrative department using the 'office journals'. Sickness funds, compulsory health insurances, the courts, Mutual Indemnity Associations, companies, and other state or semi-state institutions asked to borrow the patient journals. Outraged doctors rejected such requests. Even a gentle enquiry from the Berlin Regional Insurance Institution that 'in view of the rich materials which the Charité had available for teaching,' it 'should be quite possible to spare isolated medical records for several days', bore no fruit. Less impressive still to hospital directors was the warning that, in view of the clarity of the law on this point, the institution would contact the Ministry for Popular Welfare. The response was that the medical records were the clinic's property and needed for scientific work and were 'not intended for an outside authority' (UAHU, Charité-Direktion 1723–1945, no. 1238, p. 100f.; p. 117).[37]

The Charité files show with what rare unity clinicians resisted all attempts by administrators to fulfil their contractual obligations to transfer 'facts and evidence'. Even the children clinic's director, who admitted that his department was unlikely to face requests from pension providers, went on record as saying 'that medical records cannot be given in the original to the agency'. However, the office journals should also 'not be reintroduced'. This refusal was justified by a number of arguments which are very familiar today but were being so strongly expressed for the first time: ethical concerns regarding the disclosure of data relating to a patient; concern that the information might prove overwhelming for the patient and their relatives; the protection of the scientist's intellectual property and, finally, the rejection of demands which did not square with the idealised self-image of the physician.

It was this debate which saw the first appearance of the term which reduces the multiplicity of tasks and functions of journal- and file-keeping to the central feature characterising this institutional registry: bookkeeping. For the clinicians, this was now valued as an original achievement of clinical science to be defended at all costs (see also Ledebur 2011):

This is a fundamental principle for the development of our scientific work. Just as a merchant does not allow others to look at his ledger, but keeps (it) for his own mental orientation and business dispositions, it is also impossible that we can lend records in which our intellectual material lies (UAHU Charité-Direktion, no. 1238, p. 54).[38]

Medical histories [...] are our private account books out of which, in contentious matters, no merchant would allow extracts. Ultimately, medical histories are our intellectual property; whoever wants to use this property should reward it accordingly, i.e. request and pay for a written expert opinion (UAHU Charité-Direktion, no. 1238, p. 116).[39]

The scientific appropriation erased the final remains of what were once legal and administrative functions. It is significant that it was the psychiatrists who were most vehement in their rejection of the release of medical records whether to health insurance companies, authorities and courts or to private individuals: 'The medical histories are purely medical documents and are intended for this use alone. Psychiatric medical histories, in particular, often contain confidential disclosures concerning personal or family histories.' This is why Karl Bonhoeffer, whose first vetoed their use, even denied 'judicial authorities consultation rights' (ibid., p. 137: Bonhoeffer's veto of 21 December 1926). There was no danger of 'causing damage to the administration of justice', since in cases of doubt the psychiatrist could be asked to do a paid assessment. Thus, the registry and file-keeping had found the purpose which they serve today. The bookkeeping of madness had come to full bloom in scientific psychiatry's system of recording.

Translation Julia Stone, Berlin.

Notes

1. On the origins and the status of the patient file, see Hess (2011b).
2. The German Hospital Federation recommends preserving them for 30 years in view of the differing regulations relating to liability and insurance law (Aktualisierter DKG-Leitfaden: Aufbewahrungspflichten und – fristen von Dokumenten im Krankenhaus. Stand: Mai 2011 [legal storage obligations and time limits of hospital documents. May 2011].
3. Comparable medical records archives exist in Jena, Tübingen, Zürich, Giessen, Hamburg, Leipzig.
4. Roelcke adopts this line of argument with regard to Kraepelin und Rüdin's research programme. See Roelcke (2003).
5. This argument is mainly promoted by literary specialists as the following edited volumes clearly show: Behrens and Zelle (2012); Wübben and Zelle (2013b).
6. There has been much written concerning the form and origin of the case history in the past few years. One good example of how developments outside the United Kingdom and North-America were ignored is Reiser (1984); see Craig 1989/90; Howell (1995); Anderson (2013). See in contrast Hess (2010b), esp. 303–310.
7. Therefore, although Vienna's Bürgerhospital (Public Hospital) has no patient files, it does have the weekly reports on the highly official tasting by a „Speisekommissär" ('food inspector') of the meals prepared (Knolz 1840, 188).
8. One of the earliest examples is contained in Dross (2010).

9. General Instructions from Januar 29, 1801, quoted after Augustin 1818 2nd vol., 10. The first part of this intended purpose is often neglected (cf. Dörner (1969); 230; Braun (2009); 172.
10. Regulations of 16 April 1802, quoted after Augustin 1818 2nd vol., 28.
11. Rescript of 29 September 1803, quoted after Rönne and Simon (1846), 418.
12. Koblenzer Amtsblatt of 1824, quoted after ibid., 495.
13. See Amtsblatt der Regierung von Breslau, 1830, 129–131, quoted after ibid., 429.
14. Rescript of 1 February 1810, quoted after Augustin 1818 2nd vol., 43f.
15. The regulation for implementing the court order is found as a requirement for local authorities in the Regulations for the lunatic asylum in the Mark of Brandenburg of 16 April 1802, quoted after Rönne and Simon (1846), 451f.
16. Regulations of 16 April 1802, quoted after Augustin 1818 2nd vol., 28.
17. See also the impressive example from Bavaria in Weikl (2013).
18. See here the corresponding decrees and regulations of March 5, 25 November 1822, 16 February 1825, 21 January 1839, 1841 and 6 November 1851 Rönne and Simon (1846), 418–421.
19. Hereafter shorten to *declaration of lunacy*.
20. Rescript of 16 February 1839, quoted after (Rönne and Simon 1846), 420 (emphasis from the original).
21. It was not the authorities against the citizens, not state violence against helpless subjects in this dramatic production, but rather negotiations before an independent authority: trustee versus family. Who took which role in this performative form of proceedings is a historically largely open question.
22. Directive of 19 July 1814 relating to the Marsberg Lunatic Asylum and Hospital Von Der Heyde (1819), 126.
23. General Instructions of 29 January 1801, quoted after Augustin 1818 2nd vol., 10.
24. General Instructions of 29 January 1801 for the Provincial Lunatic Asylum at Neuruppin, quoted after Rönne and Simon (1846), 461.
25. Directive of 7 May 1859, quoted after (Eulenberg 1874), 3rd ed. Part 1, 44.
26. See, for example, the Bavarian General Instructions for district court medical officers of 1803, Mair (1869).
27. Instructions on the inspection of private lunatic asylums from 18 October 1873 [Württemberg], quoted after Grauer (2012), 143.
28. In detail: „Acta betreffend die Führung der Kranken- und und Totenjournale und der Toten-Zettel, Todes-Anzeigen" (Files concerning the keeping of journals of patient and of dead persons, death slips, death notices), university archive of the Humboldt University Berlin (UAHU).
29. See the letter from the Berlin Chief of Police to Chief Inspector Marquard (Charité Administrative Director) of 9 July 1825 on account of a file which could not be found (UAHU, Akten der Charitédirektion, No. 41, Bl. 20f.), which caused a reorganisation of the registry.
30. Letter from the Berlin Chief of Police on account of a file which could not be found (cf. fn 29).
31. This distinction follows an appeal (Schenk 2008), 12f. to differentiate it from an often 'loose use of language' (ibid.). See also (Ernst 2002; Ebeling and Günzel 2009; Horstmann and Kopp 2010; Weitin and Wolf 2012); and the journal produced by the Zentrum für Literatur- und Kulturforschung, Issue 27, Trajekte.
32. For the archive see Friedrich (2013); for the collection see Te Heesen and Spary 2002.

33. Rescript of 31 July 1841 (quoted after Augustin 1838 6th vol., 107–109), which had found its way into the Charité's self-portrayal by the mid-19th century Esse (1850), 534–537.
34. The missing patient file on merchant Schlotius, which as mentioned above triggered the 1830 reform of the Charité registry's business routine, was probably connected to psychiatric treatment, which is likely due to the size of the bill see also Hess (2010b).
35. In detail: Letter from Ladenberg to the Royal Hospital Board of 12 September 1840, UAHU.
36. See also Ideler (1841).
37. In detail: Letter from the Berlin Regional Insurance Institution to the Charité directorate of 21 December 1921, UAHU, Charité-Direktion 1723–1945, no. 1238, p. 100f.; Passow's response of 22 June 1922, ibid. p. 117.
38. In detail: Letter by Greff to the Charité directorate of 20 April 1917, UAHU.
39. In detail: Letter by Greff to the Charité directorate of 22 June 1922, UAHU.

Disclosure statement

No potential conflict of interest was reported by the author.

Funding

This work was supported by the European Research Council [Advanced Investigator Grant 295712]. The paper results from the DFG research program 'Cultures of Madness' and the ERC Advanced Investigator Grant 'How physicians know'.

References

Anderson, W. 2013. "The Case of the Archive." *Critical Inquiry* 39 (3): 532–547. doi:10.1086/670044.

Anke, T. H., and A. Michels, eds. 2007. *Auf/Zu. Der Schrank in Den Wissenschaften [Anlässlich Der Gleichnamigen Ausstellung an Der Eberhard-Karls-Universität Tübingen, 24. Oktober 2007-15. Februar 2008]*. Berlin: Akademie-Verlag.

Anke, T. H., and E. C. Spary, eds. 2002. *Sammeln Als Wissen. Das Sammeln Und Seine Wissenschaftsgeschichtliche Bedeutung*. Göttingen: Wallstein Verlag.

Ankele, M. 2009. *Alltag Und Aneignung in Psychiatrien Um 1900: Selbstzeugnisse Von Frauen Aus Der Sammlung Prinzhorn*. Wien: Böhlau.

Arnold, F. C. V. 1861. *Das Gerichtliche Verfahren Gegen Geisteskranke Und Verschwender*. Erlangen: J.J. Palm und E. Enke.

Augustin, F. L. 1818-1838. *Die Königlich Preußische Medicinalverfassung Oder Vollständige Darstellung Aller, Das Medicinalwesen Und Die Medicinische Polizei in Den Königlich Preußischen Staaten Betreffenden Gesetze, Verordnungen Und Einrichtungen*. Vol. 1-6. Potsdam: Karl Christian Horvath.

Behrens, R., and C. Zelle, eds. 2012. *Der Ärztliche Fallbericht: Epistemische Grundlagen Und Textuelle Strukturen Dargestellter Beobachtung*. Wiesbaden: Harrassowitz.

Braun, S. 2009. *Heilung Mit Defekt: Psychiatrische Praxis an Den Anstalten Hofheim Und Siegburg: 1820-1878*. Göttingen: Vandenhoeck & Ruprecht.

Craig, B. L. 1989/90. "Hospital Records and Record-Keeping, C. 1850-C. 1950. Part 1: The Development of Records in Hospitals." *Archivaria* 29: 57–80.

Damerow, H. 1840. *Ueber Die Relative Verbindung Der Irren-Heil- Und Pflege-Anstalten in Historisch-Kritischer, so Wie in Moralischer, Wissenschaftlicher Und Administrativer Beziehung*. Leipzig: Otto Wigand.

Daude, P. 1882. *Das Entmündigungsverfahren Gegen Geisteskranke, Verschwender Und Gebrechliche Nach Der Reichs-Civilprozeßordnung Und Den Deutschen Landesgesetzgebungen: Für Juristen Und Ärzte*. Berlin: H.W. Müller.

Dohrmann, O. 2015. *Die Entwicklung Der Medizinischen Dokumentation Im Charité-Krankenhaus Zu Berlin Am Beispiel Der Psychiatrischen Krankenakten Von 1866 Bis 1945*. Husum: Matthiesen.

Dörner, K. 1969. *Bürger Und Irre: Zur Sozialgeschichte Und Wissenschaftssoziologie Der Psychiatrie*. Frankfurt/M: Europäische Verlagsanstalt.

Dross, F. 2010. "Patterns of Hospitality: Aspects of Institutionalisation in 15th & 16th Centuries Nuremberg Healthcare." *Hygiea Internationalis* 9: 13–34. doi:10.3384/hygiea.1403-8668.109113.

Ebeling, M. K., and S. Günzel, eds. 2009. *Archivologie: Theorien Des Archivs in Wissenschaft, Medien Und Künsten*. Berlin: Kadmos.

Engstrom, E. J. 2005. "Die Ökonomie Klinischer Inskription: Zu Diagnostischen Und Nosologischen Schreibpraktiken in Der Psychiatrie." In *Psychographien*, edited by C. Borck and A. Schäfer, 219–240. Berlin: diaphanes.

Ernst, W. 2002. *Das Rumoren Der Archive: Ordnung Aus Unordnung*. Berlin: Merve-Verlag.

Esse, C. H. 1850. "Ueber Die Verwaltung Des Charité-Krankenhauses." *Annalen Des Charité-Krankenhauses* 1: 524–570.

Eulenberg, H. 1874. *Das Medicinalwesen in Preussen, Nach Amtlichen Quellen Neu Bearbeitet*. Berlin: August Hirschwald.

Fischer, M. 1914. "Die Ausleihung Der Ärztlichen Krankengeschichten." *Münchener Medizinische Wochenschrift* 61 (47): 2306–2308. 2274-2276.
Friedland, A., and R. Herrn. 2012. "Die Einführung Des Schizophreniekonzeptes an Der Charité." In *Kulturen Des Wahnsinns. Schwellenräume Einer Urbanen Moderne*, edited by V. Hess and H.-P. Schmiedebach, 207–258. Wien: Böhlau.
Friedrich, M. 2013. *Die Geburt Des Archivs: Eine Wissensgeschichte*. München: Oldenbourg.
Gageur, R. 1852. *Vormundschaft, Pflegschaft Und Beistand: Nach Badischen Gesetzen Und Verordnungen*. Freiburg: J. Diernfellner.
Grauer, J. 2012. "Die Privatirrenpflegeanstalt Der Wundärzte Irion Und Koch in Fellbach 1843-1891." PhD diss.,Medizinischen Fakultät der Eberhard Karls Universität zu Tübingen.
Hanke, C. 1981. "Untersuchungen Über Die Charité-Patienten Von 1743 Bis 1752: Eine Studie Zur Funktion Und Soziologie Eines Krankenhauses Im 18. Jahrhundert." PhD diss., Humboldt-Universität Berlin.
Hess, V. 2008. "Disziplin Und Disziplinierung: Die Geburt Der Berliner Psychiatrie Aus Dem Geist Der Verwaltung - Ernst Horn Und Karl Wilhelm Ideler." In *Psychater Und Zeitgeist - Zur Geschichte Der Psychatrie in Berlin*, edited by H. Helmchen, 163–178. Lengerich: Pabst Science Publisher.
Hess, V. 2010a. "Die Alte Charité, Die Moderne Irrenabteilung Und Die Klinik, 1790-1820." In *Die Charité. Geschichte(N) Eines Krankenhauses*, edited by J. Bleker and V. Hess, 41–66. Berlin: Akademie Verlag.
Hess, V. 2010b. "Formalisierte Beobachtung. Die Genese Der Modernen Krankenakte Am Beispiel Der Berliner Und Pariser Medizin (1725-1830)." *Medizinhistorisches Journal* 45: 293–340.
Hess, V. 2011a. "Das Material Einer Guten Geschichte. Register, Reglements Und Formulare." In *Fakta, Und Kein Moralisches Geschwätz. Zu Den Fallgeschichten Im "Magazin Zur Erfahrungsseelenkunde" (1783-1793)*, edited by S. Dickson, S. Goldmann, and C. Wingertszahn, 115–139. Göttingen: Wallstein.
Hess, V. 2011b. "Krankenakten Als Herausforderung Der Krankenhausgeschichtsschreibung." *Historia Hospitalium* 27: 43–52.
Hess, V. 2017. "A Paper Machine of Clinical Research in the Early 20th Century." *Isis* 109 (2018), September issue. under review.
Hess, V., and J. Andrew Mendelsohn. 2013. "Paper Technology Und Wissensgeschichte." *NTM. Zeitschrift Für Geschichte Der Wissenschaften, Technik Und Medizin* 21: 1–10. doi:10.1007/s00048-013-0085-1.
Hess, V., and S. Ledebur. 2012. "Psychiatrie in Der Stadt. Die Poliklinik Als Urbaner Schwellenraum." In *Kulturen Des Wahnsinns. Schwellenräume Einer Urbanen Moderne*, edited by V. Hess and H.-P. Schmiedebach, 19–56. Wien: Böhlau.
Horn, E. 1818. *Oeffentliche Rechenschaft Über Meine Zwölfjährige Dienstzeit Als Zweiter Arzt Des Königlichen Charité-Krankenhauses Zu Berlin*. Berlin: Realschulbuchhandlung.
Horstmann, A., and V. Kopp. 2010. "Archiv - Macht - Wissen: Organisation Und Konstruktion Von Wissen Und Wirklichkeiten in Archiven." In *Archiv - Macht - Wissen. Organisation Und Konstruktion Von Wissen Und Wirklichkeiten in Archiven*, edited by A. Horstmann and V. Kopp, 9–22. Frankfurt am Main: Campus-Verlag.

Howell, J. D. 1995. *Technology in the Hospital: Transforming Patient Care in the Early Twentieth Century*. Baltimore: Johns Hopkins University Press.

Ideler, K. W. 1841. *Biographien Geisteskranker in Ihrer Psychologischen Entwicklung*. Schroeder: Berlin.

Ideler, K. W. 1847. *Der Religiöse Wahnsinn, Erläutert Durch Krankengeschichten: Ein Beitrag Zur Geschichte Der Religiösen Wirren Der Gegenwart*. Halle: Schwetschke und Sohn.

Klöppel, U. 2009. "Das Historische Krankenakten-Archiv Der Nervenklinik Der Charité." *Jahrbuch Für Universitätsgeschichte* 12: 267–270.

Knolz, J. J. 1840. *Darstellung Der Humanitäts- Und Heilanstalten Im Erzherzogthume Oesterreich Unter Der Enns Als Staatsanstalten Und Privatwerke, Nach Ihrer Dermaligen Verfassung Einrichtung*. Wien: Verlag der Mechitaristen Congregation.

Ledebur, S. 2011. "Schreiben Und Beschreiben. Zur Epistemischen Funktion Von Psychiatrischen Krankenakten, Ihrer Archivierung Und Deren Übersetzung in Fallgeschichten." *Berichte Zur Wissenschaftsgeschichte* 34: 102–124.

Ledebur, S. 2013. "Sehend Schreiben, Schreibend Sehen. Vom Aufzeichnen Psychischer Phänomene in Der Psychiatrie." In *Krankheit Schreiben. Aufschreibeverfahren in Medizin Und Literatur*, edited by Y. Wübben and C. Zelle, 82–108. Göttingen: Wallstein.

Litschel, A. 2010. "Offenbaren Und Verheimlichen 'Vor Dem Archiv' - Schriftlichkeit, Sichtbarkeit Und Öffentlichkeit Im Spätmittelalterlichen Lüneburg." In *Archiv - Macht - Wissen. Organisation Und Konstruktion Von Wissen Und Wirklichkeiten in Archiven*, edited by A. Horstmann and V. Kopp, 89–106. Frankfurt am Main: Campus-Verlag.

Mair, I. 1869. *Handbuch Des Ärztlichen Dienstes Bei Den Gerichten Und Verwaltungsbehörden. Würzburg.* Stahel.

Oppert, F. 1883. *Hospitals, Infirmaries and Dispensaries: Their Construction, Interior Arrangement and Management*. London: J. & A. Churchill.

Reiser, S. J. 1984. "Creating Form Out of Mass: The Development of the Clinical Record." In *Transformation and Tradition in the Sciences: Essays in Honor of I. Bernard Cohen*, edited by E. Mendelsohn, 303–316. Cambridge: Cambridge University Press.

Roelcke, V. 2003. "Unterwegs Zur Psychiatrie Als Wissenschaft: Das Projekt Einer "Irrenstatistik" Und Emil Kraeplins Neuformulierung Der Psychiatrischen Klassifikation." In *Psychiatrie Im 19. Jahrhundert. Forschungen Zur Geschichte Von Psychiatrischen Institutionen, Debatten Und Praktiken Im Deutschen Sprachraum*, edited by E. J. Engstrom and V. Roelcke, 169–188. Basel: Schwabe.

Rönne, L. V., and H. Simon. 1846. *Das Medicinal-Wesen des Preussischen Staates eine systematisch geordnete Sammlung aller auf dasselbe Bezug habenden gesetzlichen Bestimmungen, insbesondere der in der Gesetzsammlung für die Preussischen Staaten, in den von Kamptzschen Annalen für die innere Staatsverwaltung und in deren Fortsetzungen durch die Ministerial-Blätter enthaltenen Verordnungen und Reskripte, in ihrem organischen Zusammenhange mit der früheren Gesetzgebung dargestellt*. Vol. 2. Breslau: Georg Philipp Aderholz, 1844–1846.

Röske, T. 1995. *Der Arzt Als Künstler. Ästhetik Und Psychotherapie Bei Hans Prinzhorn (1886-1933)*. Bielefeld: Aisthesis.

Schenk, D. 2008. *Kleine Theorie Des Archivs*. Stuttgart: Franz Steiner Verlag.

Thoms, U. 2005. "Anstaltskost Im Rationalisierungsprozeß: Die Ernährung in Krankenhäusern Und Gefängnissen Im 18. Und 19. Jahrhundert." In *Medizin, Gesellschaft Und Geschichte.Jahrbuch des Instituts für Geschichte der Medizin der Robert Bosch Stiftung, Beiheft 23*. Stuttgart: Steiner.

Vismann, C. 2000. *Akten. Medientechnik Und Recht*. Frankfurt am Main: Fischer Taschenbuch Verlag.

Von Der Heyde, W. G. 1819. *Repertorium Der Polizeigesetze Und Verordnungen in Den Königlich Preussischen Staaten: Ein Handbuch Für Die Mit Der Polizeiverwaltung Beauftragten Beamten, 1819–1822*. Vol. 1. Halle: Gebauer und Sohn.

Weikl, K. 2013. "Das Leben Eines Taugenichts Im Zeitalter Der Nützlichkeit: Eine Fallstudie Um 1800." PhD diss., Humboldt-Universität Berlin.

Weitin, T., and B. Wolf, eds. 2012. *Gewalt Der Archive. Studien Zur Kulturgeschichte Der Wissensspeicherung*. Konstanz: University Press.

Wilhelm, F. 1795. *Allgemeine Gerichtsordnung Für Die Preußischen Staaten: Prozeßordnung*. Vol. II. Berlin: Pauli.

Wübben, Y., and C. Zelle. 2013a. "Einleitung: Aufzeichnen in Pathologie, Psychiatrie Und Literatur." In *Krankheit Schreiben. Aufzeichnungsverfahren in Medizin Und Literatur*, edited by Y. Wübben and C. Zelle, 13–19. Göttingen: Wallstein.

Wübben, Y., and C. Zelle, eds. 2013b. *Krankheit Schreiben. Aufzeichnungsverfahren in Medizin Und Literatur*. Göttingen: Wallstein.

Work, paperwork and the imaginary Tarban Creek Lunatic Asylum, 1846

James Dunk

ABSTRACT
Following the injunction of the field of paperwork to look at paper, rather than through it for information, a close read of the first volumes of the New South Wales State Archives & Records series NRS 5031 discloses a surprising history. The New South Wales Legislative Council appointed a select committee in 1846 to enquire into the management of Tarban Creek Lunatic Asylum – into its work. Finding the work in order, the committee quickly turned to its paperwork failures. The Legislative Council, created in 1843, worked tirelessly through the 1840s to establish control over the penal colony, anticipating self-government. Cited as an example of its humanitarian impulses and thorough committee work, the 1846 committee's report shows parliamentarians embracing bureaucratic forms and medicine's promise to cure madness. The absence of proper records was taken up by the committee and by the colonial press as a weapon; attacking the asylum officers, they attacked also the structure of colonial government and the likeness of irresponsible government in the colonies. NRS 5031, a series of casebooks filled out from 1847, helped to create the 'imaginary' lunatic asylum on paper which was demanded by these politics.

The earliest surviving records of Tarban Creek Lunatic Asylum, built at Gladesville on the Parramatta River outside Sydney in 1838, read like any other medical registers from any number of contemporary institutions. Solid folios with thick leather binding and marbled cover pages disclose handwritten lists of names and pages ruled into columns and rows of text constituting persons as patients. They list significant features and treatments and status reports against dates and a result: either death or discharge, and if the latter, relieved or cured – or a reference to the next folio in which the patient was tracked in time and space by medical professionals, and captured by the records they created.

The precise, pre-printed columns of this case book, imported from London, completed at Tarban Creek, is now held by New South Wales

State Archives & Records in its secure and authoritative (if somewhat outdated) premises in Western Sydney. When summoned by its shelf number, the indexed case book arrives in the reading room as a sober, disinterested artefact of medical practice. The State Archives & Records series NRS 5031 Medical Case Books begins with two inconsistent volumes containing particulars of patients admitted from 1822 onwards into Tarban Creek's predecessors at Castle Hill and Liverpool, and still remaining at Tarban Creek in 1847. The image above is from the second volume, 4/7653, which covers, according to the catalogue, the period 1841-47. However, dated notes of treatment and response for each patient begin only from 1 June 1847. This is because these registers were overhauled as a result of the Select Committee on the Lunatic Asylum, Tarban Creek, appointed by the Legislative Council of New South Wales in May 1846 and reporting in October that year. Its chairman, who was responsible for writing the final report, was the indefatigable Charles Cowper; he was joined by the magistrate Hannibal Macarthur (John Macarthur's nephew), George Allen, the first solicitor trained in New South Wales, philanthropist, and sometime mayor of Sydney, the sharp civil servant and politician Henry Parker, the banker Quaker Joseph Phelps 'Humanity Robinson', Colonial Secretary Edward Deas Thompson, and medical doctor William Bland, who had been surgeon at Castle Hill Lunatic Asylum in 1814-15 while briefly serving his sentence of transportation. Established to examine the work of Tarban Creek Asylum, its management and patient conditions, the Committee quickly became preoccupied with its paperwork.

The Select Committee on the Lunatic Asylum has been cited as an example of the thoroughness of its 'committee work' in the 1840s Legislative Council, for its methodical interrogation of witnesses and setting out recommendations (Mills 2012, 147). The biographer of Charles Cowper, chairman, finds that the Select Committee led to 'great (and expensive) improvements in the organization of that Australian Bedlam', Tarban Creek, and cites it as evidence of Cowper's 'humanitarian purposes' (Powell 1977, 38). In this article I argue instead that it demonstrates the aggressive capability of this committee work, which was a species of paperwork. The work of the asylum was found to be more or less in order (Ireland 1964), but the paperwork, linked as it was with professionalising medicine and bureaucratic modernity, was taken up by the committee and by several newspapers as a weapon. It was used to attack the officers of the asylum but it was also wielded against the officers of the colonial government, and the likeness of irresponsible government – government essentially by the unelected clerks of the Colonial Office, in a striking example of the 'overgrown power' for which the term bureaucracy was coined (see the introduction to this issue). By contrast, the members of the Select Committee on the Lunatic Asylum were drawn from a Legislative Council which had been created in 1843 – after decades of colonial campaigning. I argue that they used the forms of bureaucracy, and the claims of medicine, to force institutional change at the asylum. They did so by subtly superimposing an abstraction upon the physical asylum, along the lines of that envisioned by Alexis de Tocqueville – the rational superstructure which bureaucracy, as a system of governance, presumed upon (see Kafka 2012, 34). The Council was a stomping ground for colonial leaders, and Committees provided the forum for searching inquiry into a wide range of the facets of government. The Select Committee on the Lunatic Asylum provided a superb vehicle not only to demonstrate the Councillors' capacity to manage institutions – to govern – but to attack the fundamental character of colonial government as irresponsible and opaque. This was all by reference to a perfectly rational, imaginary institution for the care of the colony's insane.

This history is inscribed in the paperwork of Tarban Creek. Case book 4/7653 may be contrasted with another book which is not held by the government archive, or by any known repository. When Thomas Lee arrived at Tarban Creek in 1840 there was a single register of admissions. He acted to supplement this so he could keep track of the medicines he prescribed to patients, recording the details of each instance on loose leaves of paper and then sewing them together. He created, by his careful labour, a prescription book. This book cannot be viewed, but if we look closely at the case book, which can – if we look at this paperwork rather than through it, as Kafka (2009) suggests – we can trace the history of both books. The burgeoning field of paperwork reframes the putting of pen to paper within the ever-more intricate webs of modern bureaucracy not as a neutral transfer of information but as constitutive of that information. Paperwork, studied closely, becomes a richly historical, material phenomenon, not least because, as Sally Swartz suggests in this issue, such writing, or recording, is a complex engagement, an entanglement of desires, anxieties, and professional encoding. Writing mediates between the work of individuals at an institution like Tarban Creek and remote contemporaries like magistrates and other official visitors, higher medical officers, and government agents, but if it is preserved, its materiality – its capture of knowledge – draws countless others into this work, in perpetuity. The accelerating encroachment of bureaucratic process from the late eighteenth century across states and empires has meant that this paperwork is stamped with the lifeless rigidity of registers and forms everywhere, with the dull ringing of modernity. Drawing close to such a series of registers, however, allows us to see them not only as sources for other histories but as objects with their own histories. In many cases it is difficult to break through the rigid formality of bureaucracy, but the brazen energy of the Select Committees of the Legislative Council of New South Wales in the 1840s opens to door for this.

Mills (2012) suggests that the frequent use of Select Committees in the New South Wales Legislative Council, from 1843 until the advent of self government in 1855, drew from the nineteenth-century 'revolution in government' identified by MacDonagh (1958) and Parris (1960). The select committee allowed governments to broaden their vision, obtain intimate knowledge of the ordinary experience of sections of society with which they, as elites, were unfamiliar. Mills argues that in New South Wales in the years up to 1855, the Select Committee served a local function of drawing up members of the colonial community into the lawmaking process. It functioned as 'a lawmaking institution' and became, 'almost immediately ... a dominant force in the colonial legislative process' (Mills 2012, 154). Historical forces, like physical forces, are applied and produce counter-actions; Mills also shows that the power of the Select Committee could be manipulated by the councillors, according to their charisma and industry. Select Committees served a range of individual purposes, both political and personal. William Wentworth and Robert Lowe, Mills shows, consistently used the interrogation of evidence by committee and the report-writing process to serve their own political ends (143).

*

In March 1846, the Visiting Magistrate to Tarban Creek, Joseph Long Innes, attacked the management's practice of not holding coronial inquests upon the unexpected deaths of patients. In May there were further, sharper accusations of a great many faults in the design and management of the asylum (Bostock 1968, 92–93). The Select Committee on Tarban Creek Lunatic Asylums was appointed on 26 May 1846 to investigate, but, after interviewing Innes and the Deputy Inspector of Hospitals, William Dawson, it fell quiet.[1] It was reappointed on 10 September, conducted a further 10 interviews, and lay its

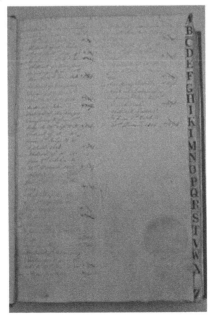

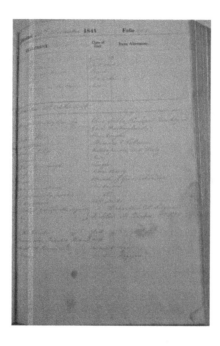

findings upon the council table in October, 1846. This five-page report and the 52 pages of minutes and appendices chart the committee's turn from the work at the asylum, and the question of abuse, to its paperwork and to an abstract idea of a repressive institution.[2] Dawson had been asked his opinion of the treatment at Tarban Creek. 'I have scarcely the means of judging,' he replied; 'the treatment is not recorded in any way'. At first the Committee did not notice, and moved on to how the asylum compared with similar establishments in England. 'I have no means of judging,' reiterated Dawson, 'as there is no record kept of cases; there is no written statement of the appearance of a patient at the time of his admission into the Asylum, or of the progress of the disease, or the treatment'. Tarban Creek could not be compared with any institution because it had no paperwork. The Committee took note. 'You consider it to be absolutely necessary that there should be a record kept, such as you have described, either by the Superintendent of the institution or by a medical man?' 'I do', Dawson replied,

> a register detailing symptoms and appearance at admission, the progress of the disease, the treatment, physical and moral, with a particular note about the use of restraint and the reasons for its being used.[3]

It would need to be kept by a medical man, since 'none other could keep it correctly'.

This represented a sidestep for Tarban Creek. The asylum, opened in 1838, was part of the vision of Richard Bourke, Governor of New South Wales from 1831 until 1837 and a pronounced Whig. He was at first reluctant to associate himself with the penal colony, but his concerns were assuaged by Robert W. Hay, undersecretary in the Colonial Office: a bureaucrat with an impressive patronage network (Laidlaw 2005). The Australian colonies were 'the most thriving Colonies of the present day', Hay wrote, 'every day increasing in importance.'[4] When he left for the colony, Bourke was under the impression that the flow of convicts would soon end (King 1971, 134), but it did not, and, indeed, increased during his administration. Some 30,000 convicts arrived in the colony in the 1830s, more than a third of the total the colony received (Robson 1965, 168). In the 1830s, with Bourke as governor, New South Wales was at its most divided. It was still a receptacle for British criminals but it was also a flourishing colonial society with a free population growing both in number and in sense of entitlement (King 1971, 196–98). Large profits were made in wool and whaling, and these fed into a land revenue windfall (Ford and Roberts 2013). 'This Colony is like a healthy Child outgrowing its Clothes,' wrote Bourke in 1836.[5] The colonists wanted to use the windfall to build local infrastructure – not for the convict department, which had a limited tenure in the colony, but for the coming free society. Bourke agreed, and planned a suite of national schools, new gaols, courthouses, roads and bridges, a new government house, and a circular quay at Sydney Cove. Even the institutions of justice were not for convicts; the new Sydney gaol was to be of a 'permanent character', servicing the colony 'long after the mother country shall have ceased to send out Convicts'. The asylum was much the same. The old one had been a rented building, funded from the military chest – the crown monies held in the Colony, recalling its original organisation. The new 'permanent Building' should be built at the expense of the Colony' since, as Bourke would later write, it was 'adapted to outlive the arrangements that now throw so large a proportion of the Expences of the Colony upon the Mother Country.'[6]

Bourke applied to the Secretary of State for the Colonies to appoint a keeper and matron in England, ideally a married couple, because 'it will not be possible to obtain in the Colony Persons well qualified for its superintendence'.[7] It was later claimed that each of Tarban Creek's two predecessors had fallen into 'a deplorable state' because of the lack of experienced, professional staff.[8] Joseph Digby was appointed from a London asylum and came with a reference from Dr Sutherland, physician at St Luke's Hospital.[9] In the interim, Bourke was replaced by George Gipps, and Digby found when he arrived, to his chagrin, that the new governor would not pay the half salary he had been promised from the time of his departure, that he and his wife were supposed to take up residence at the half-finished asylum 'to speed progress', and that Gipps strongly resisted fitting out the asylum as he wanted it (Bostock 1968, 40–41). The official disinterest in exteriors and funds was matched by a bureaucratic disinterest. Neither Digby nor his wife Susannah, matron, received any precise information about their responsibilities – a trough in the regular oscillation of official interest in the colony's asylums (see Dunk 2017). Similarly, a board of official visitors was constituted to visit the asylum regularly and report any concerns to the governor, but beyond this no details of the relative responsibilities of superintendent and visitors were provided.

The asylum was built from sandstone at Bedlam Point, on Parramatta River, in present-day Gladesville. With its beautiful, tranquil outlook over the water, it hinted at ideas of the therapeutic outlook (see Hickman 2009). For all this, and Bourke's liberality, only eight years later the Select Committee found the asylum physically wanting. There was not enough room, little facility for classifying and separating patients and insufficient access to water. The real cause for alarm, however, lay within. 'Great changes must be made in the whole establishment', the committee declared: Digby had repudiated the authority structures put in place over him, including its visiting magistrates and other formal visitors. This was seen not only as a sign of his personal idiosyncrasies, but as revealing the incorrect arrangement of knowledge and power at Tarban Creek. Their chief recommendation was that a medical superintendent should be placed over Digby, who had, by some mishap, been installed over his proper situation as chief steward or head keeper.

No abuse had been discovered during the proceedings. Apart from the concerns about the scale and quality of the buildings, with which the asylum staff were only too eager to agree and had already complained of to the government, the crucial failing at Tarban Creek was in its paperwork. 'The circumstance which most excited the surprise of the Committee', ran the report under the 'superintendent' header, 'and for which no sufficient reason was assigned, was the omission on the part of the officers to keep any books or registers, such as ought to be kept in a public establishment'.[10]

The want of paperwork, the author of the report made a point of noting, 'was felt very sensibly by your Committee'. There is an alarmism in the way paperwork was targeted by the committee which surprised the asylum officers and would later contribute to suspicions about the conduct of the inquiry. This was all the more puzzling because there was paperwork done at the asylum. Several books were handed to the Committee during the course of the enquiry, noted by italics which read like simple, prosaic, stage directions. They were touched and prodded; pages were turned. Joseph Digby took responsibility for an admission register, which had been procured by a former visiting magistrate, which included details about the patient's identity and condition at the time he or she was admitted. Digby also kept a private diary noting medical and moral treatment and the use of physical restraint. Thomas Lee, the resident medical officer, kept a case book, though without much detail, as well as his sewed prescription book. The Committee, taking up Dawson's concern, found these books so inadequate they might be ignored entirely. The Report called for a full suite of 'registers and books for public records': a register of patients; medical register; case book; and visitor's book. 'The absence of any such records in the Lunatic Asylum in this Colony', the Committee reiterated here, was 'so obvious an irregularity' that they hoped their alarm would be enough to 'induce the Government at once to require the Superintendent and Medical officer to commence a system of books and records as herein described.'[11]

The books that were kept by Digby and Lee were not public documents, which meant that authority could not be exercised remotely, by paperwork – that bureaucracy was impossible. This was a problem for Dawson, Inspector General of Hospitals, who expected to be able to evaluate the work of the asylum from his desk in Macquarie Street. This would accord with the broader history of bureaucracy, which is implemented from above to create systems which could be checked and results which could be measured. The alarm and surprise, however, suggest that this brief bureaucratic history is inflected differently in several ways. Firstly, public accountability had a special significance in a colony concerned by the executive power of a government established for convict discipline and still shaped by it. Here, new technologies and practices of record-keeping were demanded by representatives of the Legislative Council, a new, hard-won body which helped the colonists influence and check the governors installed over them. The Committee's accusation that Digby enjoyed irresponsible power and obstructed those who were meant to be overseeing the asylum – partly by failing to keep public books – suggests that the enquiry was in part a protest against this executive power.

These genuine concerns for 'regular', public paperwork, however, were transfigured into a private, underhand attack on the current officers of the asylum. The doctor's failure to keep a record of his treatment of the asylum's patients was construed as a fundamental failure in the practice of medicine and even of his 'imbecility' – which, since he was supposed to be caring for patients afflicted by this condition, was a clever rhetorical move. Digby's supposed repudiation of authorities over him was used to portray him as an irresponsible and unsuitable head of a public institution, appointed arbitrarily from London rather than for any real qualification. That is, it was a professional conspiracy of a colonial medical fraternity. It has been written of as a 'medical coup', or 'class coup' (Murray 1985) in which medical professionals triumphed over the less articulate and less elite (see also Curry 1989). But if a 'medical model' was instituted it was not, as Murray writes, 'one of cure over one of detainment' (Murray 1985, 35) – there is no evidence for this – but one suffused with bureaucratic concerns and forms. It was perhaps only in such a place as New South Wales that bureaucracy could take on such qualities; that paperwork could be a weapon in this way. The colony's paperwork was distinctive, not only in this insidious sense but also in an aspirational sense. Paperwork might underwrite colonial dreaming.

'Have you any book in the shape of a medical register?' William Bland asked Thomas Lee, the medical officer of Tarban Creek Lunatic Asylum.[12] The question seems to hold a hint of contempt, as well as consternation. The Select Committee appointed to investigate conditions at the asylum had fixed upon its paperwork. 'This is the book to which I have referred', answered Lee. 'It is called the case book'. The printed minutes which were presented to parliament with the report, and from which the bulk of these discussions about paper are derived, record the handling of paper itself during the progress of the enquiry. '[*The witness handed in the case book.*]'[13] With the case book, Lee proffered a name, and a definite article, as if the vocabulary was still in prototype. Lee's evidence suggests the unfamiliar quality of paperwork at Tarban Creek. The 'case book' – a singular, material book, rather than an iteration, or abstraction, or metaphor – had been at the asylum for longer than Lee. He described the history of 'the book' with some intimacy:

> I have the book here; it was partly written by Dr McLean, or some person for him. He was ill for some time before his death, and was assisted by a person, now a merchant in this City, who was in some branch of the profession, and some of the writing is in his hand, as I have been informed.[14]

The case book changed hands and the committee members flicked through it. Were any other records kept, they asked, and Lee told of a serendipity:

> It was only lately that I discovered this book, which was then blank, lying at the bottom of a box in the Asylum; I previously kept an account of the prescriptions on loose paper, which I afterwards sewed together. [*The witness handed in the prescription book.*]

This physical work with paper was a painstaking, delicate process, and suggests that, contrary to the tenor of the interrogation, Thomas Lee did have some regard for records. Without instruction or precedent, Lee had kept a written record of the medicines given to the patients, even before he had found McLean's presumably empty prescription book stored away. That is, Lee had a paperwork culture, even if later interrogation would show its limitations.

> Is that a complete record, as to the medical treatment of the patients? You have merely followed in the track of your predecessor?
>
> Pretty much so.

The book existed materially, but the details it was intended to record were not fully entered. Cowper asked whether the case book had been 'a complete record' of medical treatment; Lee replied 'No, it is a very imperfect one, and the record I have kept is just the same as the former one.'[15]

'Will you look through some of the pages of the medical register', the Chairman asked visiting magistrate Captain Joseph Long Innes, 'and state to the Committee your opinion as to the mode in which it has been kept.' Here, again, the paperwork was the subject, and the book changed hands. '[*The Chairman handed the book to the witness who examined it.*] Is there anything there which renders the book worthy of the name of a record?' Innes, having assessed the case book, concluded:

> This is not a medical register at all. If I had not been a military man, I might have paused before I gave my reply, but having been ten years an adjutant, I have had abundant opportunities of seeing medical registers, and I have no hesitation in saying this is not a register at all; if it is meant to serve as a medical register it is very deficient.

At one level this was unsurprising. Anderson (2013) has shown that in the United States, medical professionals learned to keep careful records from the military, in which the identification of deserters was of paramount importance. Military medicine developed precise techniques of identification and registration, and civilian medicine followed in its train. A parallel story is told about the Charité Hospital, Berlin where doctors learned record-keeping at the behest of the hospital kitchen. Precise, complete records were developed not in order to advance medicine, but in order to know how many patients had to be fed from day to day so as to prevent wastage (Hess, this issue; Hess and Ledebur 2011). This has become a common-enough story: records were developed, at least in part, to reduce costs by careful accounting.

Perhaps there was a range in focus and emphasis between the developing army bureaucracies. Thomas Lee's predecessor was Daniel McLean, an aging army surgeon who was asked by Bourke's successor, George Gipps, to take charge of the 'medical department' at Tarban Creek soon after he arrived in the colony in November 1838. The asylum had opened several months prior. McLean died in August 1840, and his obituary in the *Sydney Herald* claimed that his appointment was made 'with a view to organise its operations, then commenced on a magnificent scale'. Under McLean and Digby, declared the elegist, 'that institution has been made as complete as any similar institution in England'.[16] (Indeed, according to John Blaxland, too complete. He argued that, whatever Bourke said about the permanent needs of the colony, part of the cost should have been borne by England, whose '*aged infirm* convicts' now filled the hospitals, gaols and new asylum.[17]) Whether these claims were embellished or whether the completeness was judged by other means, McLean's medical records were 'very imperfect'. Though Lee considered McLean's record-keeping imperfect, he continued in the same manner, because his priority was patient treatment. Here was a 'case book', with entries made by at least three, and perhaps four people; a book which William Dawson and the Committee wished was a medical register.

The other key record was the admission register. It, by comparison, approached perfection. Henry Hothersall Browne, who had been the first visiting magistrate appointed to Tarban Creek under the *Dangerous Lunatics Act* 1843 and had served for six months in 1844 before being promoted to the position of commissioner of the court of requests, told how he was responsible for this register. He had found no records of the patients' cases. He told the committee that he had 'insisted upon the Superintendent keeping a register of the patients admitted – the nature of their diseases when admitted – the treatment received – and also whether a patient had improved, or the contrary'. 'Do you mean to say', the Committee pressed, 'that until you required it there was not even this journal kept?' Browne admitted there was a brief nominal register of patients admitted and discharged – details were not asked. 'Then if the Superintendent had carried out that arrangement', asked Hannibal Macarthur, 'there ought now to be a detailed history of every patient?' 'Yes, I think so', Browne replied, 'a very perfect one; I had a great deal of trouble in the matter at first.' This difficulty was that there had been no book; Browne gave them one, and by the time he left the asylum it was two-thirds complete.[18]

By 1846 there was some form of paperwork at Tarban Creek: a 'very imperfect' case book which rarely detailed patient treatment, a prescription book and a nearly perfect admission register creating an institutional identity for two-thirds of the patients. Nevertheless these records were judged urgently inadequate, failing in three key ways. The first was in its perfection, or completeness, addressed above: the ideal created by the printed books was of complete recording. It failed, secondly, to be sufficiently 'public'; and failed as a medical knowledge system – to transform patients into cases at the point of admission.

Digby kept entries about the patients in his diary, which he considered 'a private book', or 'note book'.[19] It was not official, presumably had no printed pro forma, and was not presented to the Select Committee. Nor has it survived in the asylum's formal archive. Digby kept the private diary for his own reference, and he used it to record patient treatment, including physical restraint.

> Do you make any entry of the circumstance when a patient it put under restraint?
>
> In my note book only – I keep no registry; indeed it is only within the last two or three years that it has been done in England.
>
> But you are aware that it is now done in England?
>
> Yes; it is easily done. I generally make a note of it, but do not keep a registry.[20]

Now, was there a substantive or only a semantic difference between the private and public record? Digby considered his diary or note book 'a private book, although I should not have any objections to its being seen'.[21] Captain Innes' statement shows that it was not the access itself, but its formulation that was objectionable. 'My authority is repudiated by Mr Digby', he said. 'He says I have no right to interfere; and although he gives me every information in this power, he does so out of courtesy, protesting against any right to interfere, or to do anything beyond going in, walking round, and going out again'.[22] Although this irked Innes, only one of the visitors seems to have been interested in examining the asylum's records – George Turner, an Anglican minister at Ryde.[23] Thomas Lee thought that the visitors 'do not consider it to be their duty to interfere either in the moral or medical management; they never look into the books'.[24] That is, for the asylum's officers and visitors, the work of the asylum was oral, and it was Dawson who identified an urgent need for fuller written records.

'But you do not consider it part of your public duty', the Committee pressed Digby, 'to keep such a register or diary as any visitor could have access to?'[25] Reverend Turner, the most frequent visitor to the asylum and the only one to defend its officers in his interview, wanted public books. Cowper asked 'Did you not find [the records] very defective?' He did; there was no 'public diary', 'only an entrance and discharge book with such particulars as could be obtained upon admission of a patient'. Hannibal Macarthur interjected, 'No History of the case?' 'No current history in the public record', Turner replied. He took visitation seriously, and saw the 'public record' as an important means of fulfilling his duty.[26] Encouraged by William Bland, Turner subscribed to the dream of a perfect paper regime: full case records, with disease histories, treatment notes, especially of physical restraint and confinement, and 'also the food, clothing, and every other matter connected with the health and comfort of the patient?' 'Yes', Turner agreed, 'I think you could not have too full a record of the daily transactions of the establishment'.[27]

Innes had requested to come before the Committee again to refute 'cruel innuendoes' published in the *Sydney Morning Herald* on 4 September.[28] In his first he had already spoken against the over-use of restraint, in his second, he gave some modest statistics of the use of restraint. The Committee was sceptical.

> What means have you of ascertaining what patients are or are not under restraint?
> Personal inspection.
> There is no record kept?
> None.
> Then how do you know that, during the intervals between your visits, many of the patients were not put under restraint by the keepers themselves?
> That is possible.
> Do they know the day when you are likely to visit?
> No, it is very irregular.

> If they saw you coming, might they not take the restraint off?
> I think that is hardly likely.[29]

The Committee demonstrated a profound faith in the register. There were regulations in place, which Digby had laid down and had printed and hung in the keepers' rooms. By these regulations, keepers were required to refer to the superintendent if physical restraint appeared necessary, and as Digby mentioned, this was only bypassed if urgency was paramount, and then the incident was to be immediately reported. Why, it might be wondered, would a written register be any more reliable than a verbal conference between keepers and superintendent, together with a private note in the superintendent's diary? Digby was aware that in English asylums, a register of physical restraint was now kept – a product of the non-restraint movement that had swept English asylums in the 1830s (Frank 1967; Colaizzi 2005; Bynum and Bynum 2016). The difference between diary and register for Digby, here, was negligible: it was easily done to keep a register.

The *Act for Regulating Private Madhouses* 1774 responded to reports of rampant abuse in private madhouses in England. It stipulated that madhouses had to be licensed and proprietors had to keep patient registers with certificated for legal confinement, and open themselves to inspection by magistrates in the provinces and physicians in London (Porter 1987). 40 years later, however, a parliamentary enquiry found that visits were perfunctory; visitors frequently simply checked the patient population against the number in the register. Roy Porter suggests that the 1774 Act served 'perhaps to license the abuses of the status quo, rather than eradicate them' (Porter 1987, 152–53).

Work and paperwork

It was not only an issue of transparency and efficient oversight. For William Dawson, the avatar of modern, military medicine and its notary practices, Tarban Creek did not properly exist until it was transfigured by paperwork into the public record. He rejected the 'Statement of Table' (a telling imprecision) which Digby had compiled of the results obtained during his tenure.

> As the statements contained in this paper are unsupported by anything except the private memoranda of Mr. Digby to which I have never had access, I cannot express an opinion [...] I have no reason to suppose that the numbers have been given incorrectly, but I merely say that there is no public document kept in the Asylum to support the statement.[30]

The actual work at Tarban Creek was literally immaterial, since its paperwork was private and imperfect.

The Committee quickly established that Joseph Digby and Thomas Lee could not be accused of insubordination, since they had received scant instructions as to the nature of their roles and what was expected of them, and none at all before they had requested them.[31] Tarban Creek came under the remit not of the medical department, but the central government, and all it required were an annual return of convicts to the Commissariat, and yearly returns of free paupers in the asylum as well as quarterly returns of patients received into the asylum to the Colonial Secretary.[32] Superintendents had been completing these returns in a similar fashion since the 1810s. These instructions reflect the principal concern – to keep accurate accounts so as to distribute the cost between colonial and home funds. Nor did the visitors show real interest in the asylum's books. The Committee, after a comprehensive interrogation on Lee's (and McLean's) record-keeping, finally clarified that, 'since you have been appointed, no intimation has been made to you, that you have failed in your duty, either as regards the keeping of books, or in other respects?' Lee replied simply, and surely curtly, 'No'.[33]

Joseph Digby and Thomas Lee were surprised at the strength of the committee members' sensibilities. After the enquiry, others were also taken aback: legislative councillors in debate, media commentators, one of the witnesses, and even one of the committee members were perplexed by the line of questioning and the recommendations handed down. Why did the Committee appear to be scandalised by poor paperwork in an institution, and a colony, when neither governor nor visitors had demanded it? Why, when it appeared that different recording practices were common in England and Ireland, was the record-keeping at Tarban Creek such a profound professional and moral failure? Where did this disjuncture come from?

Other paperwork was different, and consuming. When Digby was asked whether he kept a daily patient register, he replied that he had never been required to, 'and as we have a great deal of writing to do in the office I have never proposed it'.[34] Hannibal Macarthur, who had plenty of experience of paperwork as a former magistrate and prominent businessman, made an important connection at this juncture: time meant staff (see Nairn 1967). Staffing had been a vexed issue in Australian asylums for decades (Neil 1992; Bostock 1968; see Monk 2008, 2009). At the time of the enquiry there were seven free keepers and a free clerk, paid decent wages, and five convict keepers paid a pittance.[35] Digby saw this as inadequate, and Macarthur asked whether he would need another clerk if he had to keep a full register. Digby concurred, but said that he normally '[made] a clerk of one of the patients [...] most of the returns laid before the Committee' had been made out by patients under the clerk's instructions. The clerk himself was a ex-convict named Henry Flemming (Craze 1993, 406–407). To an enquiry so concerned with precise and complete records, this may have been disconcerting. No comment was made.

For Thomas Lee, the issue was more ideologically charged. Medical record-keeping was a paperwork devil which needed to be held at bay, something approaching Kafka's (2012) 'demon of writing'. The ideal paperwork conjured by Bland and Turner threatened to consume not only he, the medical man, but his notion of the practice of medicine. Asked whether the case book he inherited from his predecessor was a complete record, he replied, 'No, it is a very imperfect one, and the record I have kept is just the same as the former one'. Cowper, having flicked through the book, found it wanting. 'How is it that in the column headed "Treatment", the treatment of diseases is very rarely put down?' he asked. McLean had not filled it out, Lee replied, 'and really I have not the time to do it'. He recorded details only if the case was 'of an interesting kind in a medical point of view' – or if a private patient's friends demanded it. Cowper was unimpressed, and his displeasure shows the authority afforded to the pro forma. 'Then although this book has a form printed expressly to be filled with certain information', Cowper pressed, 'that information is in very few instances supplied?' 'Just so', replied Lee. ('JUST SO', capitalised a reporter in a long and antagonistic review.)[36] 'How do you explain that to the Committee?' demanded Cowper. 'I have not the time to take down the cases so particularly', Lee said, 'nor have the cases been more particularly stated by my predecessor'.

Lee really was time poor. 'The Committee will please to bear in mind', (he appears to have become polite when he was angry), 'that I have acted in the fourfold capacity of physician, surgeon, apothecary, and a dispenser in that establishment. I have had no assistant, not even a wardsman, and have frequently been obliged to borrow one of the keepers to turn a patient in bed, and that the average number of patients, under my care, has been double the average number of those under the care of my predecessor'. On 1 September 1846 there were 74 males and 61 females in the asylum.[37] Lee had gone so far as searching the annual reports of English and Irish asylums in recent years and, by his estimation, he could find no single officer in the United Kingdoms who had been so burdened by his medical duties.[38]

This was brushed aside as superfluous detail as the Committee returned to his dismal records. 'You admit that although you have a register book', concluded the Chairman, 'the information supplied in that register is so scanty, as to be almost useless?' Cowper expected the doctor to meet the demands of the paper in his hands. Lying beneath this expectation was the assumption that the case book evoked some higher regime of medical knowledge. The case book was printed in England and its columns reflected the cumulative gravity of that established, normative medical culture. Why else would it matter if there was an empty column? 'Not altogether useless', Lee protested, 'but it is very scanty, certainly'.[39]

In Lee's view, the recording of symptoms and treatments detracted from a doctor's capacity to observe his patients. Bludgeoned with discourteous questions about his attention to patient diets, he replied,

I may remark that in going round every day, I know every man's case on seeing him, not only as to what has been done for him, but as to the state of his mind and health. I examine every patient every day, and have never been absent from the Asylum but one day, and then, in consequence of an accident.[40]

This close observation was the core of Lee's practice, and paper had nothing to do with it, except to impinge upon it. 'A physician who has been in the habit of attending a patient for some time', he suggested, 'will at once see, upon visiting him, what has been done, and what is required; I did not therefore think it necessary to keep such a record for my own guidance, and was not required to do it by others'.[41] Paperwork should serve the needs of the doctor, and since he found it unnecessary, and his superiors had not instructed him to keep such records, he had not. Nor had he kept them in his long medical career: 'I have been attendant physician to the Royal College of Maynooth, during nineteen years, and to the Hospital and Infirmary, Jervis-street, Dublin, during eleven years', and from both had received 'a *special* vote of thanks'. At neither Maynooth nor Jervis-street had he been required to keep 'a detailed account of the cases which had come under my care'.[42]

Perhaps there was something specific at stake here. In Digby's examination there had been a succession of questions about when Thomas Lee, the medical officer, first saw patients who were admitted. After the question had been asked, and the answer given five times already, William Bland asked Joseph Digby once more, 'It is not imperative upon the medical man to see the patient upon his first admission?' 'No', answered Digby, 'we have nothing binding it upon us; it is left to our own discretion'.[43] At the core of this bureaucratic bullying there seems to have been a real consternation here. For Dawson the demands of paperwork began, precisely, at the point of admission, with a case history and assessment of the patient's 'appearance'. It was this writing that transformed a person into a patient, and it was against this written record that progress was judged – both the individual progress of the patient towards health and the progress of the officers and the institution itself, towards the fulfilment of its institutional purpose. Medical cases are built around narrative (Montgomery 2006).

Weaponising paperwork

'The reverend gentleman, instead of the polished weapons so skilfully wielded by the reviewer, avails himself of missiles of the coarsest and most barbarous kind'.[44] In the struggle for Tarban Creek Lunatic Asylum, words were understood, rightly, to be weapons as this response to Turner shows. More than specific, biting words printed and circulated, however, the paperwork at the asylum became a more powerful and far more diffuse means of assault. Paperwork was, therefore, not only a site of contest but also a means of struggle, because the contest was staged. Thomas Lee was its chief victim. However sophisticated was the critique of the sovereignty of medical knowledge, and its inscription, at Tarban Creek, and whatever people thought in Dublin, Lee's paperwork failure was construed as a fundamental failure to practice medicine. There is an interesting contradiction in the way Cowper, who with the other committee members was so concerned with the written record at the Asylum, disregarded Lee's written references: 'the Attorney-General had talked of his high testimonials', Cowper thundered in Legislative Council debate,

> but he [Cowper] could assure the learned gentleman that the certificate of the whole Bench of Catholic Bishops and of the Pope of Rome himself, would not prevent him from forming his own opinion in this matter – whether he had been an efficient man or not some fifty years ago was not the question; he contended he was not so now.[45]

Thomas Lee bore the brunt of the attacks. Inexplicably, Joseph Innes was asked to assess the doctor's capacity. 'Will you state whether you think there is such a weight of medical duties upon [Dr Lee], as to prevent his keeping a proper record of the cases?' 'I should say certainly not', Innes replied. 'There is nothing to prevent an active medical man from keeping such a record; indeed I should think he would wish to do so, for his own satisfaction for the purposes of science, setting public duty out of the question'.[46] It was a damning assessment. In its formal report, the Committee specified that a 'professional man of ability, and experience in the treatment of insane persons' must be installed as head of the institution.[47] Diplomatically, there was no direct statement of Lee's capacities, but in the minutes, an exchange canvasses the subject in disparaging terms: 'What do you think of the present doctor', George Allen asked Henry Browne, ' – do you think he is fit to take charge of the Asylum?' 'I feel delicacy in giving my opinion; he is a very old man'.[48] Lee was 62 or 63 at the time of the enquiry.[49] His age quickly became shorthand for ineptitude. Where the Committee had been circumspect, the anonymous reviewer in the *Australian* briefly quoted above (in capitals) wrote of 'the ignorance and imbecility of the officers', clearly thinking of Lee.[50]

In May 1847, Cowper moved in Council that the Committee's report be sent to the new Governor, Charles FitzRoy, urging him to implement its recommendations. This occasioned a vigorous debate of the merits of the enquiry. The fiery barrister Robert Lowe stood and said that he had promised to look into the 'censure thrown upon' Lee in the report, 'though he did not see how it could possibly be explained. If Dr. Lee was not a proper person, the Committee should have said so, and should have taken evidence to prove it'. The report had emphasised the need for *a duly qualified person*; their italics. 'It was natural', Lowe suggested, for Lee to take this to mean he was not duly qualified. Lowe objected to the 'language of insinuation or innuendo' in the report; to 'a report, implying by a side wind, what it could not on evidence affirm directly'. (To side wind is to blow, or slither, crosswise.) Charles Cowper met the criticisms bluntly. He certainly did not think Lee was qualified for the situation he held – let alone that of medical superintendent! – but the Colonial Secretary had indicated that to put it like this in the Report might compromise the separation of powers. But since the entire Committee judged Lee 'unfitted', he had made the insinuation deliberately. Cowper quoted long sections of Lee's evidence and suggested that 'a man who had displayed so great an amount of imbecility was not qualified'.[51] The roots of Lee's failure lay in his not keeping adequate records, which was transformed from a problem of time to a problem of stamina, that is age. But in his failure to admit the error, and in maintaining that he was qualified and capable, age became the more serious problem of 'imbecility', so that Lee was lambasted as incapacitated by a condition afflicting many of those he was failing to treat. The motion was successful, the recommendations passed to FitzRoy, and Lee was eventually dismissed.[52] He sailed for London in February 1848.[53]

The assault on Lee, and to a lesser extent on Digby, was almost too effective. Turner, writing in the *Herald* after the furore in the Legislative Council, claimed that it was, in fact, disingenuous.

> There has been an object floating before the eyes of some persons connected with the cause of the enquiry, separate from the mere improvement of the state and condition of the Asylum. Six somewhat *recherchées* but visionary and theoretical productions, evidently from the pen of a medical man, appeared in the *Morning Herald* some few months ago; and it is now made a paramount condition of future reformation that a duly qualified medical man should be placed at the head of the institution. On this point I will simply ask a question. Is it true that the writer of those papers has already sought his Excellency's patronage for the appointment?[54]

Three days after Charles Cowper had moved that the Legislative Council appoint a select committee to enquire into Tarban Creek, a lettrist called *Iatros* (doctor, in Greek) wrote a lengthy exhortation on the 'lunacy bill' Gipps had introduced for the *Sydney Morning Herald*.[55] In the next four months, nine long letters – nearly 16,000 words in all – followed the first in the pages of the *Herald*. They called for the overhaul of Tarban Creek asylum on the glorious, European principles of total non-restraint and for it to be placed under a medical superintendent.[56] *Iatros'* tactics were an esoteric literary style and exhaustive repetition.

Several parties had suggested that Lee was too old and tired to make note of patient treatments so that case histories could be kept. The writer of the *Iatros* letters was so demonstrably on top of his workload that had the time to stay up late compiling anti-Catholic histories of insanity and constructing aphorisms.[57] William Dawson's description of an ideal medical superintendent, dispensing physical restraint with *gravitas*, was clearly not meant to describe Lee. It does seem to describe *Iatros*. 'He should not be a common medical man', effused Dawson; 'he should be a good physician, something of a scholar, a man of the world, and possessing considerable conversational power and tact, so as to be able to lead the minds of the patients from their diseased trains of thought to more healthy ones'.[58]

After only two interviews on 1 June, the Select Committee fell silent, though it was supposed to report after a month. *Iatros*, meanwhile, scribbled furiously and the *Herald*, on 9 June, printed an editorial in his train.[59] Others, like the reviewer, joined the fray. It also seems suspicious that between the first and second round of Select Committee interviews, a recently discharged patient issued a complaint which fed neatly into the gathering critique. The patient, known as Mrs. P—, had given birth to a child whilst en route to New South Wales, with no one to attend her. She developed puerperal insanity and was admitted to the asylum on arrival. During her several months there, she was frequently violent, attacking anyone who entered her room: in one instance, 'immediately the door was opened, she struck the female keeper in the face, and threw her back against the wall'.[60] She sometimes injured herself in these paroxysms, at one point wounding her left arm and damaging the brachial nerve and causing paralysis of the hand.[61] Because of this, she was placed under physical restraint, generally a leather belt with handcuffs at the waist. Her statement alleged abuse, but the Committee was unable to corroborate this, with both officers and official visitors denying ill-treatment.

If it was, as it seems to have been, a medical conspiracy, it was effective. Francis Campbell, author of the *Iatros* letters, was appointed medical superintendent of Tarban Creek in December 1847.[62] It brought the *Herald* 'very much pleasure'.[63] It was a prestige appointment: the Report recommended that 'the Council should be prepared to provide liberally for a duly qualified person'.[64] Digby had had a salary of £200 per annum; Campbell was appointed with a salary £400 (Bostock 1968, 85). Thomas Lee, after Campbell's appointment above him, complained to the governor that 'some hostile and interested persons ... interested themselves' in his removal.[65] Joseph Digby worked as steward under Campbell, with frequent conflict, for two years, until he fell entirely from grace, and was dismissed in 1850 (McDonald 1965). 'To place the direct management of the Asylum in the hands of a medical man', wrote Turner, 'has been the obvious end for which almost all persons connected with the enquiry have been working together'.[66]

The matter did not escape other sections of the press. 'Many consider the [Select Committee] to be a well-managed scheme to oust one surgeon in order to make room for another at a much higher stipend', wrote the editor of the *Freeman's Journal* in 1851.[67] This revisitation of the Select Committee's work was in response to a letter written to the *Journal* in support of an electoral campaign by Charles Cowper. The career of Cowper, who had chaired the Select Committee, shows that straight political pragmatism may have played a part.

Cowper was elected to the Legislative Council in 1843, and resigned his seat in 1850 in response to criticism that his interests were divided between the Council and the new Sydney Tramway and Railroad Company of which he was chairman of the board, at £600 per annum. When the Company foundered, he tried to return to the Council, but struggled to gain a seat, polling lowest at the City of Sydney election in September 1851, then losing also at the Cumberland Election (Ward 1969). Cowper's biographer Alan Powell suggests that he was well suited to committee work, in contrast with the brilliance and showmanship of William Wentworth and Robert Lowe (Powell 1977, 29). Cowper sat on an intimidating number of committees – 64 in the space of 5 years, often as chair, and in that capacity 'frequently produced well reasoned balanced reports' (Mills 142). But if, as Mills argues, Wentworth and Lowe applied their charisma quite overtly to further their own agendas, perhaps Cowper simply furthered his more subtly, in his exhaustive committee work. Reformism was a key component of Cowper's political platform: the supportive letter to the *Journal* cited the 'famous enquiry' on Tarban Creek, and his 'arduous and long continued labours' on behalf of the incarcerated.[68] But Cowper, writes Hirst (2003), 'gave no impression of believing in the reforms which he effected. His opponents claimed with some justice that he was driven by the need to keep his ministerial salary.'[69] What, after all, had the ardour of Charles Cowper and others accomplished, wrote the *Freeman's Journal* in 1851. The 'repeated and unsatisfactory "investigations"' in the five short years since the enquiry cast doubt on its conduct and claims, and left a sour impression of that 'expensive and badly managed Institution', Tarban Creek.[70]

*

Bureaucracy, a technique of government, is rarely self-imposed. It came to Tarban Creek in a clandestine manner; its means for addressing substantive concerns introduced to the institution by means of conspiracy. Nevertheless, the discursive transformation which the asylum underwent between 1846 and 1848, when Campbell was appointed as medical superintendent, was also constructive. I suggest that the members and commentary pundits were not only responding to the clinical promises of medicine, but to something more nebulous, and glorious. In Campbell's fifth letter to the *Herald* he wrote that if he had the funds and power, and the political will, he would 'erect a little republic somewhat after the model of the Elysium of Homer and Virgil, but furnished with the tangible and substantial elements of a terrene paradise'.[71] His imagery burst the bounds of expectation, and possibility, in the colony. His vision, though he defended it as realistic – as metropolitan – was in fact prophetic:

> that the happy time were come when I could see added to this scene one other object, and that the most gratifying and delightful of all the ornaments with which I have yet adorned my Elysium. I wish, with the most unfeigned earnestness, to see it replenished with a crowd of living and moving statues, all hastening through the various graded of convalescence to a complete recovery of that which alone can convert the brutish animated clay into the most glorious and perfect images of all the works of God. [...] The time will come when the cure, not the imprisonment, of the maniac, even here in New South Wales, will be the policy of the statesman and the duty of the physician – [...] and when the certainty of cure shall be the rule, and the solitary failure the exception.[72]

It was a 'challenge of the most powerful type – not an exposure of malpractice, not even an appeal for justice, but the presentation of an ideal' (Ireland 1964, 91). In Berlin, at the Charité Hospital, doctors began keeping 'account' of their patients because it was demanded by their kitchen staff and by frugality. The kitchen, if not parsimony, lost its authority, but paperwork itself developed a strange, self-contained power. From the keeping of financial accounts developed the notion of accountability. Any work might be mapped, reviewed, surveilled, and corrected if it was recorded on paper, and the act of recording, as much as the records, helped to control work. The resulting paperwork had an uneasy relationship with work itself.

There is an electrifying, if terrifying logic to this which can be too easily and too generally accepted. How, this article has asked, did individuals, institutions and governments transform work structures to move away from their traditional content – that is, in the context of a nineteenth-century lunatic asylum, from good, defensible medical practices, human relationships, including vertical reporting structures, personal accounts by witnesses, visitors, magistrates, and reported cures?

Kafka (2012) wrote, of the *ancien regime*, that it created 'an imaginary society' above the real one, with all its variation and contradiction – an imaginary construction where everything was 'simple and coordinated, uniform, equitable, and in accord with reason'.[73] Accountability frameworks were erected around such imaginary structures, assuming and demanding that this rationality be expressible numerically. Kafka (2012) argues that this imaginary structure had actual, aspirational power, but perhaps it also has (and has) negative power, as a standard – not unlike the sanitised asylum model implied in the circular audit sent to the British colonies in 1864 (Swartz 2010). To take the perspective of William Dawson and later the Committee, the treatment of insanity really did operate within some imaginary, abstract ideal, conflating work and paperwork.

During the course of the committee, just such a reasonable, coherent structure was imaginatively – or perhaps unimaginatively – substituted for the actual Tarban Creek Asylum. This coherent structure, constituted by records, checks, and balances, was not, of course, imagined by everyone. The sharp disjuncture in the ideas of good asylum work between the asylum officers and certain of the witnesses and other witnesses with the majority of the select committee, suggests that some saw one and some the other. It was not a matter only of training and expertise: Joseph and Susannah Digby had been trained in London and had long exposure to a leading, physical asylum, and Thomas Lee had vast experience in Irish medical institutions. For them, the creation of paperwork patient identities and careful tracking of these identities through asylum treatment was foreign. It was a consciously modern practice, defined in opposition to former wrongdoing, and built upon a discourse of the reproach of irrationality. Here, however, this discourse was deployed suddenly, even violently, and not only by medical administrators but by politicians and journalists.

It was a powerful structure, like all iterations of Tocqueville's hovering rationalism, but if it was constituted by ordered paperwork, it was created by subterfuge – by operations working not above but beneath the level of the tangible and visible. But why as such an assault necessary? Why were bureaucratic standards deployed in this way, and not an orderly way? The use of such tactics suggests a weak faith in the basic appeal of these methods of ordering and governance, even for those in power, the receivers rather than the writers of returns and reports. One means of exploring this is to look at what these methods achieved: record-keeping practices were overhauled, to be sure, or at least appeared to be, but there were also other quite dramatic effects. The two leading officers of the actual asylum – three, if Susannah Digby, who appears to have declined into alcoholism and infirmity between 1846 and 1848, is included – were terminated by the power of the imaginary one (Murray 1985; Bostock 1968). They were dismissed in disgrace even though at no point were problems with their actual work identified.

William Dawson's sharp interest in records might be explained as an anxiety for control. So too the complicity of the medical witnesses and medical men on the Committee can be explained by the appeal of a bureaucratic conspiracy which created a prestigious, lucrative job for a medical person, helped establish the claims of medicine over the care and cure of insanity, and generally helped elevate the profession in the colonies. Charles Cowper was politically interested in reform and may have cajoled others, like George Allen, into his fold. Perhaps, however, there was also a positive force common to many of these parties. Medicine, as *Iatros* wrote in a high register, represented the promise of cure. This rhetoric left Digby's pragmatic, modest assessment of patients and asylum conditions floundering.

It was a fabulous prospect, the cure of the insane, and it was underwritten by paperwork. Persons suffering from insanity would become patients by paper rituals upon admission, and become persons again upon their discharge. It was on paper that the progress of treatment and cure would be recorded. Paper would also store the 'connected histories' of these persons, so that institutional knowledge could hover over the colony, allowing professionals to know, treat, and cure men and women wherever they presented. This was an evocation of convict department information, which fed into police information, and then into medicine. That is, the bureaucracy of New South Wales had a special shape. In other places, precise medical record-keeping developed to help allow the flow of information through the departments of complex institutions. Here this was an inheritance of penal concerns, as it was elsewhere a military concern – the identification and tracking of deserters.

Thomas Lee and Joseph Digby kept notes for themselves, to support their work. They were judged to have failed to keep the public books required by professional medicine and transparent government. The path from registers to case-files and on to detailed filing systems is well established; standardisation was demanded by centralising governments, and became a goal in itself, with the sort of amnesic rhetoric seen in the unlikely context of Tarban Creek Lunatic Asylum in 1846. The 'system of records' which the Committee recommended in strident terms initiated this other iteration of progress, towards standardised registers and case files which increasingly mandated the time and type of observations (Craig 1989–90, 61). What was eventually indexed in such systems, suggests Warwick Anderson, was 'indexicality' (Anderson 2013, 546–57). Patient experience was overlooked. Bureaucracy would take medicine, other disciplines, and government away from Lee's conception of work, in which time was spent on people rather than on their paperwork abstractions. The Select Committee on Tarban Creek exposed the point of departure within this institution – a departure thrown into relief by a conspiracy of bureaucracy.

The records discussed by the Select Committee – Digby's private diary, Lee's case book, and the medical prescription journal – have not been represented here because they are not in the archive which holds the official records of the asylum. Between the bitter politics of 1846 and after, the feelings of their authors, and the concerns of those who replaced them, this paperwork has not been retained, despite their value to historians and, it could be ventured, to nurses and doctors working in the asylum. Indeed, as deliberately private documents, the closest they came to the public gaze was during the select committee inquiry. We could wonder when and how they were lost – tossed aside by Digby, as his wife deteriorated and he contemplated what he had given up and what he had simply lost; moulding in some upper attic of his house, or Lee's house; or lost in steerage as the Digbys left the Colony in disgust for England or Ireland. Or, more suggestively, were they filed on some obscure shelf in a backroom of the asylum? Perhaps, better still, they consulted by the incoming Francis Campbell, whose belief in medical histories may have helped him overlook any theoretical inconsistency or insufficiency in these 'private' documents. We have no way of knowing, but the questions do not only remind of the problem of navigating between work and paperwork, but of the marvellous contingencies which swirl around paper in our histories.

This history reveals the registers' semblance of propriety and clarity as itself a response to the Select Committee's challenge to the interrelationship of work and paperwork at the asylum.

This history of paperwork encourages us to look askance at medical records, which incorporate the claims, or projections, of the nascent psychiatric profession of coherence. The evidence of the Select Committee (evidence obscured by Charles Cowper's report) reveals a specific history of medical professionalisation, not by the usual channels of theoretical work, sober promotion, and exclusive certification, but through underhand means. We can also, however, see the investment of an adolescent settler colony in the promises of medicine, and this changes the way we might read medical registers and case books: each page, each patient identity, is an invocation of a rational, legible superstructure which can be called to from doctors, journalists, parliamentarians and perhaps even patients, but not by everyone, because it is at odds with certain kinds of messy, detailed health work, which is in the end, unable to be abstracted. Such a superstructure, with all its correlated disciplinary and legal meanings, calls for dishonesty, or perhaps for double writing, as in the context of clinical psychology (Swartz 2006). Historians, too, can be caught in bureaucracy's web of apparent rationality, which remains stickily perilous even, or rather especially, in the climate-controlled, routinised and catalogued state archive.

Notes

1. The Deputy Inspector was the highest ranking medical officer in the colony; 'deputy' here indicated that the officer was deputised to inspect hospitals by the governor. See Cummins (2003).
2. Report from the Select Committee on the Lunatic Asylum, Tarban Creek, 20 October 1846, V&P NSWLC 1846, Session 2, pp. 291–7; Minutes of Evidence Taken Before the Select Committee on the Lunatic Asylum, V&P NSWLC 1846, Session 2, pp. 299–350 (hereafter Minutes).
3. Minutes, Examination of William Dawson, pp. 5–6.

4. R. W. Hay to Henry Prinsep, 30 July 1828, marked private, UK:CO 324/86, quoted in King (1971, 13). As early as 1829, Hay was canvassing the prospect of ending transportation to New South Wales and Van Diemen's Land.
5. R. Bourke to T. Spring Rice, 11 October 1836, Bourke Papers, vol. 9, SLNSW, quoted in King (1971, 178). 'Such prosperity became almost monotonous', writes King (1971, 178–79).
6. *Sic.* R. Bourke to T. Spring Rice, 13 January 1835, *Historical Records of Australia* (hereafter *HRA*) I, vol. 17, p. 631; R. Bourke to Lord Glenelg, 24 April 1837, *HRA* I, vol. 18, p. 737. See also Beckett (2002, 78–84).
7. R. Bourke to Lord Glenelg, 24 April 1837, *HRA* I, vol. 18, p. 736.
8. 'Legislative Council', *The Sydney Morning Herald*, 13 May 1847: 3. http://nla.govau/nla.news-article12896104.
9. Lord Glenelg to G. Gipps, 31 October 1837, *HRA* I, vol. 19, p. 142.
10. Report, Superintendent, p. 2.
11. Report, Recommendations, p. 5.
12. Minutes, Lee, p. 16.
13. Minutes, Lee, p. 16. The square brackets are reproduced from the published text of the report. These brief reports of physical action resemble, rather strikingly, stage directions in a dramatic script; they capture the theatre of the proceedings.
14. Minutes, Lee, p. 16.
15. Minutes, Lee, p. 16.
16. 'The Late Dr. McLean', *The Sydney Herald*, 31 August 1840, 5. Web. 8 May 2017 <http://nla.gov.au/nla.news-article12865486> .
17. 'Mr. Blaxland's Protests', *The Sydney Monitor and Commercial Advertiser*, 10 October 1838: 1, Morning edition, Supplement. Web. 23 August 2015 <http://nla.gov.au/nla.news-article32161490> .
18. Minutes, Browne, p. 28.
19. Minutes, Digby, pp. 11, 14.
20. Minutes, Digby, p. 11.
21. Minutes, Digby's re-examination, p. 14.
22. Minutes, Innes' re-examination, p. 25.
23. Browne knew vaguely of the case book, but had not tried to see it, nor had Innes. Dawson, while complaining of the state of the asylum's books, was not very familiar with them.
24. Minutes, Lee, p. 16.
25. Minutes, Digby, p. 14.
26. Minutes, Turner, p. 23.
27. Minutes, Turner, p. 23.
28. See Editorial, *The Sydney Morning Herald*, 4 September 1846, 2. Web. 7 August 2015 <http://nla.gov.au/nla.news-article12899249> .
29. Minutes, Innes re-examination, p. 25.
30. Minutes, Dawson, p. 6.
31. Minutes, Digby, p. 9; Minutes, Lee, p. 16.
32. Minutes, Digby, p. 12. Examples were provided in Appendices L, M, and N.
33. Minutes, Lee, p. 17.
34. Minutes, Digby, p. 14.
35. As well as the clerk, there were two senior male keepers (£40 each per year); two junior male keepers (£25 each per year); two senior female keepers or nurses (£20 per year); an under-nurse (£15 per year); two male

prisoners and three female prisoners as keepers and two laundry women (3 pence per day).
36. 'State of the Lunatic Asylum, Tarban Creek', *The Sydney Morning Herald*, 17 June 1847, 2. Web. 22 December 2013 <http://nla.gov.au/nla.news-article 12901479>.
37. Appendix D, Appendices, p. 4.
38. Minutes, Lee, p. 16.
39. Minutes, Lee, p. 16.
40. Minutes, Lee, p. 18.
41. Minutes, Lee, p. 19.
42. Original emphasis. Minutes, Lee, p. 16.
43. Minutes, Digby, p. 11.
44. 'The Lunatic Asylum, Tarban Creek', *The Australian*, 3 July 1847, 2. Web. 23 July 2013 <http://nla.gov.au/nla.news-article37131930>.
45. 'Legislative Council', *The Sydney Morning Herald*, 13 May 1847, 3. Web. 5 May 2017 http://nla.govau/nla.news-article12896104.
46. Minutes, Innes re-examination, pp. 25–26.
47. Report, Recommendations, p. 4.
48. Minutes, Browne, p. 29.
49. According to the Attorney-General: 'Legislative Council', *The Sydney Morning Herald*, 13 May 1847, 3. Web. 5 May 2017, http://trove.nla.gov.au/newspaper/article/12896104.
50. 'The Lunatic Asylum, Tarban Creek', *The Australian*, 3 July 1847, 2. Web. 23 July 2013 <http://nla.gov.au/nla.news-article37131930>.
51. 'Legislative Council', *The Sydney Morning Herald*, 13 May 1847, 2.
52. Lee was awarded one year's salary in compensation – not more than £183: *An Act for applying certain Sums arising from the Revenue receivable in New South Wales* [...] 11 Vic No. 52 (1849) s 10.
53. 'Shipping Intelligence', *The Maitland Mercury and Hunter River General Advertiser*, 12 February 1848, 2. Web. 8 May 2017 <http://nla.gov.au/nla.news-article713294>.
54. 'Original Correspondence', *The Sydney Morning Herald*, 11 June 1847, 3.
55. 'Original Correspondence. The Lunacy Bill. No I', *The Sydney Morning Herald*, 29 May 1846, 3. Web. 12 August 2014 <http://nla.gov.au/nla.news-article12887545>.
56. 9 Vic. No. 34, 1846 made the transfer of convict lunatics to Parramatta Female Factory and Liverpool Hospital legal, and defined the phrase 'legally qualified medical practitioner' in the initial act. See Shea (1999, 33–34).
57. It seems likely that at least some knew the identity of Iatros – Francis Campbell, M.D. Campbell also had time to write a long pamphlet on flax in addition to other long letters to the editor under different pen-names. John Dunmore Lang called him 'one of the ablest of our colonial literati' (Lang 1847, 320) (Campbell 1845).
58. Minutes, Dawson, p. 6.
59. 'Lunatic Asylums', *The Sydney Morning Herald*, 9 June 1846: 2. Web. 7 August 2015 <http://nla.gov.au/nla.news-article12887707>. A second editorial followed, after *Iatros* had fallen silent, which offered to reprint his letters in full. He declined. Editorial, *The Sydney Morning Herald*, 4 September 1846: 2. Web. 7 August 2015 <http://nla.gov.au/nla.news-article12899249>.

60. Minutes, Turner, p. 21.
61. Minutes, Lee, p. 19.
62. The appointment followed further politicking in the Legislative Council, and a subsidiary enquiry which convinced even those in government who had objected to the tone and content of the 1846 Report: 'Council Papers', *The Sydney Morning Herald*, 30 September 1847: 2. Web. 12 December 2014 <http://nla.gov.au/nla.news-article12898191>; 'Lunatic Asylum, Tarban Creek', *The Australian*, 21 December 1847: 3. Web. 23 July 2013 <http://nla.gov.au/nla.news-article37129741> .
63. 'Lunatic Asylum, Tarban Creek', *The Australian*, 21 December 1847: 3. Web. 12 August 2014 <http://nla.gov.au/nla.news-article37129741> .
64. Report, Recommendations, p. 4. Francis Macrae suggested that £400 should be enough: 'Lunatic Asylum, Tarban Creek', *The Sydney Morning Herald*, 7 July 1847: 3. Web. 3 September 2015 <http://nla.gov.au/nla.news-article 12889409> .
65. T. Lee to E. Deas Thompson, Colonial Secretary, 12 January 1848, with Gipps' annotation, SLNSW:48/832, quoted in Bostock (1968, 112).
66. 'To the Editors of the Sydney Morning Herald', *The Sydney Morning Herald*, 29 June 1847.
67. 'Original Correspondence', *Freeman's Journal*, 4 September 1851: 10. Web. 23 December 2013 <http://nla.gov.au/nla.news-article115767639> .
68. 'The Sydney Morning Herald'. *The Sydney Morning Herald*, 27 August 1849, 2. Web. 3 September 2015 <http://nla.gov.au/nla.news-article12913247> .
69. In 1851, the *Bell's Life in Sydney and Sporting Review* mocked the *Herald* for its too-lavish praise of Cowper, 'its own particular pet': 'The Herald on Charles Cowper', 16 August 1851, 2. Web. 3 September 2015 <http://nla.gov.au/nla.news-article59773014> . The *Australian* had earlier called out the *Herald* for its own debatable commitment to the reformism it was lauding: 'Original Correspondence', *The Australian*, 10 September 1846, 3. Web. 4 August 2015 <http://nla.gov.au/nla.news-article37155282> .
70. 'Original Correspondence', *Freeman's Journal*, 4 September 1851, 10.
71. 'Lunatic Asylums. No. V', *The Sydney Morning Herald*, 15 June 1846, 3. Web. 12 August 2014 <http://nla.gov.au/nla.news-article12887803> .
72. 'Lunatic Asylums. No. V', *The Sydney Morning Herald*, 15 June 1846.
73. The quotation is modified and reproduced in Ben (Kafka 2012, 34).

Disclosure statement

No potential conflict of interest was reported by the author.

ORCID

James Dunk http://orcid.org/0000-0002-7733-8734

References

Anderson, W. 2013. "The Case of the Archive." *Critical Inquiry* 39 (3): 541–544. doi:10.1086/670044.
Beckett, G. 2002. *Financing the Colonial Economy 1800–1835*. Bloomington, IN: Trafford Publishing.
Bostock, J. 1968. *The Dawn of Australian Psychiatry: An Account of the Measures Taken for the Care of Mental Invalids from the Time of the First Fleet, 1788, to the Year 1850, Including a Survey of the Overseas Background and the Case Notes of Dr. F. Campbell*. Glebe, NSW: Australasian Medical Publishing Company.
Bynum, B., and H. Bynum. 2016. "The Straitjacket." *The Lancet* 387 (10028): 1607. doi:10.1016/S0140-6736(16)30206-9.
Campbell, F. 1845. *A Treatise on the Culture of Flax and Hemp: Being a Reprint of the Letters of Robin Goodfellow*. Sydney: Statham and Forster.
Colaizzi, J. 2005. "Seclusion & Restraint: A Historical Perspective." *Journal of Psychosocial Nursing & Mental Health Services* 43 (2): 31–37. doi:10.3928/02793695-20050201-07.
Craig, B. 1989–90. "Hospital Records and Record-Keeping, C. 1850-C. 1950, Part 1: The Development of Records in Hospitals." *Archivaria* 29: 57–87.
Craze, L. W. 1993. "The Care and Control of the Criminally Insane in New South Wales: 1788 to 1987." PhD diss., University of New South Wales.
Cummins, C. J. 2003. A History of Medical Administration in NSW 1788-1973, 2nd ed. North Sydney: New South Wales Department of Health.
Curry, G. 1989. "The Select Committee on the Lunatic Asylum Tarban Creek, 1846: The Medicalisation of Mental Nursing in New South Wales." MA diss., University of Sydney.
Dunk, J. 2017. "Authority and the Treatment of the Insane at Castle Hill Asylum, 1811–25." *Health & History* 19 (2): 17–40.
Ford, L., and D. A. Roberts. 2013. "Expansion, 1820–50." In *The Cambridge History of Australia, Vol. 1: Indigenous and Colonial Australia*, edited by A. Bashford and S. Macintyre, 121–148. Port Melbourne and New York: Cambridge University Press.
Frank, J. A., Jnr. 1967. "Non-Restraint and Robert Gardiner Hill." *Bulletin of the History of Medicine* 41 (2): 140–160.
Hess, V., and S. Ledebur. 2011. "Taking and Keeping: A Note on the Emergence and Function of Hospital Patient Records." *Journal of the Society of Archivists* 32 (1): 22–24.
Hickman, C. 2009. "Cheerful Prospects and Tranquil Restoration: The Visual Experience of Landscape as Part of the Therapeutic Regime of the British Asylum, 1800–60". *History of Psychiatry* 20 (4): 425–441. doi:10.1177/0957154X08338335.
Hirst, J. 2003. "Cowper, Charles." In The Oxford Companion to Australian History, edited by G. Davison, J Hirst, and S. Macintyre. Oxford University Press. DOI: 10.1093/acref/9780195515039.001.0001

Ireland, A. W. 1964. "The Select Committee on the Lunatic Asylum, Tarban Creek, 1846." *The Medical Journal of Australia* 51: 90–97.
Kafka, B. 2009. "Paperwork: The State of the Discipline." *Book History* 12: 340–353. doi:10.1353/bh.0.0024.
Kafka, B. 2012. *The Demon of Writing*. New York: Zone Books.
King, H. 1971. *Richard Bourke*. Melbourne: Oxford University Press.
Laidlaw, Z. 2005. *Colonial Connections, 1815–45: Patronage, the Information Revolution and Colonial Government*. Manchester and New York: Manchester University Press.
Lang, J. D. 1847. *Phillipsland; Country Hitherto Designated Port Phillip: Its Present Condition and Prospects, a Highly Eligible Field for Emigration*. London: Longman, Brown, Green, and Longmans.
MacDonagh, O. 1958. "The Nineteenth Century Revolution in Government: A Reappraisal." *Historical Journal* 1 (1): 52–67. doi:10.1017/S0018246X58000018.
McDonald, D. I. 1965. "Gladesville Hospital: The Formative Years, 1838–1850." *Journal of the Royal Australian Historical Society* 51 (3): 289–292.
Mills, K. 2012. "Lawmakers, Select Committees and the Birth of Democracy in New South Wales, 1843–1855." *Journal of Australian Colonial History* 14 (2012): 131–154.
Monk, L.-A. 2008. *Attending Madness: At Work in the Australian Colonial Asylum*. Amsterdam and New York: Rodopi.
Monk, L.-A. 2009. "Working in the Asylum: Attendants to the Insane." *Health and History* 11 (1): Australian Asylums and Their Histories.83–101.
Montgomery, K.(2006) *How Doctors Think: Clinical Judgment and the Practice of Medicine*. Oxford: Oxford University Press.
Murray, B. 1985. "Foundation Years of Gladesville Hospital: A Medical Coup, Part 2." *The Lamp* 42 (3): 31–35.
Nairn, B. 1967. "Macarthur, Hannibal Hawkins (1788–1861)." In *Australian Dictionary of Biography, Vol. 2: 1788–1850, I-Z*, edited by A. G. L. Shaw and C. M. H. Clark, 147–149. London and New York: Melbourne University Press.
Neil, W. D. 1992. *The Lunatic Asylum at Castle Hill: Australia's First Psychiatric Hospital 1811-1826*. Castle Hill NSW: Dryas.
Parris, H. 1960. "'The Nineteenth-Century Revolution in Government: A Reappraisal Reappraised'." *Historical Journal* 3 (1): 17–37. doi:10.1017/S0018246X00022998.
Porter, R. 1987. *Mind Forg'd Manacles: A History of Madness in England from the Restoration to the Regency*. Cambridge, MA: Harvard University Press.
Powell, A. 1977. *Patrician Democrat: The Political Life of Charles Cowper 1843–1870*. Carlton, Vic.: Melbourne University Press.
Robson, L. L. 1965. *The Convict Settlers of Australia: An Enquiry into the Origin and Character of the Convicts Transported to New South Wales and Van Diemen's Land 1787–1852*. Carlton, Vic.: Melbourne University Press and Cambridge University Press.
Shea, P. 1999. *Defining Madness*. Sydney: Hawkins Press.
Swartz, S. 2006. "The Third Voice: Writing Case-Notes." *Feminism & Psychology* 16 (4): 427–444. doi:10.1177/0959353506068750.
Swartz, S. 2010. "The Regulation of British Colonial Lunatic Asylums and the Origins of Colonial Psychiatry, 1860–1864." *History of Psychology* 13 (2): 160–177. doi:10.1037/a0019223.

Ward, J. M. 1969. "Cowper, Sir Charles (1807–1875)." In *Australian Dictionary of Biography, Vol. 3: 1851–1890 A-C,* edited by N. B. Naird, A. G. Serle, and R. B. Ward, 475–479. London and New York: Melbourne University Press.

Papering over madness: accountability and resistance in colonial asylum files: a New Zealand case study

Barbara Brookes

ABSTRACT
Through an examination of New Zealand legislation governing lunacy and the files from the Seacliff Asylum, this article argues how paperwork served to uphold an elusive ideal of a compassionate society. Paper, in the form of letters, reports and forms, was sent up and down the country in order to prevent wrongful confinement and to monitor costs and cure rates. Paper provided for patients allowed them to challenge their incarceration, sometimes successfully. That maze of paperwork, generated for both statutory and institutional administrative ends, mirrored the disorder of those confined within the institution. The curating of digital exhibitions of such materials flattens out their complexity and smooths over what were often disjointed narratives.

On 18 June 1887, the clerk at the local asylum signed the statutory 'Notice of Admission' that recorded the committal of Johanna Beckett to the Seacliff Lunatic Asylum, Dunedin, New Zealand. The clerk then sent a copy of the admission form, a statement and two medical certificates, on their way to the Inspector of Lunatic Asylums, based over 900 km away in Wellington. In doing so he was fulfilling the requirements of the 1882 Lunatics' Act. The vast archive accumulated relating to asylums in New Zealand and elsewhere was a result of concern with creating accountability for two things: denying the liberty of the subject and the expenditure of state funds. At each stage of the admissions procedure, actions had to be justified and reasons recorded for detaining people in a public institution. The clerk was at the centre of this circulation of paperwork.

Historians of medicine might most often encounter the mad on paper: through the archives generated by the state sanctioned and private asylums built in throughout the British Empire, or in America, over the course of the nineteenth century. That archive, and most often casebooks, has generated a substantial body of work which has greatly enhanced our understandings of the workings of asylums and given us glimpses of the lives of those admitted to them (Tomes 1984; MacKenzie 1992; Smith 1999; Swartz 2015). Individual patient files have been translated into large data sets in order to reach broad conclusions about migration and ethnicity and madness, for example (Coleborne 2015; McCarthy 2015). The documents themselves, as Matthew Hull has argued, have often been overlooked in the belief that they give 'immediate access to what they document' (Hull 2012, 253) – in this case, insights into those deemed to be 'mad'. But if we look at the paperwork, rather than through it, as Ben Kafka suggests, we see a particular form of knowledge-making at work (Kafka 2009, 341). I speculate that we might also see paper work as an intervention between the 'mad' and those dealing with them that served to quell physical violence towards the insane.

While asylum repositories may have been well-tended and kept, James Moran in this volume has found another source of rich insights outside of the asylum walls, in lunacy investigation laws. His study makes apparent the way in which law, not medicine, defined madness. Building on the insights of Volker Hess and Moran, my aim is to examine the New Zealand legislature's ever more elaborate demands for paper proof of madness over the course of the nineteenth century. As Black (2014, 299) has outlined, the bureaucratic information state burgeoned in the nineteenth century as papermaking became less expensive. He notes that the British Foreign Office processed around 4000 dispatches in 1815, but by 1853, that number had reached 35,104. Some of those dispatches no doubt came from New Zealand. In creating the new colony, the stationers' office became the engine of instruction in search of national unity: unity that was severely tested by the New Zealand wars of the 1860s. Military force had to be brought in the attempt to compel Māori to adhere to paper laws (Macdonald and Lenihan, in this volume).

In what follows, I use New Zealand as a case study to examine the growth of paperwork governing colonial asylums. My interest lies in the role paperwork played in the business of determining the accountability of the state's agents on the ground: the officials delegated with determining madness and running asylums. In his study of the shaping of written knowledge, Bazerman (1988, 8) argues 'each new text produced within a genre reinforces or remolds some aspect of the genre' and these interventions cannot be understood unless embedded in their history. A page, he continues, is an archive 'mediating between an imagined event and a distant realization' (10).

The profusion of paperwork surrounding committal, I suggest, was a means of monitoring costs, outlining key tasks and recording the transfer and committal of patients and their treatment. As Volker Hess argues in this volume, 'the guiding principle' of the institutional files 'was not storage but mobilization'.

If bureaucracy succeeds, according to Max Weber, because it eliminates the emotions from all official business: 'love, hatred, and all purely personal, irrational, and emotional elements' (Weber 1978, 975) – this – I would argue, had the potential to work in favour in of those deemed deranged. In asylum files, the Weberian triumph of rationality came up against the disorder of madness. Officials might be repelled with the loss of bodily control evinced by sufferers, disgusted by their obscenities, appalled by their delusions of grandeur or afraid of their violence, but such responses had to be quelled in the face of the diagnosis of 'lunacy'. Filling out the paperwork was one way to restrain more visceral responses. As Paul Slade Knight of the Lancaster Asylum in England remarked in 1821, the post of asylum superintendent required 'the exertions of men greatly superior in acquirements and intellect to the general order of mankind'. That superiority required self-mastery of 'malevolent passions' in the face of 'insults and aspersions of patients': people who should be viewed with compassion (Smith, 60).

New Zealand, colonized from the 1840s, built on the developments in asylum management pioneered elsewhere, most notably in Scotland and England, the places where most of the colonial doctors were trained. Despite all hopes that the new society created in New Zealand would be free of old world ills, madness soon made itself apparent. The decade of New Zealand's founding coincided with the 1847 publication of John Conolly's foundational text: *The construction and government of lunatic asylums and hospitals for the insane* (Conolly 1847; Scull 1989). Conolly, who found his *métier* as Superintendent of the Hanwell Lunatic Asylum, became particularly concerned that asylums should collect information in a systematic way in order to forward knowledge about the incidence of madness and the efficacy of asylum practice. As a guide to others, he appended tables to his text, which were compiled from a survey of superintendents through out the country and from numbers compiled by the English Commissioners in Lunacy.

Conolly believed that much could be learned by a 'uniform system of keeping statistical tables' about rate of admissions, ages of sufferers, cures and deaths. (1847, 152). Some asylums kept poor records of numbers of patients and others failed to distinguish between the sexes. In the interests of charting the performance of asylums, Conolly recommended that routine reporting should be legally enforced. As reporting became more standardized, the bureaucratic reports from asylums demonstrated their power to generate new knowledge, allowing national population statistics on the occurrence of 'madness', for example, to be compared.[1]

Part of the process of standardization occurred through statutory requirements detailing the forms required for committal of the insane. Paper played a key role in the transition or, in Cornelia Vismann's (2008) observation, the 'transfer operation' from the community to the asylum. 'Committal papers' performed the work of denying the liberty of the subject through a series of warrants, certificates, reports, signatures and seals by constables, Justices of the Peace and medical practitioners. In paper also lay the path to freedom, through discharge papers, occasionally prompted, as we shall see, through pen and ink wielded by patients. The very blurred boundary between reason and unreason occasioned an avalanche of paper to assure New Zealand's citizens that the newly founded state was responsible and thus only prepared to incarcerate citizens found to be dangerous to themselves or others, or of 'unsound mind'.

The flurry of paper began with the 15-clause 1846 Ordinance, printed on sturdy rag paper, by the Government's contracted printer, and issued by the Lieutenant Governor with the consent of the Legislative Council. The Ordinance made provision for the 'Safe Custody of and Prevention of Offences by Persons dangerously Insane, and for the Care and Maintenance of Persons of Unsound Mind'. At the time of the Ordinance, however, the only place to which such persons could be transported was the flimsy jails. Two Justices of the Peace and two medical practitioners were to commit such insane persons but these officials were thin on the ground. And from the outset of settlement in New Zealand, there was lively debate about 'the dangerous consequences to the liberty of the subject [by magistrates] representing the Executive Government – irresponsible to and independent of the people of this settlement'.[2]

Discussion of the need for an asylum first arose in Auckland in December 1850 when the settler population stood at about 22,108 and the Maori population at 65,650. At the Mechanics Institute in January 1851, a committee of subscribers formed to push for the founding of an asylum, 'for persons suffering under this most humbling and afflictive visitation'.[3] The Governor expressed support for this plan but noted the cost of building asylums and that the particular geography of New Zealand, 'with so many small and separate settlements' meant it was impossible to provide such a facility for each town.[4] The Auckland campaign to build an asylum went ahead but was stymied by debates about where to site the building and who should oversee it. The subscribers wished to have a say in management but this was rejected; the Executive Council taking control. The building was completed in January 1853.

The extant file to do with the new asylum is a list of the cost of the necessities required for equipping the building and reminds us of the expense of this task and the sparseness of the furnishing. Accounting was the key driver for the list. The first essential was a large bell, 'to summon assistance from the Colonial hospital if required'.[5] A bucket and rope, 'iron dogs' and an iron fender for the fireplace were essential. The list continues, numbering tables, pots and pans amongst the first prerequisites. Patients are absent but not to the subscribers to the asylum who found the asylum wanting on their first visit in terms of adequate exercise areas and ventilation. They recommended a number of improvements that were deemed by the Auditor General to be 'too expensive'.[6] Humanity constantly came up against parsimoniousness, recorded in the exchanges between those on the ground and those in provincial and central government.

The first facility for the mentally ill in the southern province of Otago, the Dunedin Lunatic Asylum, opened in 1863. Two legal documents made possible one William Jenkin's committal to the new Asylum, one an eggshell blue warrant – with the local names and provincial details to be filled in – and one hand-written letter from a single resident magistrate. Jenkins was adjudged to be dangerous, both to himself and to others. Clearly the difficulty of finding enough officials to commit patients meant the letter of the law could not be observed. The threat to the community allowed shortcuts to be taken with the paperwork.

The 1860s also saw, as Sally Swartz (2010) has outlined, the development of the Imperial centre's interest in regulating colonial lunatic asylums and its ability to do so. The creation of the Colonial Office 1854 gave greater structure to colonial business, part of which was to promote a humane vision of imperialism. In the case of asylums, the advances within Britain led to a desire to promote 'humane care with order, discipline, and statistical tables, and cleanliness with civilized standards' abroad. (Swartz 2010, p.161). A scandal at the Kingston, Jamaica Asylum, revealing a practice called 'tanking' (holding patients under water) threatened to subvert any Imperial claims to humanity and led to a determination to audit colonial asylums. On the 23 July 1863, New Zealand newspapers carried the circular from the Secretary of State for the Colonies requesting information about the state of both hospitals and asylums. Staffing, income, stores, building quality and grounds, internal structure, classification of patients, number of men and women and length of stay were some of the details sought.[7] New Zealand failed to provide any information but received the resulting report from London in August 1864 that made a number of recommendations about the proper running of asylums.[8]

That year saw Charles Reade's popular novel *Hard Cash* circulating in the colony.[9] Reade's melodrama about wrongful confinement in an asylum heightened fears that people could be arbitrarily deprived of their liberty (McCandless 1978). Perhaps in response to the prompting by the Secretary of State and Reade's novel, the Otago Provincial Council instituted a Commission of Inquiry into the Constitution and Management of the

Dunedin Hospital and Lunatic Asylum. The Commission totally condemned the current arrangements in which lunatics appeared to be 'looked upon as a class of incurables, whom it was only necessary to keep from hurting themselves, and doing harm to others'.[10] The Provincial Councillors urged the government to build a proper asylum, arguing 'lunatics should be regarded by the state as the object of tender solicitude, and that no pains or expense should be spared in ameliorating their condition'.[11] The Inquiry recommended the appointment of a resident medical officer and that records should be carefully kept: 'the keeper's or head attendant's diary should be kept with strict accuracy and precision'.[12]

'In a free country such as this' Auckland's premier newspaper, the *New Zealand Herald*, thundered in 1868, 'there is no privilege which should be more jealously guarded than the personal liberty of the subject'.[13] The author warned against 'over-straining of the law' or 'making it subservient to the designs of interested parties'. The Police Court was charged with too readily committing people to the Lunatic Asylum on the 'attestation of two medical men', both of who received a fee of one guinea. Examples were given of those wrongly committed, including a man who had a monomania about Lucifer matches and another who had been committed at the behest of his wife who hoped she could then sell the farm but found she could not because his real property belonged to his young son. The author suggested that the opinion of two doctors was inadequate and should be supplemented through cross-examination of 'persons acquainted with the alleged lunatic'.

Whether or not a result of the newspaper's tirade, New Zealand's legislation governing lunacy was greatly extended by the 1868 Lunacy Act (32 Victoriae 1868 no.16) which contained 193 clauses and specified that kind of accounting that Conolly had recommended. Writing was the key to committal: resident magistrates and medical practitioners had to complete certificates and sign forms. They also had to guarantee that they or no relative had a financial interest in such a committal. The Act specified that a clerk be appointed to each asylum (s.23) to take charge of the paperwork. Their duties included keeping a 'Register of Patients' and transferring the requisite certificates for admission and discharge to the Colonial Secretary. They were responsible for recording details of any deaths and conveying these to the local coroner as well as giving notice of any escapes. Failure by the Medical Officer or the clerk to complete the necessary paperwork could result in a fine up to £20.

Medical officers of both public and private asylums were directed to maintain a 'Medical Journal' recording the name and sex of all patients, their disorders, and those held under restraint or seclusion and the reasons for this (s.25). The Act also directed that a 'Case Book' be held, charting the history and condition of each patient, the treatment and medicines supplied, and, in the case of death, 'an exact account of the autopsy (if any) of such patient' (s. 25). An outline of the patient was therefore transferred to paper where they could be considered in the absence of the sentient person; they became a 'case' for consideration rather than an individual.

The casebooks were to be available for the Inspector of Asylums to view from time to time. Medical officers failing to keep up casebooks could be fined. Inspectors and Official visitors could inspect the paperwork and then create their own: an 'inspector's book' where they would record their inquiries and a 'patients' book' where they would enter any observations on patients (s57;58). In order to ward off imagined cruelty towards the insane, the Act specified that the 'Medical Journal' should record any patients held under restraint or seclusion and the reasons for such treatment. Every instance of death, injury or violence was to be noted (s.25).

The Act did not succeed in allaying all fears of wrongful confinement. Such a charge was brought to the Dunedin Magistrate's Court in 1876 by one John Burt who alleged ill-treatment. Counsel argued that Burt had been 'improperly and illegally detained'.[14] The magistrate argued that it was 'quite right that full enquiry should be made into any alleged abuses in public institutions, particularly where the liberty of the subject is affected'. He believed that the superintendent should be pleased with his findings that the committal was just and conducted in the right manner. According to the magistrate's findings, the plaintiff suffered 'delusional insanity' and that his complaint resulted from that condition.[15]

From 1870, reports from the inspectors of asylums, accompanied by tables of numbers, were printed in the Appendices to the House of Representatives. The numbers of admissions, discharges and deaths were recorded as were the conditions of the wards, the diet of the patients and the numbers of staff and their wages. Perhaps in response to the prompting of the Colonial Office, in 1871, a Joint Committee held an inquiry and issued a report on the state of the country's lunatic asylums. Medical men from throughout the country forwarded their views as to the kind of improvements the colonial government should undertake to enhance Asylum provision. They were divided on the question of whether a large central asylum should be established but supported the recommendation that 'a duly qualified Medical Officer from the United Kingdom', experienced in the treatment of the insane, be employed to oversee the asylum system.[16]

Sufferers from lunacy, as the Resident Surgeon at the Auckland Asylum reminded politicians at an 1871 Inquiry, were the 'victims of mental disease, to which the most amiable, intellectual, and religious members of a community are, without any offence or fault of theirs, liable to be subjected'.[17] Paperwork, therefore, helped control and police the instinctive and sometimes violent responses of the family, the police, the medical profession and asylum staff, to the incomprehensibility of lunacy. It was constitutive of an elusive ideal of a compassionate society.

In that society, patients also had a right to paper and freedom to correspond. Opening, delaying or detaining the letters of another person could lead to a fine or imprisonment under the 1858 Act to regulate the Postal Service of the colony of New Zealand. Opening a letter meant for another constituted a misdeameanour.[18] Clause 62 of the 1862 Lunatics Act stated

> Every letter written by a patient in an asylum hospital of licensed house and addressed to any responsible minister of the Crown Judge of the Supreme Court Inspector or an Official Visitor shall be forwarded to the person to whom it shall be addressed unless the keeper or licensee of such asylum or licensed house ... prohibit the forwarding of such a letter by indorsement to that effect ... they shall lay the letter so indorsed unopened before the Inspector of the Official Visitor ....

Letter writing was a well-established part of colonial culture, where settlers' only link with those they had left behind was by paper and many asylum patients were firm participants in the practice. A gold rush in Otago in the 1860s gave impetus to the expansion of New Zealand's postal services so that, by 1870, the post office handled over 5 million letters annually for the country's settler population of approximately 250,000.[19]

Letters, Konstantin Dierks argues of his study of the eighteenth century American sources, 'did not reveal – they *made* history'. By the act of writing, people could create new futures (Dierks 2009, p.xiii). The power of letter writing took on a special significance when the writer was incarcerated in a lunatic asylum. Letters allowed asylum residents to demonstrate their agency while under restraint. A social practice, in which by the late nineteenth century most were well-schooled, took on particular resonance in a cultural domain designed to deny the liberty of the subject.

What drove patients to write letters? Allan Beveridge's analysis of over 1000 letters by patients in Edinburgh's Morningside Asylum analyses a range of reasons in-depth: to express their outrage at confinement; to complain about asylum hours, food and routine; to criticize the behaviour of attendants and other patients (Beveridge 1998). Cathy Coleborne has interrogated letters to the asylum that express the emotional states of patients and those of family members affected by the 'calamity' of insanity (Coleborne 2010). Sally Swartz has noted how the letters of white patients in the Valkenburg Asylum in South Africa 'were read and responded to' and dealt with 'respectfully and meticulously' (2008, 296).

The isolated nature of the Seacliff asylum, on the coast outside of Dunedin, meant letters were crucial for the administration, from the mundane acts of ordering supplies to questions of policy, and to patients in order to maintain contact with family and friends. Letters flew back and forth to the Southern city of Dunedin ordering farm supplies, articles of clothing and general supplies, and to the seat of government in the northern city of Wellington. Seacliff was to become the largest of New Zealand's network of publicly funded asylum system, which by 1883 consisted of seven institutions with three in the North Island at Auckland, Wellington and Napier, and four in the South at Nelson, Hokitika, Christchurch and Dunedin. Dunedin was also the site of New Zealand only private asylum, Ashburn Hall, which in 1883 housed 15 residents.[20] The governance of these widely geographically spread asylums depended on correspondence with the Inspector General of Asylums, the head of the Lunatics Asylums Department in Wellington, after the abolition of the Provincial governments in 1876.

By the 1880s, the number of forms had multiplied, as detailed in schedules by 337-clause 1882 Lunatics Act. Inspectors and Official Visitors were to audit the asylums, by paper bringing into being, as Hull suggests, 'a presumptive ethical subject' a 'society' passing judgement on the care of the insane (Hull 2012).

The engine room of the Colonial government, the Government Printing Department in Wellington, which had 47 rooms devoted to print and stationery, provided the paper necessary to commit, to certify, to record and to discharge patients. The expense of the paper required more than quadrupled after the 1882 Act.[21] The government was prepared to track its investment in caring for those deemed to be insane. Caring for the insane, and removing them from the gaols, appeared to be a mark of a civilized society.

In 1887, seven forms were required for the admission of 40-year old Johanna Beckett who will serve as my key example.[22] Each printed form addressed the issue of accountability: giving specific reasons why Johanna should be committed to the asylum. As the sequence unfolds, we see how the paper trail builds a coherence around the constantly singing and talking Johanna. Each of these forms was made for mobility – to be transferred between the certifying agents and registered with the Superintendent of Asylums in Wellington.

Form 55A of the Constabulary Department was a return that the arresting constable, in a case of lunacy, had to present to the committing magistrate. Four points mattered. First, Johanna is named so that her previous identity is captured. Second, her 'Condition of life, previous occupation, and amount of personal property' are recorded: she is a married housewife, with no property. Third, the 'Date and place of Committal' recorded: 16 June 1887 in Invercargill. And perhaps the most important point comes last: the 'Name and address of relative or other person liable to contribute towards the maintenance of the patient': Henry Beckett, husband, Goldminer, from Waimumu, Near Mataura.

This paperwork made Henry Beckett liable for the upkeep of his wife in a public institution; he – like all other relatives – was brought within the margins of the state to cooperate with or to contest its demands for payment. Paper kept alive the relationship between the struggling gold miner in Waimumu and the asylum sheltering his wife.

Form 2, prescribed under the 1882 Act, provided the Certificate 'that a person is a Lunatic'. Two doctors independently filled out forms noting the 'Facts indicating Lunacy' which they observed, and reported additional 'facts' communicated by other people. Incoherence and delusion were at the heart of the observations of both doctors – in this way, garbled thoughts and incomprehensible actions – became 'facts'. Mrs Beckett had been 'going about almost naked' and attempted to spread hot ashes on the neighbour's floor. Sixteen particulars were required on the statement which included – Religious persuasion, Whether it was the first attack, Age at first attack, Supposed cause, Whether subject to epilepsy and Whether suicidal. The singing and loquacious Johanna could be pinned down by these categories. While neither of the doctors gave an opinion as to the cause of her illness, the constable, who also filled out the particulars, gave a confident diagnosis that the cause of lunacy was 'heredity', and noted Johanna was a member of the 'Christian Disciples'.

Next form no.7 had to be completed: the order for 'Conveyance to an Asylum'. The mobility of paper facilitated the mobility of people to be conveyed across the country. The Invercargill Resident Magistrate named the doctors who satisfied him 'that the said Johanna Beckett is a lunatic and not under proper care or control' and directed her to be taken to the Seacliff Asylum.

Once Johanna had made the long journey of 234 km to Seacliff, the clerk of the asylum filled out Form no.10 the 'Notice of Admission' which was then forwarded to the Inspector of Lunatic Asylums along with the medical certificates attesting to her condition. Finally, the Acting Medical Officer of the Asylum examined Johanna and certified that she was insane and suggested that perhaps the 'climacteric' was the cause but with respect 'to bodily health and condition she is anaemic but otherwise in fairly good health'.

Mirroring her relocation and movement – from freely wandering the hills – to restrained within the asylum, Johanna's record then moves from the unbound separate 'statutory papers', into the bound, heavy asylum casebook: a book whose centrality to asylum life is signified by the leather spine with the tooled labels. The index takes us to her pages, where we find that the incarceration might be a form of liberation. 'She cheers up suddenly when relating how "he" was unkind & maltreated her' but 'when it came to beating her she thought it was unbearable'. The inference is that 'he' is the husband. Four months later, Johanna was determined by the Medical Superintendent to be well enough to leave the Asylum and the resident magistrate filled out an Order of Discharge – another mobile paper – to that effect on 18 October.

Five months later, in March 1888, a similar series of statutory papers were filled out to convey Johanna, found 'wandering about, naked and excited, in the rain and acting with purposeless absurdity' again to Seacliff.[23] Her incoherent talk had now become 'violent, obscene and abusive'. She believed she was born 'ages ago'; was a 'sprite' and could go through the ceiling; that she was in heaven; and that she was the Queen of May. The constable suggested that the cause of her lunacy was 'ill treatment by her husband'.

This time a few lines about Johanna Beckett are entered into the casebook compiled by the new Superintendent of the Asylum, Frederic Truby King who appears to have taken a census of those resident in the Asylum upon his arrival.

In this casebook, Johanna is bound alongside those she may well have been physically separated from in the asylum which had separate male and female accommodation.

One of these is John Frost who Truby King interviewed in the presence of another doctor. The transcript of the interview is carefully pasted into the casebook. Frost's own paperwork – his letters – proved to be his undoing. Dr King interrogated him about his supposed wife who could not be traced. He then asked:

> Why did you write to Mr Paniock letters such as men only write to women with whom they are deeply in love and speaking of his attractions and your devotion and love for him and your desire to be always with him and beside him?[24]

Frost protested that he meant no harm, but the words captured on paper incriminated him. Labelled a sexual 'pervert', Frost was allowed to work outside only under the closest supervision – not close enough however – because he eventually escaped after nine years in the asylum.

While Frost's ink marks on paper were taken to evince criminal proclivities, John McGowan's neatly written letter, dated 24 December 1888 on plain cream writing paper, had the opposite effect:

Dr King, Sir,

> I would feel very grateful could I only obtain my discharge as a cured patient. I am now about six years an inmate of the Asylum I am of the opinion that at least the past four years I am capable of mixing amongst sane men and women.

> Dear Sir, As to my conduct for the past years I would refer you to Mr McDonal, Mr Wolly, Mr John Bucanin, Mr Alex Robinson. – to all of whom I have been known since I first came to Seacliff. Hoping you will pay some little attention to this letter

I am Sir

Your Obt Sert

John McGowan.

A few days later Truby King wrote, and inserted in the casebook,

> This patient for a long time has been perfectly well behaved and some months ago Mr Torrance tried to get him a situation but people objected to a man who had been in an Asylum. McGowan having written me the attached letter I do not feel justified in detaining him longer especially as he is confident he can find employment outside.[25]

McGowan was Discharged, Recovered, on 31 December 1888.

At least two other patients similarly wrote to King requesting their discharge, which he granted. Their letters were judged to be coherent and rational. Other patients' letters were inserted into the casebook as evidence of their delusional state. And some patients, the Chinese, most notably, and others with limited English, or completely illiterate, could not write in a way that appeared coherent to those in charge.

Internal evidence from the Seacliff Asylum files suggests that many letters were forwarded to families and copies were kept. One 26-year old, for example, wrote a very abusive letter about the superintendent but the doctor's notes recorded it was 'sane enough in parts to be sent'.[26] In 1915, 21-year old Joseph Gilfedder said to be suffering 'delusions of persecution' wrote to the Minister of Justice about the 'very grievous [sic] injustice' done to him by his detention in Seacliff and the abuse he experienced from other patients. Three months later, he was regarded as having made a 'remarkable recovery' and was discharged.[27]

Not all letters were sent; some were censored and retained in the casebooks. When Jessie Wright composed a letter to her family charging that she had been 'kicked, cursed and beaten even my eyes have been kicked black and blue' and that she was covered with bruises, the doctor immediately examined her in the presence of the matron and charge nurse and noted she had not a single bruise or 'any sign of injury' on her body.[28] The doctor on staff later noted Jessie's complaint that he had detained her letter, and when he next saw her writing she said 'this one will go, you devil.'[29] He replied, 'certainly if it is decent'. She then ran to him and slapped him over the face. The same patient was devoted to the Medical Superintendent, Frederic Truby King, writing to him as 'Darling and Only Truby' and 'Dear Old Socks' and signing off 'lovingly and devotedly yours'.

In the Medical Superintendent's Letterbook we find requests to relatives and friends, maintaining relationships. 'Your wife', Truby King wrote to Mr Beckett of Matuara, on 22 December 1888, 'I am happy to say is recovered and can now be discharged. When will you come for her?' King also wrote to a Mrs A.D. Hall of Clydesdale, Mataura, to inform her that 'Mrs Beckett is recovered and leaving the asylum – her husband will be requested to call for her.'[30]

In Truby King's census casebook of 1888, three new means of rendering disorder intelligible appear. First, the asylum now had specially printed Seacliff Asylum Diet and Thermic charts to keep track of individual diets and temperature – matters that had once been general and merely observed, now became strictly measured and recorded. Second, generic charts for temperature, respiration, etc. (meaning bodily evacuations) – appear. Third, the standardized admission form first becomes evident, with its list of questions about history and behaviour, and special section for women noting menstrual and childbearing history.[31]

In 1890, new insertions were made in the casebooks: patients began to be photographed (Brookes 2011a, 2011b). Johanna Beckett is photographed three times on her next 1890 admission, the photographs were pasted on a sheet of lined paper and inserted separately into the file. The albumen prints create a typology: from madness to recovery. This new kind of paperwork became more systematic overtime. Photographs may have informed doctors' decision-making, but it is more likely they allowed a mobile workforce of staff to recognize the patients under their care. The files, as Weber has noted, assisted stability in an institution where the long stays of many of the patients exceeded that of most of the staff. Here, we can see how the paperwork assisted knowledge as a form of control: it enabled staff to access unfamiliar histories on paper which were well known to many residents through experience.

Released in April 1891, Johanna Beckett's January 1897 road back to the Seacliff Asylum began with her husband's letter, written on robust cream, red-lined paper, to the local constable:

Dear Sir,

> This wife of mine refuses to be ruled by me and goes to the neighbours and annoys them & their children by using bad language I here [sic] yet they appear to refuse to inform of her. She is now in your hands to do to her as the Law directs.[32]

This letter led to Johanna being delivered to the Gore police station and then back to the asylum. One of the local constables reported that he had 'repeatedly found her wandering about the hills naked', while the other noted her constant hymn singing and praying and annoyance of her neighbours with 'abuse and foul language'. Her husband noted that she became 'decidedly insane every now and then' for about three weeks and then regained composure.

In reply to a letter requesting payment for his wife's care, Henry Beckett, an occasional preacher for the Disciples of Christ, revealed something of his own state of mind, saying that he could not undertake to send a remittance every four weeks for a number of reasons such as bad roads and wet weather. 'Secondly', he stated, it is altogether contrary to the word of God that a believer should make any such promises, what if God's son comes and takes away his own .... Could I come down out of heaven and put it into the Bank?[33]

Johanna was again discharged from the Asylum, 'recovered', on the 23 July 1897.[34]

In December of that year, she was readmitted and never, apparently, saw her husband again. Paper provided the means for the dissolution of the intimate contract of marriage. At the divorce proceedings instigated by Henry Beckett in 1910, Johanna was present only as a simulacrum: her photograph in the asylum register was produced, allowing Henry Beckett to affirm that the patient was indeed his wife.[35] Asylum paperwork could then undo marriage.

While undoing marriage was a rare mediation for asylum files, dealing with death was relatively common. Handwritten notes recorded death and who was present. Attendant Bowie noted his presence at the death of John Lindgren who had spent 40 years in the asylum and died aged 69 in 1904. Lindgren's nearest relative could not be found so his body, together with stamped paperwork, was sent to the medical school for dissection. A separate piece of paper recorded the size of the coffin – 5'9" long and 18" wide – ordered to transport the corpse.

Paperwork could also, miraculously, restore the dead to life. One man, in a case of bureaucratic misadventure, was advised of his wife's death in an egregious paperwork error. He visited Seacliff and identified the corpse as that of his spouse. Later, the Medical Superintendent wrote to advise him that his wife was still alive in the asylum. Not only the woman patient, but also her husband, had forgotten who she was. The knowledge contained in the files had to power to maintain individual identity in the face of the estrangement wrought by lunacy.

Paperwork errors, as this incident illustrates, could also lead to loss of identity.

Paperwork signified the asylum's power to the community – its letterhead conveyed an authority: it was an authority stamped on more and more forms and memos as the asylum population grew and the Superintendent has less time to write personal letters. Patients were drawn into the preservation of paperwork. J. Caradus, Official visitor, commented on a 'useful form of employment for some of the patients' in 1896. A bookbinding department had been created where patients bound the report books to be used by each Official Visitor and Inspector. The work produced in that department, he noted, compared 'favourably with the products of more pretentious establishments'.[36]

By 1911, the clerk's typewriter was in evidence on the paper files; carbon copies made the transmission of information ever easier.

If we look carefully at asylum paperwork, rather than through it, we can see a counter-narrative to those bleak histories that see in those files only the 'manufacture of madness' and asylum doctors as agents of oppression (Swartz 2008, 302). The files show how the accretion of marks of paper, demanded for the purposes of state accountability, laboured to translate incomprehensibility into coherence. This worked in the state's interest, allowing it to tabulate diagnoses, ethnicities, recoveries, ages, lengths of stay and operating costs, and to compare New Zealand's incidence of insanity with figures from other nations. A form of coherence also worked in the interests of families complicit in committing their relatives. It provided a way of dealing with estrangement; making suffering legible so that all parties to the encounter with madness, including the person who 'had taken leave of their senses', might find comfort in a diagnosis.

Johanna Beckett's noisy ravings became transposed into a diagnosis of 'simple mania'. Her condition was understood, in part, to be a result of 'ill-treatment' by her husband. Her dishevelled state, photographed on one admission, signifying madness, was translated into a demure and tidy appearance on a departure, signifying cure. In using Johanna's file, I have made her extraordinary and in the process elided the stories of others. Yet the plethora of paperwork is replete with blank spaces: patients who could not write, whose voices were not heard or resisted any kind of coherence of word or action, and became reduced to the description of 'chronic incurables, dirty, noisy, restless creatures'.[37] The absence of these voices from the asylum files has led to their historical absence: what can be said about those adults who required care of a kind usually reserved for infants? The daily cleaning and feeding rituals that such patients required, and that families were often unprepared to do, were performed by others in asylums.

Once hidden and still protected by a 100-year rule governing access, some Seacliff patient files now have a curated online life in one exhibition entitled 'Being at Seacliff Lunatic Asylum' and some Flickr sites, one entitled 'Seacliff Case History Johanna Beckett' where the statutory papers, photographs and divorce papers may now be found.[38] In the archive, the bundles of tied statutory papers lie separately from the casebooks and the medical superintendent's letter books. One has to know where to look to follow the sequence of events from admission, to casebook, to discharge. In the digital exhibition space, these documents are laid alongside each other giving the appearance of a coherent chain of events. Whereas once archives saw their main duty as one of preservation, they are now under an imperative to reach a wider public to justify their existence. Those paper files of tragedy become a digital enticement to a public interested in the out of kilter world of the mentally ill.

That original paperwork, captured in government files, attempted to make the incoherent coherent, to translate the multiplicity of symptoms –

from shouting to silence, from violence to complete passivity – into legible signs. Those signs were then used first, by the state to account for – and count up – both the people and the costs of incarceration. Second, the personnel involved – doctors and nurses – used the signs to classify mental states. Third, these signs, or diagnoses, were sought by those in the community who wished to understand the afflictions that transformed their loved ones into strangers. Madness robbed individuals of their history. By enquiring as to their history from others, relations and friends, doctors could reconstruct lives forgotten. The paperwork recorded this act of restitution.

The act of committal by paper captured individual misery but it did so because it was part of a system of accounting for the act of denying the liberty of the subject. That system attempted to create method in forms, casebooks and charts, but the suffering of individuals resisted neat categories just as the paperwork eluded order with pasted-in pages, letters and drawings attached with pins, writing spilling beyond margins and cases moving between books. Digital curation removes that disorder and hence changes the impact of the paper files. The unruliness and fragility of the paper mirrored the very disorders of the people it sought to contain.

Notes

1. 'Report on the Mental Hospitals of the Colony for 1906', *Appendices to the Journals of the House of Representatives* [hereafter *AJHR*]1907, H-07, 7. https://atojs.natlib.govt.nz/cgi-bin/atojs?a=d&cl=search&d=AJHR1907-I.2.4. 2.7&srpos=7&e=———-10-1—bySH—0-AJHR_1907_I_H-.
2. *Nelson Examiner and New Zealand Chronicle*, 8 April 1842, 17.
3. *New Zealander*, 18 January 1851, 3.
4. *Wellington Independent*, 26 July 1851, p.3.
5. IAI 118 1853/1422, William Davies, Colonial Surgeon Auckland to Colonial Secretary, Auckland, 2 June 1853. Archives New Zealand [hereafter ANZ], Wellington.
6. IAI 118 1853/1422, William Davies, Colonial Surgeon Auckland to Colonial Secretary, Auckland, 2 June 1853. ANZ, Wellington.
7. *Otago Daily Times*, 23 July 1863, 6.
8. LA1 255 [13] 1864, ANZ, Wellington.
9. The first newspaper advertisement for Reade's novel appears in the *New Zealand Herald*, 28 March 1864, 2 and it is advertised widely thereafter.
10. 'Report of the Commission of Enquiry into the Constitution and Management of the Dunedin Hospital and Lunatic Asylum', Province of Otago, New Zealand, *Votes and Proceedings of the Provincial Council*, Session VIII, Dunedin, 1864, 6.
11. Ibid.
12. Ibid. 7.
13. *New Zealand Herald*, 5 May 1868, 2.
14. 'The Lunatic Asylum Case,' *Otago Witness*, 4 November 1876, 10.

15. Ibid.
16. *Report of the Joint Committee on Lunatic Asylums, AJHR*, 1871 Session I, H-10, 3.
17. Thomas Aickin, Resident Surgeon, Auckland Asylum, 6 October 1871, *Report of the Joint Committee on Lunatic Asylums, AJHR*, 1871 Session I, H-10, 17.
18. http://www.nzsgb.org.uk/postofficeacts/1858PostalServicesAct.pdf.
19. https://teara.govt.nz/en/mail-and-couriers/page-2.
20. 'Report on Lunatic Asylums of the Colony for 1883',*AJHR*, H-7, 1884, 1.
21. Report of the Government Printing Department, *AJHR*, 1881, II, H-10, 5 lists amount spent on printing for Lunatic Asylums in 1880 as £32 4s 3d. Report of the Government Printing Department, *AJHR*, 1883, III, H-12, 5 reports the expense for 1882 as £140 3s 0d.
22. The following forms are drawn from this file: Statutory Admission Papers Nos. 2046–2140, DAHI D266 19850 Box 17 ANZ Dunedin.
23. Statutory Admission Papers Nos.2141–2250, 1887–1889, DAHI D266 19850 Box 18, ANZ, Dunedin.
24. DAHI D265 19956 Box 1, p.461, ANZ Dunedin.
25. 24 December 1888 & 29 December 1888, DAHI D265 19956 Box 1, p.461, ANZ Dunedin.
26. Barry Bradley admitted 18 August 1888, DAHI D265 19956 Box 1 ANZ, Dunedin.
27. DAHA D264 19956 Box 74, no.34, case 5501, ANZ, Dunedin.
28. DAHA D264 19956 Box 73, no.33, case 5564, ANZ, Dunedin.
29. DAHA D264 19956 Box 73, no.33, case 5564, ANZ Dunedin. The rest of the paragraph is drawn from this file.
30. Medical Superintendent's Letterbook vol. 1A DAHI 19828 Acc D264, ANZ, Dunedin.
31. Such a form may be seen here: http://archives.govt.nz/gallery/v/Online+Regional+Exhibitions/Archives+New+Zealand+Dunedin+Regional+Office+Gallery/Being+at+Seacliff+Lunatic+Asylum/Being+a+Patient/Patient+2947/Medical+Casebook/DAHI-19956-D264-48+-+Case+2947+-+page+3.jpg.html?g2_imageViewsIndex=1.
32. DAHI D266 19850 Box 25, ANZ, Dunedin.
33. DAHI 19850 Acc D266 Case no. 2984, ANZ, Dunedin.
34. SLA–DAHI/19850/D266/25, Statutory Admission papers, patient 2984, ANZ, Dunedin. She remained in Seacliff from December 1897 until her death in 1918. In 1910, Henry Beckett successfully sued for divorce and Truby King gave evidence 'that there was no chance of Mrs Beckett's recovery'. *Evening Post*, 29 June 1910, 3.
35. Divorce Files, Notes of Evidence, DAAC D437 21220 1045, ANZ, Dunedin.
36. Seacliff Hospital Report Book, J. Caradus Official Visitor, 16 November 1896–1 January 1907. DAHI D264 19826 Box 2, ANZ, Dunedin.
37. 'Report on Lunatic Asylums of the Colony', for 1887, *AJHR*, 1888, Session 1H-08.
38. http://archives.govt.nz/gallery/v/Online+Regional+Exhibitions/Archives+New+Zealand+Dunedin+Regional+Office+Gallery/Being+at+Seacliff+Lunatic+Asylum/Being+a+Patient/Patient+2947/Medical+Casebook/DAHI-19956-D264-48+-+Case+2947+-+page+3.jpg.html?g2_imageViewsIndex=1 https://www.flickr.com/photos/archivesnz/albums/72157685717615381/with/36904965876/.

Acknowledgments

I want to thank Tony Ballantyne and Craig Robertson for first asking me to consider asylum paperwork. Thanks to the Centre for Research on Culture at the University of Otago which funded that initial workshop and made our 2017 workshop possible. The input of all participants has been crucial and I thank them.

Disclosure statement

No potential conflict of interest was reported by the author.

Funding

This work was supported by the University of Otago Research Grant [14406 2740].

References

Legislation 1858. "Lunatics Ordinance Amendment 1868 Lunatics Act." http://www.nzlii.org/nz/legis/hist_act/la186832v1868n16232/
1882. "Lunatics Act." http://www.nzlii.org/nz/legis/hist_act/la188246v1882n34189/

Books and Articles

Bazerman, C. 1988. *Shaping Written Knowledge. The Genre and Activity of the Experimental Article in Science*. Madison: University of Wisconsin Press.
Beveridge, A. 1998. "Life in the Asylum: Patients' Letters from Morningside, 1873–1908." *History of Psychiatry* 9: 431–469. doi:10.1177/0957154X9800903602.
Black, J. 2014. *The Power of Knowledge. How Information and Technology Made the Modern World*. New Haven: Yale University Press.
Brookes, B. 2011a. "Pictures of People, Pictures of Places: Photography and the Asylum." In *Exhibiting Madness in Museums: Remembering Psychiatry through Collections and Display*, Eds. C. Coleborne and D. MacKinnon, 30–47. New York: Routledge.
Brookes, B. 2011b. "The Asylum Lens: Photographs in the Seacliff Asylum Case Files." In *Early New Zealand Photography: Images and Essays*, Eds. A. Wanhalla and E. Wolf, 98–103. Dunedin: Otago University Press.
Coleborne, C. 2010. *Madness in the Family: Insanity and Institution in the Australasian Colonial World, 1860-1914*, 88–106. Basingstoke: Palgrave Macmillan.

Coleborne, C. 2015. *Insanity, Identity and Empire: Immigrants and Institutional Confinement in Australia and New Zealand, 1873–1910*. Manchester: Manchester University Press.

Conolly, J. 1847. *The Construction and Government of Lunatic Asylums and Hospitals for the Insane*. London: John Churchill. https://archive.org/details/constructiongove00cono.

Dierks, K. 2009. *In My Power. Letter Writing and Communications in Early America*. Philadelphia: University of Pennsylvania Press.

Hull, M. S. 2012. "Documents and Bureaucracy." *Annual Review of Anthropology*. doi:10.1146/annurev.anthro.012809.104953.

Kafka, B. 2009. "Paperwork: The State of the Discipline." *Book History* 12: 340–353. doi:10.1353/bh.0.0024.

MacKenzie, C. 1992. *Psychiatry for the Rich: A History of Ticehurst Private Asylum, 1792–1917*. London: Routledge.

McCandless, P. 1978. "Liberty and Lunacy: The Victorians and Wrongful Confinement." *Journal Of Social History* 11 (3): 366–386.

McCarthy, A. 2015. *Migration, Ethnicity, Madness: New Zealand 1860–1910*. Dunedin: University of Otago Press.

Scull, A. 1989. *Social Order/Mental Disorder: Anglo-American Psychiatry in Historical Perspective*. Berkeley: University of California Press.

Smith, L. D. 1999. *'Cure, Comfort and Safe Custody'. Public Lunatic Asylums in Early Nineteenth Century England*. London: Leicester University Press.

Swartz, S. 2008. "Colonial Lunatic Asylum Archives: Challenges to Historiography." *Kronos* 34: 285–302.

Swartz, S. 2010. "The Regulation of British Colonial Lunatic Asylums and the Origins of Colonial Psychiatry, 1860 to 1864." *History of Psychology* 13 (2): 160–177.

Swartz, S. 2015. *Homeless Wanders. Movement and Mental Illness in the Cape Colony in the Nineteenth Century*. Cape Town: UCT Press.

Tomes, N. 1984. *A Generous Confidence; Thomas Story Kirkbride and the Art of Asylum-Keeping, 1840–1883*. New York: Cambridge University Press.

Vismann, C. 2008. *Files. Law and Media Technology*. Stanford: Stanford University Press. Trans by Geoffrey Winthrop-Young.

Weber, M. 1978. *Economy and Society*. Vol. 2. edited by G. Roth and C. Wittich. Berkeley: University of California Press.

Paper Soldiers: the life, death and reincarnation of nineteenth-century military files across the British Empire

Charlotte Macdonald ⓘ and Rebecca Lenihan

ABSTRACT
From the moment a man took 'the king's shilling' and was sworn to serve as a soldier in the nineteenth-century British Army, his life proceeded as a file as well as a fighting man. Disorder and desertion drove the utilitarian purposes of discipline and tracking, while constant pressure to account for expenditure in lives and money added further impetus to the copious industry of military record-keeping. Individuals were enumerated, named, appraised and allocated pay. Such archives produce a disorderly silence where men are present but without voice. Carefully archived and always public, military files have a continuing currency through the post-army lives of soldiers into the twenty-first century for descendants and historians. Tracking the life of 'files' over time, the paper reflects on the shifting forms of knowledge produced. In particular, it notes the tensions between the densely written form of the files in a population of rank and file soldiers who were partially literate; the highly detailed individuation of the files within a heavily conformist institution, and the modernity of post-1850s record-keeping in an institution bound by tradition. It ends with a reflection on the limitations and opportunities presented by digital access to this substantial archive of imperial-colonial conflict.

Abbreviations: AJCP: Australian Joint Copying Project TNA: The National Archives, London WO: War Office

Introduction

From the moment a man took 'the king's shilling' and was sworn to serve as a soldier in nineteenth-century Britain, his life proceeded as a file as well as a fighting man, a number as well as a name; his identity inked on paper as firmly as the redcoat on his person. By the nineteenth century, tens of thousands of men comprising 'the thin red line' of Britain's rank and file army appear by name and some detail in the copious written records of the

War Office, an early manifestation of 'big data'.[1] The scale of the military archive is vast; its reach into the labouring class and sparsely documented levels of society, remarkable.[2] The extensive War Office archive testifies to the military as an engine of knowledge production at a time of unparalleled British expansion as an imperial and 'information state' (Higgs 2004). The 'archive story' it tells, as Burton (2005) and Perry (2015) remind us, is of a technology central in the creation of an imperial world rather than simply 'a window into it' (Perry 2015, 1).[3] The status of paper and writing, together with the accomplishment of elaborate bureaucratic machinery, underscore clerical mastery as both the instrument and demonstration of Victorian imperial power and culture.

Our work on these files is part of a larger investigation into the military's social and cultural reach, as well as its significance as an institution of enforcement. We are interested in putting a face to troops of the line sent to quell indigenous resistance to Britain's global expansion. In particular, we are seeking to identify the 12,000 or so redcoat soldiers sent to combat Māori resistance in 1860s New Zealand. Building mobility, occupational and epidemiological profiles for individuals in uniform provides a means to explore the local, variable and connected nature of the British garrison world. Balancing a qualitative or micro-level interest in individuals with a quantitative macro-level of analysis of trend and pattern is our goal. The global reach of Britain's empire during the years spanning the Crimean war, the Indian Rebellion and the Morant Bay massacre forms the backdrop of the wider research project.[4]

Military records are the oldest form of personal archival file. Defending the state was the first call on a population and is thus the link between state and record that reaches longest in time. Nineteenth-century soldiers were subjects but not citizens. This makes them, and records relating to them, very different from those of the rights-bearing soldier citizen of the twentieth century. In rethinking these archives as producers of colonial as well as military knowledge, we are asking new questions of what might be considered conventional residues of the formal, hierarchical, even archaic, institution of the British Army: War Office papers which form one of major collections in a national archive in a metropole that has despatched its imperial past to the archive while embracing a national present (Colley 2002; *JICH* special issue 2011). The paper places the nineteenth-century military files within the textual construction of empire. Doing so recognises coercion as an essential part of empire's functioning. It also underlines the post-Crimean War's army's reliance on modern paper and record-keeping systems as much as on its developing technology of rifles over muskets, chloroform and sanitary practice. Within the bureaucratic filing system was the imposition of a fiscal, hygienic, and disciplinary order over a mass of men whose bodies, behaviour and mobility were, in many ways, pressing at the bounds of control.

We are considering the development and functioning of these paper technologies across the years of transition from information recorded on the body (skin) through brand markings to a record on paper with a stable enumerated and nominal identity (a number and a name). The army was part of the creation of what has been termed a 'legible people' – a population known to itself and the state via the written record. The discussion also asks what happens when the files generated by the growth of a paper bureaucracy and advancing literacy are released from the handwritten pages of bound volumes of their nineteenth-century originals into digital forms accessible at any time from any locality at the stroke of a few keys. Where do such digital archives reside, how are they discovered, what is their form and meaning as reincarnated or reconfigured traces of a past?

The article first considers the context in which mid-nineteenth-century military files were created, their immediate uses – focusing particularly on identity, character and finance – and then turns to the various afterlives of files through the later careers of soldiers, and into the realm of memory, archive and the digital present of historical investigation.

Writing war

By the late 1850s and early 1860s, the British Army was located to a greater degree across the globe than it was at home. Of the 120,000–200,000 men serving in the army through the middle decades of the nineteenth century, more than half were abroad at any one time (Spiers 1980; Strachan 1984; Burroughs 2003; Darwin 2012). In these circumstances, a portable, reliable and centralized filing system was imperative, and contemporary technologies of communication and transport made it possible. Regimental headquarters, the army command at Horse Guards and the War Office all generated huge quantities of letterbooks, ledgers and folios, consuming ink and paper by the gross.

Yet, the limits of such government machinery were exposed by the management – or mismanagement – of British forces in the Crimean war of 1854–1856. Official information was at the forefront of public attention through scandals surrounding the failure to equip or feed soldiers sufficiently, and in the catastrophic toll of lives taken by disease. The reorganisation of the War Office in 1855 occurred under a blaze of political controversy and public scrutiny. Calls to hold logistical and military incompetence to account by journalist W. H. Russell and campaigner Florence Nightingale amounted to demands for moral responsibility, as well as efficiency of 'the information state' (Higgs 2004; Hadley 2016; Kopf 1916; Woodham-Smith 1950 ; Smith 1982; Baly and Matthew 2011). Charles

Dickens' (1855–57) satirical 'Circumlocution Office' was a direct response to these events.[5] Army reforms in the mid-1850s bringing supplies and the autonomous and often opportunist commissariat subworld under stronger centralized political and administrative control were part of the broader formation of a bureaucratic British state (MacDonagh 1961; Higgs 2004). Counting and accountability were central functions, yet the balance between the mastery possible through a rational and quantified bureaucratic machinery, and the vagaries of living human bodies and souls, produced an uncertain fulcrum. It was, as Elaine Hadley (2016) suggests, an era of 'Nobody, Somebody, and Everybody'.

Army records evolved considerably over the course of the nineteenth century, becoming more substantial and elaborate than their eighteenth-century predecessors. In 1768, Captain Bennett Cuthbertson suggested an improvement by way of specialisation. From the one compendium documenting all matters of interest, he recommended four distinct volumes: a registry of casualties, deaths, discharges and desertion; a volume of orders; a volume of annual reviews and returns; and a volume of 'March Routes and Returns of Arms, Accoutrements, Ammunition, Cloathing [sic], Camp-equipage, and Forage, received by, and delivered to the Regiment' (Steppler 1988, 8). In this elaboration, we see the beginnings of what came to be a proliferation in record series: notably, a demarcation between military and administrative domains, and further specialisation in areas such as pay, equipment and sanitary conditions.

Rank underscored every aspect of the nineteenth-century military record, the archive mirroring formal army hierarchy. Officers and men entered the army via different routes, ate at different messes and were remunerated in different ways. In most circumstances, it was an offence for a private soldier to directly address an officer. Officers and men exist in separate archive series and were separated within files. The record of officers is a great deal more full, more indexed and more likely to be made accessible through digitisation or by other means than records relating to the mass of rank and file men who served as privates.[6] In death, rank still mattered. Reporting on losses at Rangiriri, for example, Deputy Quarter Master General Colonel D. J. Gamble followed the established convention in listing Lieutenant-Colonel Austen (severely wounded) before Captain Phelps (since dead) – along with five unnamed 'men' killed and seven wounded of the 2/14th regiment (Crawford 1990).[7]

Enlistment was the point at which men first entered into lives in the line – becoming soldiers on paper and on the parade ground. Attestation forms captured a man at this first step, recording the basic details enabling him to be accurately identified from thereon: name, regiment, regimental number, previous trade and birthplace, as well as physical characteristics. When

Liverpool-born Stephen Waterson joined up with the 68th regiment in the spring of 1858, he was given the number 351 and noted as a 22-year-old carpenter, the duty clerk recording his light brown hair, grey eyes and height of 5 ft, 4½ inches.[8] Name and regimental number were the predominant identifiers carried across to other records.[9] The regimental number was not only the number assigned *to* men but also the number known and used *by* them. A military life was one of enumerated identity.

For all its scope and methodical arrangement, the military record is also riven with the tension of a system comprised of individuals yet designed to function as 'a body'. Military files show us a process of individuation in a context, and institution, whose purpose was to create conformity and whose mode was uniformity. While the records that are our focus pertain to individuals, the chief purpose of the files when they were produced was not to create a personalised record, per se, but to detail individuals as constituent parts of the broader organisation.

The careful identification of each man who signed up was especially important because information about any individual was not concentrated in any one central file but fragmented across multiple records serving distinct purposes (and often located in very disparate parts of the world). Army records were structured in serialised form dictated by the quarterly muster, monthly returns, campaign returns, discharge applications, medal lists, pension records, court martials and more (see Spencer 2008).[10] These files are not organised biographically. Bringing together the linked but fragmented entries relating to named men is laborious but does enable some reconstitution of specific lives.

The state's interest in the vast majority of soldiers who served as rank and file was utilitarian and minimal, while also continuous, efficient and systematic. The overriding imperatives were less to do with social efficiency and more with fiscal accountability. At the time of its creation, the massive paper record created by the army and War Office served the purpose of maintaining order and discipline – over expenditure and the behaviour of men whose backgrounds and living circumstances produced a reputation of rough physicality and social vulgarity. Establishing and maintaining a specific and unique paper identity for each man, and ensuring that identity continued to correspond to the men physically present at any one place or time, was a constant challenge. Counting and tracking soldiers was necessary as a check against men absconding. Army service was rarely popular. Through most of the period under discussion, life in the army was a choice of last resort. The nineteenth-century army often struggled to hold on to those who had once been persuaded to swear allegiance. Military records are, in this sense, a disciplinary record. Identifying individual men and counting them was a daily, weekly, monthly and quarterly undertaking. Such regular tracking and enumeration was also necessary in the highly dispersed mid-nineteenth-century empire with thousands of men in India, Australia, the Caribbean, Canada and in the 1860s in New Zealand. The centralised record-keeping system was the machinery that held it together.

Regimental numbers were important, but names provided the core element in tracking individuals. The nominal value of the military record, to contemporaries, and for historical enquiry, cannot be overestimated. Names of those serving were public knowledge at the time, and have remained so; it is public information, a matter of disclosure, even proclamation. Confidentiality is not a feature of military files as it is for hospital, asylum, welfare or even electoral records. The recording of men's names, place of birth, and physical appearance at the point of enlistment brought large numbers of men from low social strata into the written record of the state. Alongside other innovations of the early-to-mid-nineteenth century such as censuses, state registration of births, deaths and marriages, and social surveys, what we see is the development of an 'official culture of written records'. Writing individuals into a government record on this mass, universalising basis created what James Scott has termed a 'legible people' (Caplan and Torpey 2001, 2). Such processes of 'writing' individuals into a government record made the specification of individual identity fundamental to the operation of the modern state.[11]

Establishing and maintaining personal identity in the nineteenth century were more proximate processes before photography, fingerprinting or even very reliable production of paper 'proofs' of identity came into use. Evidence of birth (such as a birth certificate or baptismal entry) and the link between that 'proof' and an individual adult person were modern practices made possible by state, as well as church registration, technologies of paper, literacy and record-keeping. But distances in time and space precluded recourse to, or the production of such information when asked to verify the question: who are you? Such difficulties provided opportunities for the less scrupulous. As Kirsten McKenzie's work (2004, 2009a, 2009b) shows, the possibility of invention and reinvention was especially rife across the late eighteenth and nineteenth century, and nowhere more so than in the motley, mobile and uncertain milieus of colonial societies.[12] The 'self-made man' of colonial opportunity (including the deserting or discharged soldier) could be taken to the full extent of adopting a new identity. It is not uncommon to encounter 'aliases' in military files – men who were known to authorities under more than one name. We must assume that for those that *were* known to contemporaries, there were others whose guise was not exposed and who changed name, or used more than one identity across their lives.

For the nineteenth-century army, descriptions of the bodies of men offered the best means of fixing individual identity. Bodies were understood as stable entities (or more so than other surfaces) and thus 'could be linked to themselves across time and space' through a clerical record (Anderson 2004, 2). Physical appearance (height, eye colour, distinguishing marks) was valuable to the nineteenth-century army primarily as a means of securing identity, rather than, as it became in the twentieth century, a record of men's eligibility for military service, or information used for monitoring fitness within an ongoing medical regime. The nineteenth-century army's interest was more limited: the soldier's body was a means of identity, an accounting unit (someone who had to be paid), a commissariat unit (a unit to be provisioned in food, rum and clothing) and a unit of force (to be armed and drilled).

The bodies of soldiers also operated as military files, as surfaces upon which the army 'wrote' its own disciplinary record. Like prisoners and convicts in other places across the global empire, the practice of tattooing or branding recalcitrant soldiers was part of the army's system of discipline well into the nineteenth century. Our period of study sits within the transition in the categorisation and tracking of subordinate groups from physical marking to the paper record. Clare Anderson's (2004, 4) discussion of efforts 'to render the bodies of prisoners, convicts and habitual offenders legible' through 'the use of visible signs to connect individuals to their written record' in the south Asian colonial setting also applies to the nineteenth-century army.[13]

Both military and carceral power relied on systems of information that tracked the bodies of those under their control (Kent 1997, 78–88). The branding and tattooing of bodies was a form of information that existed alongside paper in upholding order, in marking identity and in tracking individuals in situations where people were moving from place to place (and in which they were subject to direct state power, as transported convicts, for example, in the courts and penal system). The marking of the body by tattooing could also be a practice of self-fashioning (Caplan 1997).

Desertion was a constant threat to army discipline, and a temptation to men riling under the brutal regime of a regiment. Notifications of deserters relied on physical descriptions of offenders. When John Morrisey of the 65th regiment deserted on 19 December 1861, he was described in the *New Zealand Gazette* as being marked with an eagle on his right arm, a bracelet on his left wrist and an anchor on both of his thumbs (Sexton 1984, 75). John Newby, deserting on 20 August 1862, is noted as having lost the first joint of the forefinger of his right hand (Sexton 1984, 97). Desertion was a serious offence; those caught risked wearing their offence for life. Until 1871, men found guilty of deserting were often branded on the left side of their chest with a 'D', or with 'BC' for those Bad Characters who had deserted with premeditation (Burroughs 1985, 570). Alexander Mann, Charles Rolfe and William Johnson were all deserting for the second time when notified, and all were reported as marked with a 'D' (Sexton 1984, 36, 37). Flogging, the common mode of punishment for rank and file, left marks – 'stripes' – on the bodies of those on whom it was inflicted.[14] 'Marks of corporal punishment' are recorded alongside the letter D in the description of Andrew Archer when noted for desertion for the third time on 26 January 1863 (Sexton 1984, 83). The royal commission on courts martial and punishment in 1869 endorsed branding as a method of punishment. It was only abandoned in 1871 in order to reduce the unattractiveness of soldiering (Burroughs 1985, 570).[15]

Bodies were the most important thing the army had at its disposal: the brute force exercised by men as enforcers. The files we are concerned with are, at their essence, an accounting of the supply, use and expiry of this core 'material'. They chart the fates of those 'materials' from the moment they become something the army can use, to the moment that resource becomes 'non-effective'. In the medical records that survive – usually for those who became 'non-effective' due to a medical condition – we see wounds and other injuries sustained on and off the battlefield, as well as deaths due to active engagement, accidents and disease. The files thus fulfil a fiscal purpose through their charting of the consumption of body-power. The nineteenth-century army regarded the individual man as a resource to be tracked, to be supplied, to be transported and also to be expended. There is little expectation of maintaining a fitness for service beyond certain minimums. Instead, the military operated on the basis of 'using up' the vigour of a man during his period of duty, and on the assumption that the supply of men available for service could be easily replenished from the numerous labouring poor, especially from rural Ireland. Hence, the common discharge 'medically unfit for further service' for a man in his late 30s and the summary medical statement noting a man as 'worn out'. The army took a man's best years.

At various points in their career, soldiers were categorised as to their 'Character' on a scale that ranged from 'Exemplary' to 'Very Good', 'Good', 'Indifferent', 'Bad' and 'Very Bad'. Transgressions such as insubordination, drunkenness, dereliction of duty, falling asleep on duty or being absent without leave were all noted, as were rewards in the form of good conduct badges. Character ascriptions were a quick and readily comprehended set of categorisations, transferable across time and place, and from commanding officer to commanding officer, or across different parts of the same institution. They had a utility in a context where educational measures were either non-existent or non-applicable. 'Character' was a measure of compliance and performance within a rigid structure; a disciplinary rather than a developmental tag, and one with tangible consequences. The behaviours that led to a man being labelled as a bad character had an impact on the effective strength of the force. When men were in civil or military prison for misdemeanours, when they were absent without leave, when they were in hospital – or simply not on duty – due to drunkenness, the force was down a man.

Good behaviour was rewarded with medals, pensions, pay and testimonials (see Figure 1). Good Conduct badges added between 1 and 5 pence per day to a man's pay. However, the number of good conduct badges a man was in possession of appears not to have a direct correlation with how good his character was ultimately judged; there was not a neat calculus of virtue. While the discharge files for Private James Brien record that he had received five good conduct badges, his character is recorded only as 'Good', while Private Michael Burke was the recipient of no good conduct badges but is described as having 'Very good' character.[16] After 21 years of service with the army, Private Richard Pendergast of the 65th regiment wore four good conduct badges, and his character and conduct was recorded as having 'been that of a good and faithful soldier'.[17]

Less favourable character designations often left a more indelible mark in the archive than did good behaviour. The character and conduct of James Carty upon discharge was described as having been 'Latterly good'. He was 'not in possession of any good conduct badges' and had 'been tried twice by Court Martial one of which was for desertion'.[18] Notably, given our earlier discussion of a punishment for desertion being branding, Carty is recorded as having no marks on his body. This aligns with Burroughs' (1985, 570) note that while over two-thirds of deserters in the 1840s were branded, this did not include 'young men of previous good conduct who had behaved impulsively and who might thus be thought capable of mending their ways'. Bad conduct was often linked with drunkenness, as was the case for Private John Prescott of the 68th Regiment whose discharge records state that his conduct was 'Bad – principally drunkenness'.[19] While bad conduct appears mostly to have been punished with deduction of pay, imprisonment, or corporal punishment, in cases where the soldier's behaviour was beyond redemption they were also simply discharged. Such was the case for Joseph Hammill and Thomas William Preston of the 43rd Regiment who are recorded on the New Zealand medal list as having been discharged in June 1869 as bad characters; they are simply entered as 'incorrigible'.[20]

The overarching administrative purpose of all army files was accounting. Military files were financial records, part of an elaborate bookkeeping system at a time when war was the most important and most expensive activity of the state. Soldiers cost money, even in the crude, minimal and brutal conditions in which the majority subsisted. The files record financial obligations to individuals, the ledgers recording days served, pay distributed, supplies issued (including the calculation of pay and 'stoppages' – i.e. deductions for food, accommodation); and summative reports in numerous tabulations of the expense and liability of detachments, regiments, etc.

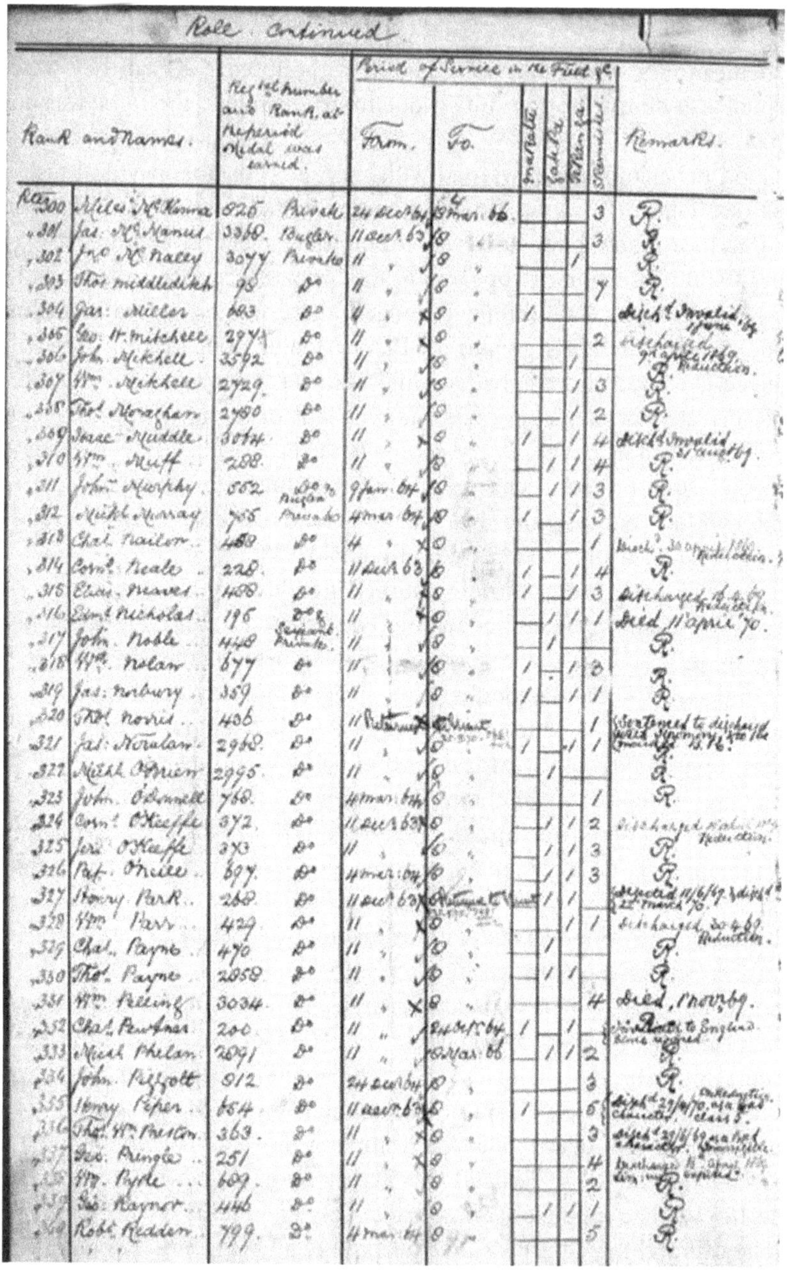

Figure 1. The New Zealand Medal Roll (WO 100/18) for the 43rd Regiment shows the rank and names of all men serving in that regiment in New Zealand, with their regimental number and rank at the time of the period the medal was earned, their period of service in New Zealand, and which fields of battle they served on (Maketu, Gate Pa, Te Ranga and other skirmishes), accompanied with a column of remarks – R signifies that the medal has been received by the man. Other notes refer to discharge and death details between their period of service and when the medal was awarded in 1869. Fifth from the bottom of this page is Thomas William Preston, Regimental number 363, noted as having discharged on 29 June 1869 'as a Bad character. Incorrigible'. 43rd Regiment, WO 100/18, TNA.

Equipping and supplying thousands of men, transporting and housing them, was an expensive business, especially as technological innovations (such as the 1853 Enfield rifle, and post-Crimea sanitary standards) raised the cost of keeping men in the field. Commissariat records tally the scale and cost of feeding, clothing, equipping and transporting soldiers across the empire. In New Zealand, these costs were substantial – in 1865 alone, the army had 26 contracted bakers producing over 300,000 loaves of bread per month.[21]

While quarterly muster rolls (WO 12) provided the army command and Secretary of State for War with a constant measure of the force available (see Figure 2), the record that mattered for a man anticipating leaving his life in uniform was the discharge application (see Figure 3). Discharge marked the exit of men from service, just as enlistment marked their entry. Applications brought together information from across a man's life

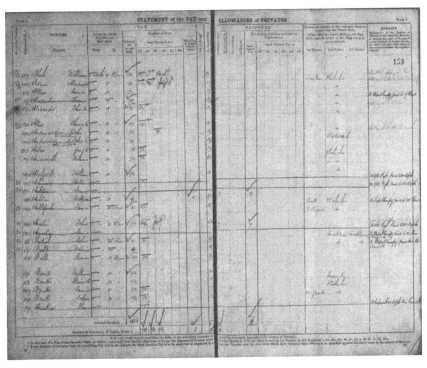

Figure 2. The WO 12 statements of the pay and allowances varied a little by rank. This one, for privates, records regimental number, names, period for which the payment has been made, ordinary and additional pay, pay forfeited, days on board ship, in confinement, or in hospital, reasons for absence at each monthly muster in the quarter, and other remarks. WO 12, 50th Regiment, Period from 1 October 1863 to 31 December 1863, Statement of the Pay and Allowances of Privates (Form 5), AJCP Reel 3803.

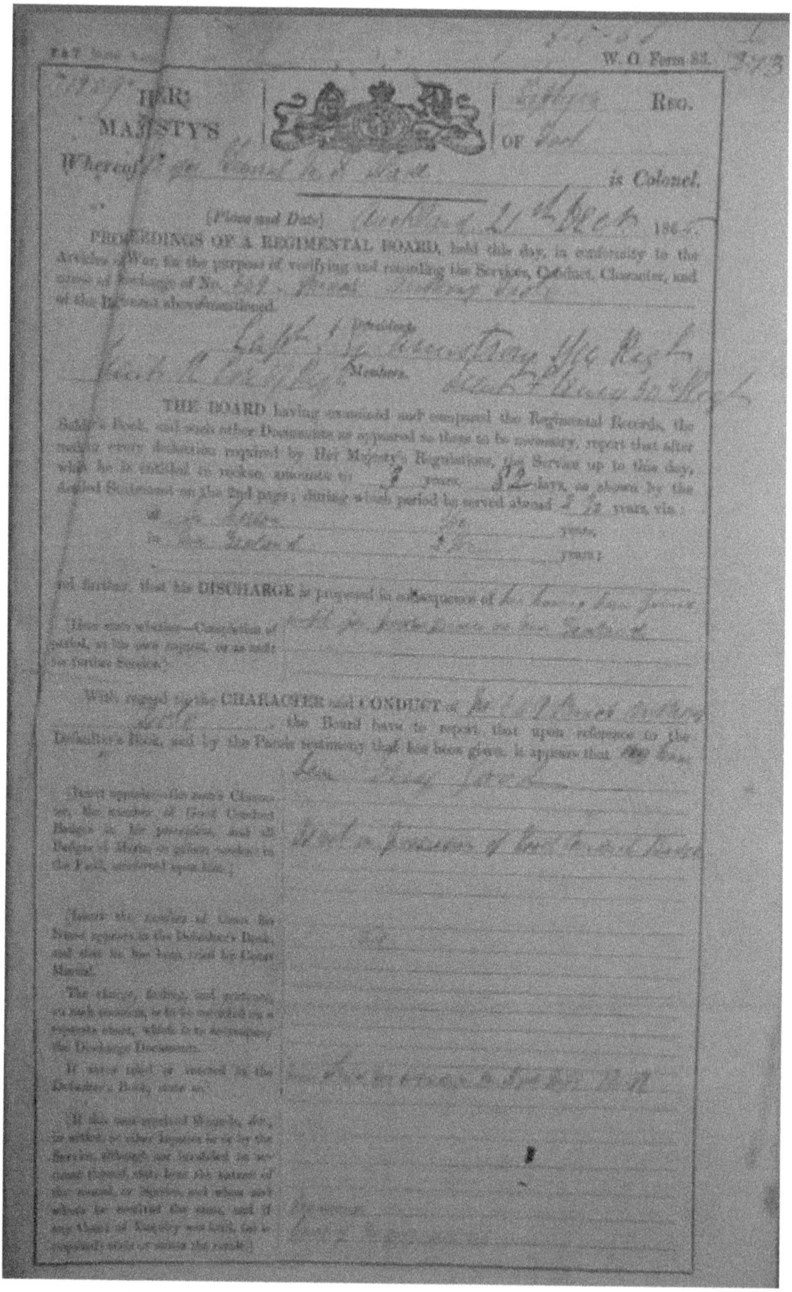
W. O. Form 83.

HER MAJESTY'S REG. OF

is Colonel.

[Place and Date] 186

PROCEEDINGS OF A REGIMENTAL BOARD, held this day, in conformity to the Articles of War, for the purpose of verifying and recording the Services, Conduct, Character, and cause of Discharge of No.

THE BOARD having examined and compared the Regimental Records, the Soldier's Book, and such other Documents as appeared to them to be necessary, report that after making every deduction required by Her Majesty's Regulations, the Service up to this day, which he is entitled to reckon, amounts to years days, as shown by the detailed Statement on the 2nd page; during which period he served abroad years, viz.:

and further, that his DISCHARGE is proposed in consequence of

With regard to the CHARACTER and CONDUCT of the Board have to report, that upon reference to the Defaulter's Book, and by the Parole testimony that has been given, it appears that

Figure 3. The format of each WO 97 discharge form is the same. The front page of this one, for Private Anthony Toole, records that he had served for 3 years and 82 days, 2 years and 1 month of which was served in New Zealand, and that he was discharging unfit for further service, his character and conduct having 'been very good' though he was 'not in possession of Good Conduct Badge'. WO 97/1546, TNA.

in service, sometimes also with a medical inspection. The outcomes of these examinations determined eligibility and payment rates for pensions. Private Anthony Toole of the 50th Regiment was discharged 'unfit for further service' on 8 May 1866 after receiving what the inspecting medical officer recorded as an accidental gunshot wound received while on duty. 'The ball entered in front passed through the forearm coming out of the centre of same', leaving the injured arm 'quite useless and not likely ever to be of much utility', the examiner nevertheless noting that he should still be able to partially contribute to his livelihood.[22] Pension records could reach long after men's years in service, leaving lengthy trails as people moved around the world and as dependents continued to make claims on the basis of a relative's service.[23] In the case of Private Toole, it also tracked behaviour after the period of service. On 15 August 1888, Toole's pension was suspended due to a conviction on the charge of being drunk and disorderly.[24]

The financial content of military files was also the chief place in which women and children appear in what is otherwise a highly gendered, masculine set of records. Women and children appear as the auxiliary obligations of men: as wives, children or mothers, recipients of remitted pay or pension, and sometimes as next of kin. In the quarter ending 30 June 1864, for example, we see Private Hugh Hylands sending a £3 remittance to Mrs Elizabeth Hylands who, without further information, we might infer is his wife or mother.[25] In that same quarter, Mary Hogan of Lismore parish, Waterford, Ireland is recorded as next of kin as the sister of Private William Hogan who died at Pukerimu on 4 June 1864.[26] From 1868 onwards, the WO 12 records include a 'Roll of the Married Establishment' with the names of wives and ages of all children under 14 in years and months. Mary Anne Barnes and her five children aged 1 month to 13 years are recorded in the roll as the wife and children of Private Charles Barnes of the 18th Regiment (Hughes and Hughes 1988, 22). The wives and children of men who had been given permission to 'marry on the strength' (i.e. with entitlement to live in barracks and draw rations) were also recorded in paybooks of those men (see Figure 4). The entries in James Hill's paybook record his marriage to Sarah Anne in Enniskillen on 13 February 1849, and their children born in Kilkenny, Corfu, Malta, Poona and New Plymouth between 1851 and 1862.[27] While slight and scattered, appearances of women and children offer some evidence of the regiments' cognisance of marriage and parental obligations – even as, overall, the army in the 1850s–1860s remained deeply ambivalent in its policy and practice towards marriage. In this regard, the army stands in an anomalous relation to what had become prevailing mid-nineteenth century notions of marriage, domesticity and respectability (see Trustram 1984; Tosh 1999; Davidoff and Hall 2002).

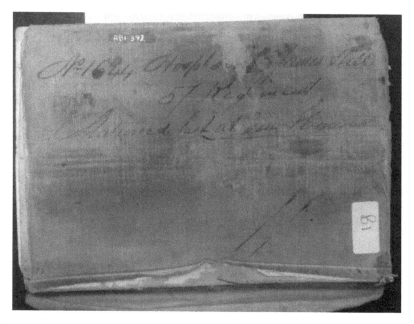

Figure 4. Cover of the paybook of James Hill, ARC 2002-401, Puke Ariki.

For the historical researcher, the archival series produces a thicket of traces, a kind of strobe effect, in which individuals are glimpsed across a shattering light of fractured, serialised records. First encounters with this archive are exhilarating. The profusion of the record, of specificity in detail about people ordinarily beyond the historical reach, of individuals described through the physical traces of hair colour, height, marks on the body, imparts a thrill. The pages contain an orderly, if silent, assemblage of men devoid of sweat, smell, cursing, blistered feet, amputated limbs or quivering fear in moments of action, yet thickly present in the words carefully entered on pages. Military files in this way impart the allure of enumerated precision: History that can be measured, counted, made certain and thereby *known*. Yet that initial excitement, the thrill of 'touching the past', can also turn to ennui, fatigue and disconsolateness in facing the task of making sense of it all, creating a coherent narrative of historical knowledge. It is as if the first rush of the discotheque dance floor, alive with glitter and beat, becomes the out-of-control giddiness of a relentless, flashing thump. As the excitement and adrenalin turn to bewilderment, oppression and hangover, the dream has turned to night-time dread.

What is the remedy to such archive affliction?[28] One is to back away, retying the string around the bundles of paper, replacing lids on boxes of files, rewinding the microfilm reel or keying out of the digital site. In some circumstances, this might be the right option, letting sleeping archive dogs lie – either to continue their repose for a future researcher with greater stamina or different questions, or to leave this record of colonial coercion in monumental obscurity. Another response is to select, either with a systematic sample or with what has been described as the 'cameo method' – focusing on a small number of individuals for whom there is a fuller existing record that 'can stand for' thousands of others (Haines et al. 1998, 262 & abstract). The dangers here lie in the issue of representativeness, and the difficulty of making sampled records 'speak' in ways that convey convincing 'flesh and blood' historical actors (Haines et al 1998, 262). A further option is to look for patterns. All of these are methods and approaches by which the historian seeks to impose or derive their own order of knowledge. What method is chosen depends on what the historian is seeking to create.

Knowledge that represents the historian's order is different from the information contained in sources now designated 'historical' by their status as archives housed in a repository of national significance and underwritten by public expenditure and legislative protection. But the line of value, and capacity for interaction between visitor/reader and files, is infinitely various. Residues of the past, now designated as 'archives' (by legislation, accommodation and custody) and serving as 'sources' for the historian, do not and cannot 'speak' the past in and of themselves. Their meaning is latent, activated by the historian's question, interpretation, meaning and new ordering into historical knowledge.

Afterlives

The transition of contemporary record to historical archive is, in the case of the military, one of continuity, intention and totality. Nineteenth-century military records did not survive accidentally or selectively but very deliberately. Their retention marks a recognition of the centrality of defence to the state. Unlike many other official records, military files and, in particular, records of individual service never went 'out of date'. A man's service record continued to matter, both to him and to the army after his term of duty ended.[29]

Claims for pensions, medals, land grants and for such things as prostheses (most commonly, wooden legs) proliferate in official correspondence. Almost always such claims required reference back to the War Office files. Former soldiers now living as civilian settlers in New Zealand wrote to the local Army Department who referred queries back to London and then relayed their response back to the original correspondent. Such applications include those made in the 1880s through the 1910s from, or on behalf of, elderly men who had lost their discharge certificates and were now eager to regain copies. Daniel Coughlan was one who wrote to the

New Zealand Secretary of Defence in 1888 explaining that he had served in the 50th regiment but had lost his discharge certificate and medals while crossing the Waipawa River.[30] Other claims for 'lost' certificates unearthed chequered histories. War Office investigations reveal men whose files record desertion, 'bad character' and other grounds of ineligibility. In 1911, Patrick Bedford, a former soldier in the 18th regiment, claimed a copy of his discharge certificate and associated pension. Enquiries showed he had deserted to New South Wales and later returned to New Zealand. His appeal was rejected.[31]

Honouring military service through the award of medals was the most conspicuous way in which men were recompensed for the adversity, brutality and corporeal nature of soldiering. Medals for ordinary soldiers multiplied following the Crimea where the redcoat soldier emerged from disrepute to become an object of pity and even some regard. The Victoria Cross, now the highest recognition for bravery, was first awarded at the Crimea. Medals, issued in metal on the basis of content in paper files, bestowed honour in a public and highly tangible manner. Worn as 'decorations' on the body, they displayed and proclaimed a man's service as an emblem of pride and esteem.

When the War Office came to award the New Zealand Medal to all those who had served in the New Zealand campaigns in 1869, each regiment was required to compile a list of eligible men. Name, rank, dates of service and presence at key engagements in New Zealand are the vital elements in the resulting WO 100/18 series. Regimental variation indicates some diversity in ordering culture and practice across the army; a tension between regimental autonomy and consistency being upheld across all units. Even these utilitarian lists continued to be important after their initial purpose as further claimants emerged, and, even more significantly, because claims for honour in service exist in eternity. There is no point in time when this file, this listing, is 'expired' and ceases to have a function. Those who were adjudged as entitled to a medal continue to hold this claim for life, and that claim continues into subsequent generations; honour is a currency that endures.[32]

As signalled at the outset, nineteenth-century military files have largely stood beyond the making of 'modern memory'. Victorian redcoats were subjects but not citizens; the wars in which they were engaged in securing British sovereignty in diverse parts of the globe were not moments of national formation. Military records were carefully transferred to the public archive at the metropolitan centre, but the obligation to retain records of service was not premised on the creation of prominent public memorials. In the second decade of the twenty-first century, new questions are arising around these events, with a call for more remembering and identification of protagonists. Family history – and national history – in this context has new and different reverberations of memory.

While the primary user of this vast archive of files at the time of their creation was the Army bureaucracy, two documents of vital importance, paybooks and discharge certificates, were carried by men as valued personal possessions. The paybook, issued to every soldier as part of their kit, had a linen cover, a sign of the document's intended durability. Paybooks were also the place where soldiers recorded the receipt of their allocated allowance of clothing: two pairs of trousers, a tunic and a pair of boots every 6 months (the cost deducted from their pay as a 'stoppage').[33]

Discharge certificates (WO 64), similarly designed to last, were produced on parchment (see Figure 5). The certificates proved the holder's legitimate

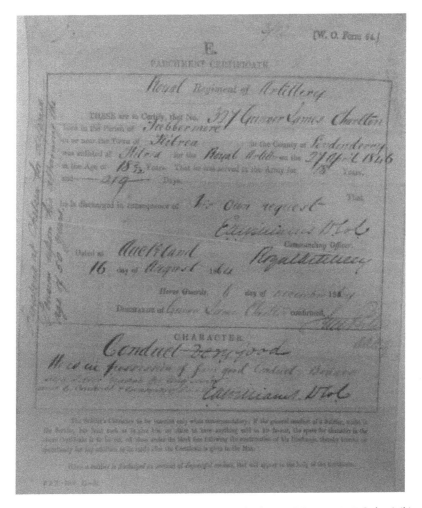

Figure 5. WO 64, discharge certificate of James Charlton, ARC 2002–257, Puke Ariki.

exit from army duty: that he had not deserted but had formally discharged by, for example, reaching the end of his term of duty, by being proved medically unfit for further service, or by purchasing his discharge. The certificate confirmed his entitlement to medals, a pension and recognition as a 'former soldier'. Because these records were kept by individual men, far fewer of them survive. Some have been retained within family collections, while others have subsequently moved from family custody to form part of public historical collections.[34]

Many soldiers serving in the mid-Victorian army had no, or minimal, literacy. The question of who had access to the knowledge produced by and contained within military documents then is interesting. While literacy and education were becoming priorities with schooling often provided within regiments for soldiers, the majority of rank and file men in the 1850s–1860s were not literate (Spiers 1980; Skelley 1977).[35] The technologies and purposes of paper and writing were still the preserve of a minority in the 1860s army as a whole. Even when men were carrying the documents themselves, as in the case of discharge certificates and paybooks, many had no means of personally checking the information presented to them in these written documents. They relied on intermediaries for interpretation. When the intermediary was a superior officer, what reliance was placed on the paper record?

While paybooks and discharge certificates remained in the hands of the men, most of the paper record stayed with the regiment and found its way to depots in England, and to capacious premises at the War Office, and Horse Guards. Military and clerical lives sometimes ran together. George James Colquhoun spent 1855–1865 as schoolmaster with the 65th regiment in New Zealand. On his return to England in the mid-1860s, both he and his 19-year-old son were employed in the War Office: as clerk and messenger boy, respectively.[36] From the War Office, records were subsequently transferred to The National Archives (formerly known as the Public Record Office) where they became available as part of the wider public record for all manner of enquiry including historical knowledge production. Occasionally, records were left behind such as the garrison order books now held at Puke Ariki, or records themselves became casualties in the field of action.[37] In the Waikato in March 1864, Mrs Reay – married to the Adjutant of the 18th regiment – drew the admiration of officers when she fled from a burning hut, clutching only her baby and the Regimental Papers. Her husband was out shooting at the time.[38]

In the 1960s–1970s, some of the War Office series were identified as priorities to be microfilmed for use in Australia and New Zealand by the Australian Joint Copying Project (a collaboration principally between the State Library of New South Wales and National Library of Australia but also supported by other institutions, including the National Library of New Zealand and the then National Archives of New Zealand).[39] The extensive microfilming project gave researchers in Australia and New Zealand access to materials that were held in London (for the most part) – an expensive and inconvenient distance away. The growth of national histories in both societies, together with expanding scholarly research communities, and a burgeoning curiosity amongst family historians, gave these records a value to antipodean researchers. By the second half of the twentieth century, these records were probably of greater interest and value to Australian and New Zealand researchers than to those in Britain, where the focus had turned away from an imperial past.[40] While the AJCP project encompassed a range of records, the military comprise a substantial portion.

A swathe of access projects have followed, particularly from the 1990s, exploiting the capacity of digital formats to increase the span of archives available to readers and to extend access beyond the reading rooms of physical repositories. Digitisation is necessarily selective. It is expensive to initiate and to sustain. In the setting of selection priorities, the convergence of new technologies with heightened public and political interest in World War I has brought the records relating to modern warfare to the fore. The records of nineteenth-century soldiers occupy a much less clear place in either the national memory or national history of Great Britain or of its former colonial societies (O'Malley 2015; Macdonald 2015). Soldiers serving in colonial conflicts are not a priority in either place. In the former colonies such as New Zealand, knowledge production has focused much more heavily on modern war of the twentieth century than the uncomfortable conflicts of nineteenth-century imperial expansion and its associated legacies of colonialism, dispossession and subordination. Nineteenth-century records have consequently taken a backseat.

The transformation of 'the archive' from a discrete place of material objects (or their microfilm surrogates) accessed via series lists and specialist cataloguing conventions, to a digital platform accessed via searches conducted through a few key strokes at any time and any place has been revolutionary. But its impact on knowledge production is more complex than a simple equation of more access and 'more available archive' resulting in more knowledge.

The way in which digital archives collapse space and time, dissolving distance between the reader/viewer and the material object of the paper file, is both astonishing and perplexing to creators of historical knowledge trained to consider context, provenance, selection, silence and position in the 'sources' they consult to 'make' history. The utility of digital archives is huge, while surprisingly, perhaps, also limiting. Even with ongoing digitisation, only some portions of the vast nineteenth-century War Office archive is available by remote access, a fact that shapes the narrative we ultimately tell. When digitised files have been made available by custodial repositories, the archive, though in electronic format, retains much of its original order, as a set of electronic images of largely handwritten files which constitute the original paper documents. The work of transforming its content into structured form for aggregate analysis remains a huge undertaking in transcription and ordering. Such rendering of 'raw archive' into organised historical 'data' opens material to new uses, including the capacity to search and access across names and fields impossible in the archive's original form. In so doing, it offers new provocation to the imagination of the researcher, and the casual browser. Australian artist Thea Constantino (2016) describes this new archive as an 'atmospheric expanse of networked digital space, producing an impression of unlimited, immediate access' to 'the laptop tourist'. Instead of seeing digital access as a simple expansion of the existing physical archive, Constantino and Wolfgang Ernst argue that in digital space it takes on a fundamentally different form, the 'permanent storage facility of the archive' becoming the 'dynamic memory system' of the computer (Constantino 2016, 59). Neither level of 'digitisation', however, substitutes for or performs the work of analysis necessary for historical interpretation.

Some of the archive that has been digitised is available only through commercial providers such as FindMyPast or Ancestry.com, who have undertaken the mammoth task of transcription and digitisation of select records but have curated them in such a way as to best facilitate family history, which is the target market of their business. The path to the records is by names. In actuality, access by modes other than name is virtually impossible. A side effect of this feature is that the records are fragmented further – as well as linked records about individuals not being in one file, individuals are also disconnected from the series they are found in, with files fragmented in favour of the individual. When the questions at hand are not about one man in particular but of a group as a whole, defined by place, event or time of service, this creates additional fragmentation. While the service life of one man might be relatively easily reconstituted, this is not so for a group or a regiment of individuals en masse, and taking a systematic or random sample is likewise difficult. For those whose interest is in social or cultural history of a broader scope, for whom a particular name is not the prime access, such digitisation has, in effect, limited access to these records. Repositories holding original records are disinclined to issue the originals when the records are digitised, and so special permissions must be sought, where previously such records were open.

Digitisation, then, is shaping our 'dreaming' of the archive, and subsequently shaping the narratives we create about the past (Swartz 2018). Digitisation of archive files, and subsequent transformation of records by transcription and organisation into a managed set of fields, has enabled us to build a database of nineteenth-century soldiers. The database, in turn, supports systematic analysis, and rapid location of identified individuals. In so doing, it goes some distance towards making visible a group of men who would otherwise languish in the obscurity that is the lot of most of their contemporaries.[41] Gathering together in a database as much information as possible about individuals from across the fragmented sources brings to the fore a group of historical actors. In aggregating their experiences, patterns can be discerned in the composition and character of the group as a whole. It is worth considering how this historical exploration could have unfolded if these sources were not digitised, and if digital methods were not being employed in their manipulation and analysis. For one, a much smaller selection of men would likely be chosen for focused attention, to stand in as 'representative' of the larger group, and this selection would probably be made based, at least in part, on how the paper archive was accessed, and as the researcher worked their way through it, 'dreaming' the archive and choosing (consciously or not) their path as they did so. Probably more would be known about that select group of men, as the researcher was forced to go deep rather than wide by the difficulty in navigating the vast archive (Haines et al. 1998). Is either approach better or worse when it comes to creating an account of the past? There is a place for them both. As historians, we are cognisant of how our narratives are formed by the archives that survive. We are wary of the potential for biases in the interpretations we offer as a result of the uneven nature of the clues we are left. It is important, as researchers and the archives we work with are propelled into the digital age, that we are also aware of the way in which access to these sources alters our interaction with the archive, the narratives we tell, the knowledge we produce. It is the mode of access as well as the mode of the archive that shapes the outcomes of our research.

Conclusion

Considering the 'paper soldiers' of the nineteenth-century record reminds us that the nineteenth-century British Army was generally interested in the individual but not the 'person'. A soldier was valued for his brute force, his physical vigour and endurance. The record produced concerning him probed little beyond accounting for his use as a resource, and the cost of maintaining that resource. What we have in the files are fragments of individuals, traces rather than full contours. Nevertheless, as a source of historical knowledge the War Office files offer a remarkable view into a layer of nineteenth-century society not easily accessed by other means. It was the systematic and continuous collection of data that was of primary use in the knowledge production undertaken by the army at the time, in tracking the men as individuals that needed to be fed, paid and clothed, and in tracking men as fighting units who could be moved around the empire and utilised as a force. The detailed record that continuous and methodical process produced offers highly valuable information to the twenty-first-century researcher – whether in the identification and mapping of an individual person, or in information that can be aggregated for larger analysis.

Fruitful comparisons could be made between these records and those of nineteenth-century migration and convict transportation, both large-scale movements of people across the globe variously connected to state machinery. Land records are another important kind of file created from the histories of nineteenth-century imperial expansion and colonial resistance, especially in settler colonies where a paper filing system underlies the transformation of 'territory' into exchangeable property, soldiers into 'settlers' (Wolfe 1999).

Setting the nineteenth-century military archive alongside other forms of record under discussion in this issue, we can see areas of similarity and difference. In their longevity (war being a core activity of states), durability (never going out of date) and public nature, military records stand apart from many other series. Unlike hospital, asylum and many welfare records, nineteenth-century army records do not provide biographical coherence. There is no equivalent of the 'patient' or 'case' record which generates a biographically coherent narrative. Military files reflect their institutional setting as 'top-down' records structured by the dynamic of command and by the precedence of organisational purposes over individual circumstances. Moreover, the military archive is one that survives through a high degree of deliberation – it is a conscious archive kept by the state as a continuing obligation to those who served and of its central function in defence. Yet, there are similarities in the methodical, rational and quantifiable ordering of information and the technologies required to maintain paper-based systems. Tasks of tabulation and enumeration are found across military and other forms of archive. So too, is the emergence and application through the mid-nineteenth century of means of tracking and conveying individual identity across spans of place and time. As in the Berlin Charité Hospital discussed by Hess and Ledebur (2011), food drives record-keeping: soldiers, like patients, need daily rations, and those rations demand a budget. Fiscal oversight was a powerful instigator of systematic record-keeping and its resulting knowledge production. Significantly, in the Berlin hospital, it is military surgeons who are in training, and their education requires a capacity in administration alongside medical understanding. Record-keeping as an integral aspect of expertise and professionalism underlies both institutions. Yet, unlike the Berlin hospital and, even more, the Valkenberg Asylum considered by Sally Swartz (2008), the military record is one of public proclamation rather than confidentiality. Names of soldiers were known to their contemporaries and remain public, declared items of information. Indeed, the names of individuals serve as the prime means of access to these records. Nevertheless, there is little space in these archives for the voice of the named – and thereby known – individuals to be heard; the original subaltern is a subject without a voice.[42] Military files kept, and keep, men in 'the lines' in which they served.

Notes

1. War Office series, The National Archives, London (hereafter TNA) described as 'Records, created or inherited by the War Office, Armed Forces, Judge Advocate General, and related bodies' spanning time period 1568–2007. There are 417 record series. http://discovery.nationalarchives.gov.uk/details/record?catid=259&catln=1. 'Thin red line' comes from line in poem by Rudyard Kipling 'Tommy'. The phrase entered popular parlance by way of the hugely popular 1881 painting by Robert Gibb 'The Thin Red Line' depicting action at Balaclava in the Crimea nearly 30 years earlier.
2. The closest other late eighteenth/early nineteenth century equivalent in documentation of this level of society are the records of transported convicts, and especially the ship indents. Kent (1997) notes 'The convicts transported to Australia were probably the best documented working-class citizens of the nineteenth-century British empire'. See also Maxwell-Stewart (2016) and The Digital Panopticon, https://www.digitalpanopticon.org/.
3. See also Bayly (1999), Laidlaw (2005), Ballantyne and Burton (2008).
4. For further information about the larger project, see www.soldiersofempire.nz. The research is supported by the Marsden Fund, administered by the Royal Society of New Zealand.
5. See lovely exegesis on Circumlocution Office at British Library: http://www.bl.uk/learning/histcitizen/21cc/lang/control1/circumlocution1/circumlocution.html.
6. In an era in which officers still purchased their commissions, and spent a career trading commissions, the WO 25 files (the equivalent of what we might later describe as personnel files) are records of patronage, sponsorship and commerce.
7. 'List of casualties in the Engagement at Rangiriri, New Zealand, on the 20th and 21st November, 1863' Journals of the Deputy Quartermaster General in New Zealand from 24 December 1861 to 7 September 1864, p. 75, WO 107/7, TNA.
8. Stephen Waterson (68th Regiment, 315), WO 97/2133, TNA.
9. WO 12, 50th Regiment, Period from 1 October 1863 to 31 December 1863, Statement of the Pay and Allowances of Privates (Form 5), AJCP Reel 3803.
10. WO 12; WO 17; WO 33/16; WO 107/7; WO 97, WO 25 and WO 121; WO 100; WO 22; and WO 90/3, respectively.
11. Caplan and Torpey's *Documenting Individual Identity* (2001) reminds us of the circumstances and processes by which identification practices were developed, their varying capacities, provisions and purposes, the broader frameworks of modern notions of subjectivity and self, and the enabling as well as subordinating power that they unleashed.
12. In early nineteenth-century New South Wales, imposture could be a lucrative, even stylish, lifestyle. McKenzie's 'swindler', John Dow aka Edward, Viscount Lascelles, pretender to an aristocratic lineage and heir to a huge fortune, used the trappings of dress as well as the demeanour of a 'gentleman' to make his way in the world. McKenzie (2009a) – see also McKenzie (2004, 2009b).
13. Anderson here also notes the frequent failure of such efforts.
14. Flogging or corporal punishment was still routinely used as punishment in the British Army and navy in 1840s–1870s. It was not abolished in the British

Army until the 1880s. Instances of flogging in New Zealand were reasonably common.
15. Burroughs notes that branding was 'a cheap, quick method of identifying deserters and unmanageable rogues, preventing fraudulent enlistment, and protecting the public from criminals'.
16. James Brien (65th Regiment, 1776), WO 97/1586, TNA; Michael Burke (50th Regiment, 4225), WO 97/1544, TNA.
17. Richard Pendergast (65th regiment, 3759), WO 97/1587, TNA.
18. James Carty (65th Regiment, 3159), WO 97/1586, TNA.
19. John Prescott (68th Regiment, 434), WO 97/1596, TNA.
20. 43rd Regiment, WO 100/18, New Zealand Medal List, TNA.
21. WO 33/16, TNA.
22. Anthony Toole (50th Regiment, 649), WO 97/1546, TNA.
23. See, for example, the records to be found in T9, Archives New Zealand, Wellington, recording payments of imperial pensions to former soldiers, and dependents, now living in New Zealand – some of whom served in the colony but many others who did not but who had subsequent to their military career, become resident in the colony.
24. Anthony Toole (50th Regiment, 649), WO 97/1546, TNA.
25. WO 12, 50th Regiment, Period from 1 April 1864 to 30 June 1864, Soldiers' Remittances (Form 29), AJCP Reel 3803.
26. WO 12, 50th Regiment, Period from 1 April 1864 to 30 June 1864, Effects and Credits (Form 25).
27. James Hill, ARC 2002-401, Puke Ariki.
28. See Farge (2013), Derrida (1996).
29. By the 1850s–1860s, more men were living to see a period of civilian life following their lives as soldiers. This was due to shorter periods of service, improvement in mortality rates and the changing nature of warfare.
30. 'Daniel Coughlan, 50th Regt, returns War Office parchment discharge certificate, cannot find address 1890', R24327766, AD1/238, M&V1890/1519, Archives New Zealand; see also 'Mr Frank Courtney, Lake Sumner, 25 May 1882 sends Post Office order for 7/6 to purchase NZ War Medal to replace one accidentally lost', R24279773, AD1/161, M&V1882/957, Archives New Zealand; and 'Claim of Edmond Healey to a pension. His claim was refused because he had no good conduct badges', R24327723, AD1/238, M&V 1890/1453, Archives New Zealand.
31. 'Bedford, Patrick – H. M. 18th Royal Irish Regt'. LS69/3/126, Archives New Zealand; AD 32/3/100, Archives New Zealand.
32. See New Zealand Defence website as example of precise guidance on who can claim for medals beyond lifetime of service person: http://medals.nzdf.mil.nz/default.htm#about. These honours continue to act as actual currency too. See, for example, Dunbar Sloane auction catalogue, 27 September 2016.
33. James Carty (65th Regiment, 3159), WO 97/1586, TNA.
34. James Hill, ARC 2002-401, Puke Ariki; Patrick Grace, ARC 2002-401, Puke Ariki; Edward Byrnes [Byrne], ARC 2002-117, Puke Ariki; see also James Charlton, ARC 2002-257, Puke Ariki.
35. See also 'uneducated men' in 'Report of the Naval and Military Settlers' and Volunteers' Land-Claims Committee'. 1889. *Appendices to the Journals of the House of Representatives*, I-7, 1.

36. George James Colquhoun (65th Regiment, 1647), WO 97/1586, TNA; 1871 census of England and Wales.
37. 1864 Garrison Order Book, ARC2002-811, Puke Ariki.
38. Williams, Edward Arthur, 'Sketches on the Waikato', Misc-MS-1085, 78–79, Hocken Library.
39. The AJCP began in 1945 and lasted until 1993. Initially, the records copied were solely those from the Public Record Office; from 1960, the scope expanded to include sources from other repositories. The scope of records included in the AJCP widened throughout its life. Part 4 contains papers from the War Office at the Public Record Office/The National Archives. https://www.nla.gov.au/research-guides/australian-joint-copying-project.
40. There are many commentaries on this subject; an indication can be found at Colley (2002), Fieldhouse (1984), see also Peers (2002). Perry (2015) comments on a similar path of archives, copied from British repositories to Canadian holdings in the early twentieth century, moving as she notes, 'from the space of empire to the space of the nation'.
41. See the related project to bring the names and brief identifying details of all 25,566 women convicts transported to Australia to contemporary attention through the Roses from the Heart convict women bonnets project. Part of the project was on public exhibit in Hobart 2016. Christine Henri, 'Roses from the Heart', https://embroiderersguild.com/index.php?page_no=327.
42. The Subaltern Studies critique took its cue from the military: the dominant mode of power in colonial India. Giving voice to those groups and perspectives silenced and subordinated by that power was its goal.

Disclosure statement

No potential conflict of interest was reported by the authors.

Funding

This work was supported by the Marsden Fund [VUW1414].

ORCID

Charlotte Macdonald http://orcid.org/0000-0003-0511-3904

References

Anderson, C. 2004. *Legible Bodies: Race, Criminality and Colonialism in South Asia.* Oxford: Berg.
Ballantyne, T., and A. Burton, eds. 2008. *Moving Subjects: Gender, Mobility and Intimacy in an Age of Global Empire.* Urbana: University of Illinois Press.
Baly, M. E., and H. C. G. Matthew. 2011. "Nightingale, Florence (1820-1910)." In *Oxford Dictionary of National Biography.* Oxford: Oxford University Press.
Bayly, C. A. 1999. *Empire and Information.* Cambridge: Cambridge University Press.
Burroughs, P. 1985. "Crime and Punishment in the British Army, 1815–1870." *The English Historical Review* 100 (396): 545–571. doi:10.1093/ehr/C.CCCXCVI.545.
Burroughs, P. 2003. "An Unreformed Army 1815-1868." In *Oxford History of the British Army*, edited by D. G. Chandler and I. Beckett. Oxford: Oxford University Press.
Burton, A., ed. 2005. *Archive Stories: Facts, Fictions, and the Writing of History.* Durham: Duke University Press.
Caplan, J. 1997. ""Speaking Scars": The Tattoo in Popular Practice and Medico-Legal Debate in Nineteenth-Century Europe." *History Workshop Journal*, no. 44: 106–142. http://www.jstor.org/stable/4289521.
Caplan, J., and J. Torpey, eds. 2001. *Documenting Individual Identity. The Development of State Practices in the Modern World.* Princeton: Princeton University Press.
Colley, L. 2002. "What is Imperial History Now?" In *What is History Now?* edited by D. Cannadine, 132–147. New York: Palgrave.
Constantino, T. 2016. "Ruination and Recollection. Plumbing the Colonial Archive" In *Visual Arts Practice and Affect. Place, Materiality and Embodied Knowledge* edited by A. Schilo, 55-79. London and New York: Rowman and Littlefield.
Crawford, J. A. B. 1990. "Gamble, Dominic Jacotin." *Dictionary of New Zealand Biography. Te Ara – The Encyclopedia of New Zealand.* Accessed April 18, 2017. http://www.TeAra.govt.nz/en/biographies/1g1/gamble-dominic-jacotin.
Darwin, J. 2012. *Unfinished Empire: The Global Expansion of Britain.* London: Penguin.
Davidoff, D., and C. Hall. 2002. *Family Fortunes: Men and Women of the English Middle Class, 1780–1850.* Rev. ed. London: Routledge.
Derrida, J. 1996. *Archive Fever: A Freudian Impression.* Chicago: Chicago University Press.
Dickens, C. 1855–57. *Little Dorritt.* London: Bradbury and Evans.
Farge, A. 2013. *The Allure of the Archives.* New Haven: Yale University Press.
Fieldhouse, D. 1984. "Can Humpty Dumpty Be Put Together Again? Imperial History in the 1980s." *The Journal of Imperial and Commonwealth History* 12 (2): 9–23. doi:10.1080/03086538408582657.
Hadley, E. 2016. "Nobody, Somebody, and Everybody." *Victorian Studies* 59 (1): 67–68. doi:10.2979/victorianstudies.59.1.03.

Haines, R., M. Kleinig, D. Oxley, and E. Richards. 1998. "Migration and Opportunity: An Antipodean Perspective." *International Review of Social History* 43: 235–263. doi:10.1017/S0020859098000121.
Hess, V., and S. Ledebur. 2011. "Taking and Keeping: A Note on the Emergence and Function of Hospital Patient Records." *Journal of the Society of Archivists* 32 (1): 21–33.
Higgs, E. 2004. *The Information State in England: The Central Collection of Information on Citizens since 1500*. Basingstoke: Palgrave Macmillan.
Hughes, H., and L. Hughes. 1988. *Discharged in New Zealand: Soldiers of the Imperial Foot Regiments Who Took Their Discharge in New Zealand 1840–1870*. Auckland: New Zealand Society of Genealogists.
Kent, D. 1997. "Decorative Bodies: The Significance of Convicts' Tattoos." *Journal of Australian Studies* 21 (53): 78–88. doi:10.1080/14443059709387318.
Kopf, E. 1916. "Florence Nightingale as Statistician." *Publications of the American Statistical Association* 15 (116): 388–404. doi:10.2307/2965763.
Laidlaw, Z. 2005. *Colonial Connections 1815–45: Patronage, the Information Revolution and Colonial Government*. Manchester: Manchester University Press.
MacDonagh, O. 1961. *A Pattern of Government Growth, 1800–60: The Passenger Acts and Their Enforcement*. London: Macgibbon.
Macdonald, C. 2015. "The First World War and the Making of Colonial Memory." *Journal of New Zealand Literature* 33 (2): 15–37.
Maxwell-Stewart, H. 2016. "The State, Convicts and Longitudinal Analysis." *Australian Historical Studies* 47 (3): 414–429. doi:10.1080/1031461X.2016.1203963.
McKenzie, K. 2004. *Scandal in the Colonies: Sydney and Cape Town, 1820–1850*. Carlton: Melbourne University Press.
McKenzie, K. 2009a. *A Swindler's Progress: Nobles and Convicts in the Age of Liberty*. Sydney: University of New South Wales Press.
McKenzie, K. 2009b. "Social Mobilities at the Cape of Good Hope: Lady Anne Barnard, Samuel Hudson, and the Opportunities of Empire." In *Moving Subjects: Gender, Mobility, and Intimacy in an Age of Global Empire*, edited by T. Ballantyne and A. Burton. Urbana: University of Illinois Press.
O'Malley, V. 2015. ""Recording the Incident with a Monument": The Waikato War in Historical Memory." *Journal of New Zealand Studies*, no. 19: 79–97.
Peers, D. M. 2002. "Is Humpty Dumpty Back Together Again?: The Revival of Imperial History and the Oxford History of the British Empire." *Journal of World History* 13 (2): 451–467. doi:10.1353/jwh.2002.0049.
Perry, A. 2015. *Colonial Relations: The Douglas-Connolly Family and the Nineteenth-Century Imperial World, Critical Perspectives on Empire*. Cambridge: Cambridge University Press.
Sexton, R. 1984. *The Deserters: A Complete Record of Military and Naval Deserters in Australia and New Zealand, 1800–65*. Magill: Australasian Maritime Historical Society.
Skelley, A. R. 1977. *The Victorian Army at Home*. London: Croom Helm.
Smith, F. B. 1982. *Florence Nightingale: Reputation and Power*. London: Croom Helm.
Special issue on Kenya and Mau Mau. 2011. *Journal of Imperial and Commonwealth History* 39 (5).
Spencer, W. 2008. *Army Records: A Guide for Family Historians*. Kew: National Archives.
Spiers, E. M. 1980. *The Army and Society, 1815–1914*. London: Longman.

Steppler, G. A. 1988. "Regimental Records in the Late Eighteenth Century and the Social History of the British Soldier." *Archivaria* 26: 7–17. http://archivaria.ca/index.php/archivaria/article/view/11489.

Strachan, H. 1984. *Wellington's Legacy*. Manchester: Manchester University Press.

Swartz, S. 2008. "Colonial Lunatic Asylum Archives: Challenges to Historiography." *Kronos* 34: 285–302.

Swartz, S. 2018. "Asylum Case Records: Fact and Fiction." *Rethinking History* 22: 289–301.

Tosh, J. 1999. *A Man's Place: Masculinity and the Middle-Class Home in Victorian England*. New Haven: Yale University Press.

Trustram, M. 1984. *Women of the Regiment: Marriage and the Victorian Army*. Cambridge: Cambridge University Press.

Wolfe, P. 1999. *Settler Colonialism and the Transformation of Anthropology: The Politics and Poetics of an Ethnographic Event*. London: Cassell.

Woodham-Smith, C. 1950. *Florence Nightingale*. London: Contstable.

Red ink, blue ink, blood and tears? War records and nation-making in Australia and New Zealand

Kathryn Hunter

ABSTRACT
Despite the rise of comparative and transnational history writing, histories of the Great War have remained remarkably bound by the nation-state. This is especially the case in Australia and New Zealand, where there has been, arguably, a recent entrenchment of the view of the Great War as a nation-making moment. This article offers the provocation that the creation of vast numbers of records during the war did make the nation: files demanded a new bureaucracy and they made the state material. The files also became materials for historians who went on to equate the national army with the nation at war. Another foray into the archives, however, suggests that despite military files being designated national heritage, they can reveal the tensions of belonging and exclusion present during and after the war.

Abbreviations: AIF Australian Imperial Force ANZ Archives New Zealand BR Base Records NZEF New Zealand Expeditionary Force

Did the Great War make the nations of Australia and New Zealand? Historians and polemicists have expended much ink (usually black) debating the question, with historians from a range of perspectives being suspicious of the idea of a national moment. But what if approximately 400,000 members of the Australian Imperial Force (AIF) and 110,000 New Zealand Expeditionary Force (NZEF) recruits and conscripts *did* establish the nation, not through their deeds but through their paperwork? What if Australia and New Zealand had their nationhood conferred and their state-ness made material, tangible and visible to historians through the records of more than half a million men produced in a time of war? I am not suggesting that the men's lives documented in military files were extraordinary in some way (although statistically, many of them must have been), but that the many hundreds of linear metres that their records comprise signify a powerful bureaucratic articulation of the nation's power. This article then pursues this provocation: that the existence of massive amounts of coherent paperwork around one event brought the men named therein into a special relationship with governments, created records for history writing and formed the first significant body of paperwork that made material the new nations of Australia and New Zealand.

At the launch of the National Archives of Australia's project to digitize over 400,000 World War I (WWI) personnel files in 2007, the Prime Minister John Howard asserted that 'Things like this [project] help more than you can imagine in bringing about an understanding of Australia... [The Great War] has left an indelible character imprint that has stayed with us' (Howard 2007). For those familiar with Australia, the linking of the Great War with the understanding of the nation and the national 'character' is unremarkable and, perhaps, even expected at occasions such as this. The WWI-nation nexus in Australia has been resistant to almost every critique of its inherent masculinism and militarism. Indeed, the centennial has resulted in an explosion of publishing in both Australia and New Zealand, of local and national histories, as well as national exhibitions at National Museum of New Zealand Te Papa Tongarewa and the Australian War Memorial (including a travelling exhibition). While some of these books and exhibitions challenged the masculine focus of remembrance, or the 'white' remembrance, the national focus of such histories and connections has remained much less challenged. Despite the shift to transnationalism, comparative frameworks and other border-busting frameworks in almost every other area of inquiry, histories and commemorations of the Great War in Australia as well as New Zealand have, if anything, consolidated their national focus.

Pursuing the question about the weight of paperwork in creating national histories requires, first, looking at WWI files seriously as paper, rusted pins, annotated scraps and forms, as well as microfilm and, now, their digital presence. The files are slightly different in Australia and New Zealand because their survival has taken a different form, but the bureaucratic context within which they were created is remarkably similar. Second, I want to consider the files in light of the burgeoning field of family history and how this endeavour has driven access to military files in particular ways and embedded the nation's past into families' identities. Finally, a glance at another set of files from the same war provides another perspective on the co-option of the personnel files into the national narrative. The Base Records files are much less kempt and curated than the personnel files. They too connect families to the army through correspondence and much of this reveals tensions between armies administered on a national basis and the more sentiment-driven imperial war service in which many Australians and New Zealanders were engaged during the war of 1914–18.

Paper and rusted pins

Armies, like asylums, are institutions: they have culture and hierarchies signified by rules and codes governing processes and behaviours, and by uniforms and language. They also have paperwork to enrol and induct, and then to surveil and track those within the institution. As institutions, nineteenth- and early-twentieth-century armies and asylums have broad bureaucratic parallels and cultural connections. Those within the institution were there through a mixture of voluntarism and compulsion; file-keeping was used to maintain food and clothing rations and acted as a brief record of movement and care. Discipline, routine and regimentation were also important to the cultures of both institutions. In personnel, the careers of medical doctors often took them into asylums and certainly into medical training institutions as instructors. They were often exposed to the same broad range of mental, as well as physical illnesses as doctors in asylums, and indeed soldiers themselves crossed over from army to asylum as patients.

The lives of asylum files and army files, however, especially in the present, could not be more different. Available in public repositories since the 1950s and 1960s, WWI personnel files now are, arguably, the most publicly available government records in Australia and New Zealand. In the mid-2000s, the Australian Government provided funding to digitize all 400,000 personnel files held in National Archives of Australia and, while New Zealand's digitization project was more ad hoc, it too was completed to coincide with the centenary of the conflict. While asylum files tend to be anchored to place, to the hospital or institution, army records are organized by surname shaping the way they can be searched and requested. As well as being available online, access to the files is free (unlike records of births, deaths and marriages for example, for which there is a fee). Asylum records, on the other hand, are governed by privacy legislation of various sorts, and permission is required if researchers want to access them and publish about them. Any records relating to patients in New Zealand, for example, are generally sealed for 100 years after the closure of the file. Clearly soldiering is something that can be visible, while commitment to that other kind of institution is not.

Military service files vary slightly between Australia and New Zealand, but have several features in common. Modelled on the British army bureaucracy, personnel files generally contain an attestation form including the results of a medical examination. Details of the occupation and address of the man enlisting were recorded along with his previous military experience, and physical attributes such as chest measurement, height and eye colour. Religious affiliation and next-of-kin details were important given the possible outcomes of enlisting in the nation's army. Crucially, a man's file also recorded his unique army service number, essential for keeping track of individuals within the mass experience of military service. Added to men's files as their service progressed were service details: where the man's unit was posted and when; any wounds received or time in hospital recorded on a buff or blue Casualty Form; a conduct record and any punishments or confinement that man received or any mentions or decorations awarded along with their citations; sometimes a will; and possibly details of his death, the disbursement of his effects; and, after the war, records of campaign medals dispatched. New Zealand files often are topped with a summary 'History Sheet' attached to the file at the end of the war

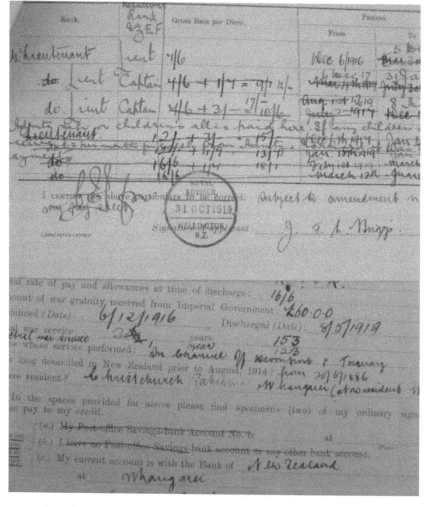

Figure 1. Military files captured details of men's lives at the time of enlistment and tracked changes in their circumstances. Author photograph.

including red ink annotations detailing the soldier's death, burial at the time of death and relocation to an Imperial War Graves Commission plot after the war (Figure 1). The microfilming of defence records in the 1960s robbed files of their colour. Australian files also contain correspondence relating to the man that was received from family members, friends or agents on behalf of family. Such correspondence does not usually survive in the New Zealand files. It was jettisoned during the transfer of the files from the army to National Archives in the 1960s, reminding us of the vagaries of archival survival as well as the agency of bureaucrats. Indeed, the original paper files themselves were sometimes destroyed after microfilming. A pencil-written note on bright yellow paper on the cover of George Bollinger's original personnel file signals the vulnerability of the files even in the 1980s. Dated 8 September 1988, New Zealand defence force historian John Crawford instructed: 'Please note, this file is of considerable historical importance and must not be purged.'[1]

While the personnel files themselves survive in slightly different ways in Australia and New Zealand, it should be noted that their survival as virtually complete records of those enlisted in the Great War is remarkable by international standards. It is estimated that somewhere between 40–60% of British personnel files survive, while German, French, Russian, Turkish and Austrian files have not fared well over a century of political upheaval, a second war that resulted in massive damage to infrastructure in the capital cities (and hence to bureaucratic repositories), and the development of very different cultures of remembrance (http://www.nationalarchives.gov.uk/; Stibbe 2014).

Great War enlistment occurred in a changing bureaucratic context. The outbreak of war closely followed both Australia and New Zealand becoming self-governing dominions. Their new responsibility for their own defence proved significant for file creation. Just as constitutional powers transferred from the Crown to the national governments, the bureaucratic functions of the Imperial War Office transferred also: the dominions could raise their own armies. Thus, the personnel files were a product of a mushrooming local defence bureaucracy measured in both paper and people. In New Zealand, a country of just over 1 million people, the public service expanded from a pre-war base of approximately 5000 employees (including, of course, all postal and railway workers, and state school teachers) by employing more than 3000 temporary clerks. By 1917, the Defence Department alone employed 337 men and 597 women (Henderson & Nicholls, 397–8; Report of the Public Services Commisioner 1917, 5). In Australia, the number of public servants in the Defence Department at the time the federal government took over the department in 1901 was a mere 185; by 1918, MPs were asserting that there were more than 2500 men in the Defence Department eligible for service (meaning younger than 45 years), giving some sense of the growth of the department (https://historichansard.net 22 August 1905, 1193; 25 June 1918, 6331; 23 October 2017). In addition to public servants, paperwork and processes contributed substantially to the strengthening of the state in the dominions. The production of military personnel files expanded exponentially the material presence of the state while creating a special relationship between certain men and that state. This new relationship between soldiers and the nation-state has been remarked upon and investigated by historians of both warfare and welfare (Lake 1992; Garton 2015; Nolan 2000; Scates & Oppenheimer 2014; Parsons 2008).

By 1914, both Australia and New Zealand had armies over which their governments were sovereign – even if the declaration of war was one made by the King – and national welfare provisions attached to military service, such as separation allowances and pensions, were extended to those who enlisted and their dependants. These provisions were substantially different in nature to other welfare measures extended in the colonies which were predicated on various conditions including birth, residency, enfranchisement, good character and race. The Old Age Pension Acts in both Australia and New Zealand, for example, stipulated a residency requirement of 25 years in order to qualify, and both governments excluded Chinese residents entirely.[2] The fact that military welfare provisions applied only to enlisted men excluded civilian war workers and other citizens who enlisted in imperial forces from the special relationship with the state. Regardless of country of birth or length of residency, those who enlisted in the AIF or NZEF became the responsibility of that nation's defence department: armies were administratively organized according to geographical location of enlistment. For soldiers this was an important change from earlier colonial participation in both the repression of the Sudanese uprising (1885) and the South African War (1899–1902), in which troops from the Australasian colonies were distributed among British troops and administered by the Imperial War Office.

There was a critical coincidence then, between the granting of dominion status to Australia and New Zealand and the bureaucratic eruption instigated by the outbreak of the Great War. Australian historian Alan Atkinson suggests this coincidence created a 'primary' national narrative similar in power to the American Revolution in US history. 'While more reverence has… been paid to the Anzac "legend" [than to federation]', Atkinson comments, 'the two phenomena combined, taken as a single creative process, exert a magic which seriously distorts our understanding of the past' (Atkinson 2013, 264). Certainly, from the official histories that emerged in the interwar period in both Australia and New Zealand through to the new military histories of the 1990s, there has been an alignment of those who served in the nation's forces, the nation's war with the nation's character. The impact of Australia's multi-volume official history of the war, and of its chief author Charles Bean, is well known (Thomson 2015; Coulthart 2014; Atkinson 2014). Even within the less coherent effort of the New Zealand histories, which emphasized local unit identities and relationships with 'the Motherland', the importance of the national 'type' as the NZEF serviceman emerged. While restrained in their discussion of 'the men', authors nonetheless agreed that New Zealand soldiers were 'steadfast and stubborn in defence' (Waite 1919, 300). They laid the foundations of the national legend, describing the source of the NZEF as a 'young and virile people... of unusually fine physique, a race of horsemen farmers musterers athletes and Rugby footballers [sic]' (Stewart 1921, 619). With the rise of new military history in the 1990s, campaign histories were humanized with the letters and diaries of soldiers. This conflation of army and nation has become standard, with New Zealand military historian Glyn Harper, for example, stating sweepingly in his 2011 *Letters from Gallipoli* that it was 'undeniable' that 'the Gallipoli experience is a pivotal part of their [Australia's and New Zealand's] journey to nationhood and has become essential to their national make up and character. (30). More materially – or virtually in this case – the Australian Government's decision to digitize all WWI personnel files held in National Archives of Australia was described purely in national terms, as preserving 'Australia's heritage' (Gibbs 2007). The identification of the AIF and NZEF as those who constituted the nation also cascaded into archival and curatorial collection policies that confirmed the AIF and NZEF as the embodiment of the nation at war. Although official war historians at the Australian War Memorial instigated the collection of personal papers in order to 'supplement the frigid records of the [unit] diaries with the warm, personal narratives of the men' (Bean in Luckins 2010, 26), most WWI personal papers in Australasian public collections were acquired from the late 1960s onwards.[3] Both New Zealand's Ministry of Culture and Heritage and the Australian Department of Veterans Affairs made concerted efforts in the late 1990s to encourage 'families to preserve the records and ephemera of soldier forebears as part of a national heritage' (Ziino 2010, 132).

Red pen, blue pencil

Before this generalized 'heritage' purpose, however, personnel files fulfilled their important bureaucratic function as proof of service and entitlement beyond the war, thereby linking soldiering men and their families to the state. Medal distribution, and access to medical care and pensions, all kept the files as working documents complete with red ink and civil service blue pencil annotations of change of address, next-of-kin details and death dates. The absence of a file made accessing entitlements very difficult and the Base Records files are dotted with requests from men for duplicates of lost discharge papers, or from hospitals claiming costs of treating veterans. The absence of files had serious consequences for individuals that could be felt decades after the war. Dorothy Raff, for example, was one of many Australian nurses who served with the British nursing corps, but she struggled to claim medical benefits from the Australian repatriation department because her service records were not held in Australia. Unlike members of the Australian Army Nursing Service and New Zealand Army Nursing Service, whose records were poorly kept and preserved but were, at least, housed locally, Raff's British service record had been vulnerable to destruction during the Blitz. In such cases, sworn affidavits had to be provided by retired nurses giving their service history and, even then, it is unclear whether or not they received assistance they had requested (Raff 1958). Marginalia and instructions in red pen and blue civil service pencil record decisions that had significant effects on ex-servicepeople (Figure 2).

The files became more than functional from the late 1960s when the coincidence of the social history movement and the deaths of men who had served in the Great War made their stories more precious and the collection of personal papers and ephemera more urgent (Ziino 2010, 130–131). The explosion of family history at the same time gave the files new purpose as the link between individuals, their families and the 'Anzac legend'. Many families still retained correspondence, diaries and ephemera of their soldier or nurse relatives and the files provide a scaffold of service details: the *where*

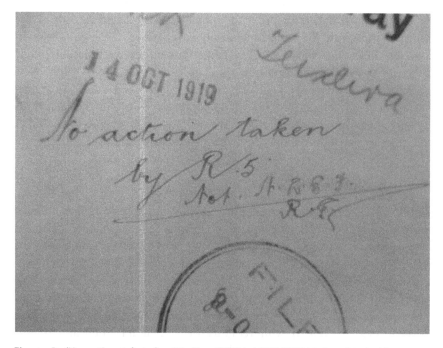

Figure 2. 'No action taken by R5. Not NZEF.' AABK W5614 Box 95 Archives New Zealand. Author photograph.

and *when* of a soldier's or nurse's time with the forces, and sometimes beyond. As well as giving physical locations to the ubiquitous 'somewhere in France' at the head of so many letters, the files also provide other details that family historians thirst after. If family historians use one of the many guides and online sources to decipher military and medical abbreviations, nomenclature and shorthand, their soldier-relative's movements, time in hospital, disciplining and rewarding can be laid out. Just as Swartz argues in this volume, it is the 'fiction of accuracy that gives statistics their authority over us', military files hold the same promise of accounting for soldiers' experiences. Physical details recorded in the medical examinations such as height and eye colour 'are highly valued by descendants because they can draw perceived links between generations' (Wallis 2015, 30). Ziino (139) points additionally to the important constellation of family actors who can appear in files (in Australian ones, at least) as next-of-kin and as 'anxious parents, sweethearts or siblings, soldier friends or others who wrote to military authorities for information'. Even for historians, as Alistair Thomson has noted (Thomson 2015, 283ff), the bare details of a service record have the power to recast oral narratives delivered decades after the end of the conflict.

Evidence that military files have the power to disrupt family narratives, however, is never far away. When a student in my class on WWI investigated the history of a treasured family object, the bugle kept by her grandmother, she discovered that the files told a different story to the family narrative. The bugler, Arthur, was uncle to Beryl, the student's grandmother. He had died on the western front, one of the thousands of New Zealanders who had 'fallen' in those terrible campaigns. His letters home and the bugle sent back with his effects had been kept as memento mori within the family, and Anzac Days were religiously attended in his honour. The local war memorial listed Arthur under 'Killed'; the local newspaper, on the other hand, had recorded his death as 'died of disease' but the family Bible recorded Arthur's death as 'in the field'. Arthur's early letters revealed a young bugler, proud to serve his empire and represent his family, narrating camp life in Egypt with humour. When mobilized to the western front after April 1916, the letters became more troubled: there was no role for buglers in the French trenches making the stalemate of the conflict even more pointless for the musician, and his busy life in camp had left him feeling undertrained and unprepared for combat. He wrote from France,

> 'you ask about being a bugler, well it is alright until the hard work comes, and then one finds himself incompetent to carry on with a Private's duties, for he has not the training a Private gets and as you know buglers are a thing of the past once one gets into the firing line' (Dyett cited in Burgess 2013).

The file, however, was quite clear: Arthur had not been killed in battle, but had taken his own life. The family narrative had always been one of death 'in the field', nothing more. The file disrupted the family narrative, changed the reading of the bugler's letters and the shape of family memory.

Scraps and scribbles

National narratives too can be disrupted by defence files. Taking a broader view of defence records beyond the curated, digitized personnel files bring a wider set of conversations between families and the army into view. The Base Records files are scrappy records, sometimes only single pieces of paper with a few lines, but sometimes containing letters to officials. The reason such letters were not transferred to a personnel file was because one did not exist: the correspondence remaining in Base Records files referred to men and women serving with a range of British services, not with the Australian or New Zealand armies.

Imperial service was very common. A further segment of the shifting bureaucratic context within which defence force files were created was that of 'nationality' and despite its vague definitions, it was interlocked with enlistment in the nations' armies in complex and contradictory ways. As legal historian John Torpey argues (2000 13, 6), identities are 'anchored in law and policy' as well as sentiment, and these policies and the files they create are key to the creation of nation-states. In order for 'state-ness' to be implemented, 'the notion of communities must be codified in documents rather than merely "imagined"'. Australia's and New Zealand's positions as self-governing dominions in the empire created swirling and complex currents of codification and documentation. By the turn of the twentieth century, both had expanded their democratic base through the enfranchisement of white women, and Maori in the case of New Zealand, setting themselves apart from the rest of empire. The passage of the *British Nationality and Alien Status Act 1914*, however, bound them by cementing the British nationality of all individuals born within 'His Majesty's dominions and allegiance' (Baldwin 2001, 527). In the absence of Australian or New Zealand nationalities, before the passing of distinct citizenship acts after World War II, members of the 'white dominions' understood themselves to be, at some level, Britons (Bridge & Fedorowich 2003, Woollacott 2001, Bell 2007).

It is not surprising then that WWI British dominion armies were made up of a significant proportion of men born elsewhere. The NZEF, approximately 110,000 men, was 30% 'foreign-born'; the AIF comprised 20% British-born soldiers and approximately 5% (16,500) men born in other dominions (Inwood et al 2010, 271; Robson 1973, 739). Other indicators of the mixed character of national forces include more than 8500 files created by AIF Base Records of Australians by birth serving in other armies about whom some correspondence was required.

The empire was a fluid place in the early twentieth century and this extended to movement between the colonies as well as between the metropolis and the outposts. That men of colonial origin enlisted in imperial forces reflects in large part this mobility: bodies were in motion at the outbreak of war. The realities of such mobility were played out administratively in other ways when, for example, in 1916 Miss Todhunter, who headed the Christchurch-based Enquiry Bureau for Missing and Wounded Soldiers in New Zealand, took steps to 'amalgamate with the New South Wales Bureau' because so many New Zealanders 'were serving with the Australian forces, and it would be more easy [sic] to trace missing men' (North Canterbury Red Cross Minutes, 7 June 1916, cited in McNamara n. d., n.p.). Reinforcing this idea was the report in the *New Zealand Red Cross Record* (17 August 1916, 26), of the 'great number of enquiries' being made by the New South Wales Bureau of men whose next-of-kin lived in Australia but who had enlisted with the NZEF.

This ecumenical approach to the war effort did not survive the war. Instead, national remembrance and history writing dominated. Yet, the imperial endeavour of war was clearly visible in wartime propaganda messages, contemporary newspapers, family correspondence and enlistment patterns of men and women who served with a wide range of military and civilian forces, and was clearly in evidence in a few corners of the bureaucracy such as Base Records departments in Wellington (for the NZEF) and Melbourne (for the AIF). Base Records was the point of contact for civilians seeking news of their friend or family member in the services. While correspondence from civilians does not survive in the NZEF personnel files, the Base Records files are intact, and files from both sides of the Tasman indicate significant tensions between the administration of the defence force at a national level and continuing popular understandings of the war as an imperial effort (Figure 3).

In 1916 Royes Sherriff was returning home to New Zealand after crash-landing his aeroplane. Sherriff had gone to England at the outbreak of war, securing a commission in the Royal Flying Corps. While Royes sailed back to New Zealand, his father Arthur wrote to Base Records in Wellington requesting a next-of-kin railway pass to enable him to meet the boat at Auckland. Base Records denied the request because Royes had not served with the NZEF. Arthur wrote immediately to Minister of Defence Sir James Allen to protest, emphasizing the claim that 'my son is a New Zealander'. Allen's department drafted two replies: one acceding to the request and one denying it. In the end, Allen sent the letter granting the request, re-stating the policy set out by the defence department but acquiescing in a somewhat scolding tone: 'As, however, your son has been injured in the service of the

Figure 3. Base Records files at Archives New Zealand. Author photograph.

King though not in the NZEF, I have instructed the Director of Base Records that an exception will be made in this case' (Sherriff 1916). That an exception had to be made for Arthur probably came as a shock to him. An enormous amount of British propaganda had reinforced politicians' messages that New Zealand was one of the 'young lions' standing with the 'Old Lion' in the face of German aggression.[4] Just like Royes Sherriff, thousands of Australian- and New Zealand-born men and women enlisted in allied military forces and joined overseas civilian organizations during the Great War.

Letter after letter in the Base Records files demonstrates the divide between national bureaucracy and imperial realities. As Australian or New Zealand residents, families expected local agencies would be able to assist them but Base Records was not usually able to help. For example, the wife of Lieutenant O'Donnell Forster had lost track of her husband after he was wounded while serving with the Highland Light Infantry Lahore Division (Indian Expeditionary Force) at La Basse in October 1915, and she hoped Base Records could assist her, but they could not (O'Donnell, BR37/56, ANZ). A soldier's father WJ Rees wrote in July 1916:

> I see by today's *Herald* that the British losses at La Boiselle are very heavy, the East Lancashire's suffering especially. My third son Joe is in the 7th Kings Lancashire Regiment and has been in the advance trenches for months. I feel very anxious regarding him.

Mr Rees had found himself in a situation, not uncommon to parents of New Zealand- and Australian-born soldiers, of having been struck out in the file. Rees wrote that,

> Having married since he went to England his [Joe's] next of kin now is his wife in Liverpool. Can the Defence people here get information for me, or arrange that I be communicated with in the event of his being wounded or killed?' (Rees, BR37/68, ANZ)

These queries, as with hundreds of others, were not answered by Base Records beyond directing families to contact other countries' officials; Base Records kept records of the AIF or the NZEF, not of Australians and New Zealanders.

The national administration of armies privileged military service over all other forms of war work and cut across people's ideas of imperial unity. Other sources such as newspapers provide evidence that imperial loyalty could be expressed without recourse to national service, and public and family opinion supported service in any of the allied forces or organizations (Hunter 2017). Base Records correspondence makes clear that a gap existed between national administration and popular understandings of the war effort.

Conclusion

Despite the openness of the files in Australia and New Zealand, military files are visible in very particular ways. The files contain history: they bring artificial order to the messiness of the imperial world, to the chaos of the conflict and the emotional turmoil of wartime. Similarly, the existence of such a large body of records has made WWI the subject of an astonishing amount of research and scholarship. The creation of the archive, its preservation combined with the openness of files, has shaped the history of the conflict and created a cycle of collecting and archival acquisition that re-inscribes the importance of war in these nations' pasts. Files had the effect of making local a foreign conflict: the soldiers might be in France or in the Middle East, but their files were in Melbourne (then Canberra) and Wellington, and they now online, available intimately and immediately. This is not, in any way, to argue against the impact of the war on families and communities, but to attempt to explain such anomalous history-making. Why, for example, has the impact of the war has been remembered far more than the influenza pandemic that killed thousands on the 'homefront' just as the war was ending (Youde 2017, 360–362).[5] It is the exclusion or diminution of some families' wartime suffering because of administrative infrastructure and regulations that raises a question about the extent to which it was the prosaic growth of bureaucracy, rather than the heroic deeds of Anzacs, that came to define the 'nation' at war in Australia and New Zealand.

Notes

1. George Bollinger, digitized original paper personnel file. Accessed at http://ndhadeliver.natlib.govt.nz/delivery/DeliveryManagerServlet?dps_pid=IE10640133 13 October 2017.
2. The *Old Age Pension Act 1908* in Australia superseded all state legislation in this area and originally required residency for 25 years and all 'natives' of Australia, Africa, Asia and the Pacific Islands except New Zealand were excluded. Later amendments reduced residency requirements to 20 years. The New Zealand *Old Age Pension Act 1898* specifically excluded any Chinese residents, and the residency requirement was also 25 years.
3. My own survey of more than 250 collections of personal papers in the Alexander Turnbull Library, Wellington, in 2011, for example, revealed that more than 80% of them had been acquired or donated after 1965.
4. Wardle, Arthur. 1915. 'The Empire Needs Men'. Accessed at https://collections.tepapa.govt.nz/object/1020691 2 June 2017.
5. The death toll in Australia was 12,000 from influenza and 60,000 during the war; in New Zealand 8600 died from the flu and 18,000 at war.

Disclosure statement

No potential conflict of interest was reported by the author.

References

Atkinson, A. 2013. "Federation, Democracy and the Struggle against a Single Australia." *Australian Historical Studies* 44 (2): 262–279. doi:10.1080/1031461X.2013.791709.

Atkinson, A. 2014. *The Europeans in Australia, Volume 3: Nation*. Sydney: UNSW Press.

Baldwin, M. P. 2001. "Subject to Empire: Married Women and the British Nationality and Status of Aliens Act." *Journal of British Studies* 40 (4): 522–556.

Bell, D. 2007. *The Idea of Greater Britain: Empire and the Future of World Order, 1860–1900*. New Jersey: Princeton University Press.

Bridge, C., and K. Fedorowich. 2003. "Mapping the British World." *Journal of Imperial and Commonwealth History* 31 (2): 1–15. doi:10.1080/03086530310001705576.

Burgess, M. 2013. Unpublished Paper on Arthur Dyett's Bugle.

Coulthart, R. 2014. *Charles Bean*. Sydney: Harper Collins.

Garton, S. 2015. "Demobilization and Empire: Empire Nationalism and Soldier Citizenship in Australia after the First World War – In Dominion Context." *Journal of Contemporary History* 50 (1): 124–143. doi:10.1177/0022009414546505.

Gibbs, R. 2007. Speech at the launch of 'Gift to the Nation' Accessed 2016 May 17. www.naa.gov.au/collection/publications/papers-and-podcasts/war/index.aspx

Hansard 1905, 1918. House of Representatives Accessed 2017 October.https://historichansard.net/23

Harper, G. 2011. *Letters from Gallipoli: New Zealand Soldiers Write Home*. Auckland: Auckland University Press.

Henderson, Alan with Roberta Nicholls. 1990. *The Quest for Efficiency: The Origins of the State Services Commission*. Wellington: State Services Commission.

Howard, J. 2007. Speech at the launch of 'Gift to the Nation' Accessed 2016 May 17. www.naa.gov.au/collection/publications/papers-and-podcasts/war/index.aspx

Hunter, K. 2017. "National and Imperial Belonging in Wartime: The Tangled Knot of Australians and New Zealanders as British Subjects during the Great War." *Australian Journal of Politics and History* 63 (1): 31–44. doi:10.1111/ajph.12321.

Inwood, K., L. Oxley, and E. Roberts. 2010. "Physical Stature in Nineteenth-Century New Zealand: A Preliminary Interpretation." *Australian Economic History Review* 50 (3): 262–283. doi:10.1111/aehr.2010.50.issue-3.

Lake, M. 1992. "Mission Impossible: How Men Gave Birth to the Australian Nation." *Gender and History* 4 (3): 305–322. doi:10.1111/j.1468-0424.1992.tb00152.x.

Rees, WJ. Letter to Base Records 1916 July 8, BR37/68, Archives New Zealand.

Luckins, T. 2010. "Collecting Women's Memories: The Australian War Memorial, the Next of Kin and Great War Soldiers' Diaries and Letters as Objects of Memory in the 1920s and 1930s." *Women's History Review* 19 (1): 21–37. doi:10.1080/09612020903444635.

McNamara, A. n.d. Centre on Many Fronts. A History of the Red Cross in North Canterbury. Typescript, New Zealand Red Cross Archives. Wellington.

Nolan, M. 2000. *Breadwinning: New Zealand Women and the State*. Christchurch: Canterbury University Press.

O'Donnell, F., 1915 AABK W5614, BR37/56, Archives New Zealand.

Parsons, G. 2008. "'The Many Derelicts of War': Great War Veterans and Repatriation in Dunedin and Ashburton, 1918–1928". PhD thesis, University of Otago.

Raff, D. 1958. MT1487/1, National Archives of Australia.

Report of the Public Services Commissioner. 1917. *Appendices to the Journals of the House of Representatives*, H–14.

Robson, L. 1973. "The Origin and Character of the First AIF: Some Statistical Evidence." *Historical Studies* 15 (61): 737–749. doi:10.1080/10314617308595502.

Scates, B., and M. Oppenheimer. 2014. "'I Intend to Get Justice': The Moral Economy of Soldier Settlement." *Labour History* 106: 229–253. doi:10.5263/labourhistory.106.0229.

Sherriff, R. P., 1916 AABK W5614, BR37/33, Archives New Zealand, Wellington.

Stewart, H. 1921. *Official History of New Zealand's Effort in the Great War, vol. II: The New Zealand Division 1916–1919*. Auckland: Whitcombe and Tombs.

Stibbe, M. 2014. "Remembering, Commemorating and (Re)Fighting the Great War in Germany." In *Nation, Memory and Great War Commemoration: Mobilizing the past in Europe, Australia and New Zealand*, 205–222. Wellings, Ben and Sumartojo, Shanti eds. Bern: Peter Lang.

Thomson, A. 2015. *Anzac Memories: Living with the Legend*. 2nd ed. Melbourne: Oxford University Press.

Torpey, J. 2000. *The Invention of the Passport: Surveillance, Citizenship and the State*. Cambridge: Cambridge University Press.

Waite, F. 1919. *Official History of New Zealand's Effort in the Great War, vol. I: The New Zealanders at Gallipoli*. Auckland: Whitcombe and Tombs.

Wallis, J. 2015. "'Great-Grandfather, What Did *You* Do in the Great War?' The Phenomenon of Conducting First World War Family History Research." In *Remembering the First World War*, edited by B. Ziino, 21–38. London: Routledge.

Woollacott, A. 2001. *To Try Her Fortune in London: Australian Women, Colonialism and Modernity*. Oxford and New York: Oxford University Press.

Youde, J. 2017. "Covering the Cough? Memory, Remembrance and Influenza Amnesia." *Australian Journal of Politics and History* 63 (3): 357–368. doi:10.1111/ajph.12402.

Ziino, B. 2010. "'A Lasting Gift to His Descendants': Family Memory and the Great War in Australia." *History & Memory* 22 (2): 125–146. doi:10.2979/his.2010.22.2.125.

A tale of two bureaucracies: asylum and lunacy law paperwork

James Moran

ABSTRACT
This article offers a comparative analysis of two well-developed bureaucratic systems at work in the production of files connected to the response to madness in colonial contexts. The first, more familiar and well known to those who have dug into the archival records to write about the history of madness, is the bureaucratic legacy of the lunatic asylum.

The second, less familiar bureaucratic system is lunacy investigation law. This was a body of law had a much longer file-generating history than that of the asylum, but it has drawn much less attention from those interested in the history of madness. Although this 'tale of two bureaucracies' is one of overlap between the paperwork of the asylum and of lunacy law, the therapeutic turn in approaches to madness seems to have contributed to the marginalization of the legal, and to an over privileging of the medical. The recent digitization of paperwork has partially rescued legal bureaucracies of madness from obscurity. So too has recent interest in the paperwork of legal responses to madness by some historians. This article considers how taking the paperwork of lunacy law into account leads to a rethinking of the history of madness.

Introduction

In 1842, Charles Dickens took a tour of the Boston State Hospital for the Insane. He was impressed by how well run the 3-year-old asylum was, and was especially complimentary about the resident physician's humanity in his interactions with the patients. In his account he made the following observation:

> 'Evince a desire to show some confidence, and repose some trust, even in mad people,' – said the resident physician, as we walked along the galleries, his patients flocking round us unrestrained. Of those who deny or doubt the wisdom of this maxim after witnessing its effects ... I can only say that I hope I may never be summoned as a Juryman on a Commission of Lunacy whereof

they are the subjects; for I should certainly find them out of their senses, on such evidence alone. (Dickens 1996).

Here, the mid-century master of social criticism likened his experience at the asylum to being a witness at a civil trial in lunacy, suggesting not only his familiarity with the role of civil law in the response to madness, but also indicating that the asylum and the civil law – along with the bureaucratic structures that accompanied both – operated in tandem.

In both Massachusetts where Dickens took his tour of the Boston State hospital, and in several other North American jurisdictions, one can trace parallel trajectories of institutional and legal responses to madness. However, it took longer for asylum development to take root in North America, perhaps leaving lunacy investigation law to generate more paperwork and to play a more prominent role in defining and regulating madness.

In the state of New Jersey, south of Boston, Massachusetts where Dickens took his tour, evidence of the two bureaucracies of madness represented by the asylum and by lunacy trials is plentiful. To take but one example, on 26 June 1865 Mary Ann Mulford sent a paper petition to the New Jersey Court of Chancery explaining that her 26-year-old son, Benjamin F. Mulford, was 'so far deprived of his reason and understanding that he is rendered altogether unfit and unable to govern himself or to manage his affairs' (New Jersey State Archives, Trenton (hereafter NJSA), Chancery Court [hereafter CC], 1865–8). The petition included more paper – a letter signed by Mulford's brother in law, Stephen Perch, and his friend, Wallace Taylor, who further testified that Mulford had been 'insane' for at least 8 months leading up to the petition. Perch noted that he had been frequently called by Mulford's mother to assist in calming Mulford down during his delusional episodes, which included the conviction 'that he had been mesmerized: that his brain had been taken away and his mind lost' (NJSA, CC, 1865–8). According to these witnesses, Mulford's 'conduct became so violent that he was removed to the state lunatic asylum of New Jersey where he has since remained and where he still continues without any material change in his mental condition' (NJSA, CC, 1865–8).

The act of writing a petition set in motion the organization of a civil trial in lunacy. Like many other lunacy trials in New Jersey, this one was held on the premises of the local innkeeper and it consisted of a 12-member jury of property holding men, a judge, witnesses accounts of Benjamin Mulford's mental state, and a verdict. In this case, the burden of testimony led the judge to declare that Mulford was *non compos mentis* at the time of the trial (mentally incapable of governing his property or his person). In fact, the trial found that Mulford had been mentally unsound for the past 5-years. This finding set in motion a legal guardianship process whereby Edward Mulford, Benjamin's brother, was appointed guardian of Benjamin's person and his large farm property. By law this meant that Edward was responsible for protecting his brother and for ensuring that his property was safely taken care of until such time as Benjamin Mulford recovered his sanity and his mental status. In the event that he recovered mentally, Mulford could regain his legal status as a sane person by petitioning for another trial that followed the same process as the one that had found him insane. This retrial of mental status was referred to as a *supercedas*.

According to his guardian, Benjamin Mulford spent three years 'off and on' at the Trenton Asylum. The State Lunatic Asylum at Trenton was the first asylum in the state, established in 1848. By the time of Mulford's asylum committal in 1864, the Trenton Asylum was treating about 320 patients and was a well-established institution whose superintendent, Horrace Buttolph, was a commanding presence. It is hard to evaluate the effects of Mulford's intermittent stays at the asylum over a 3-year period on his mental state, but the Trenton Asylum was archetypal in so far as its superintendent, Horrace Buttolph, insisted upon the usual prodigious amounts of paperwork in the certification, processing, evaluation, treatment, and release of his patients.

By 23 December 1867, Mulford was composing a petition to the Chancery Court for a new lunacy trial in which he aimed to re-establish that he had regained his mental capacity to govern himself and his property, including his large and prosperous farm. According to Mulford: 'some time after taking said inquisition your petitioner was restored to his reason and understanding: that he has and still hath to some extent, the management of and oversight of his farm and of his affairs; that he transacts all his own business [but] that a large portion of his property such as bonds, notes, and mortgages are in the hands and possession of his said guardian' (NJSA, CC, 1865–8). Mulford's guardian and witnesses in the trial of *supercedas* agreed that he had recovered mentally enough to take back control of his person and property despite having 'odd warps' from time to time. On 11 February 1868, Mulford won his retrial and was legally deemed mentally fit again to govern himself and his property.

Two bureaucracies of madness

Benjamin Mulford's experiences with asylum committal and the civil trial of his mental status, so familiar to Charles Dickens at mid century, reflect two well-developed bureaucratic systems at work in the production of files connected to the response to madness. The first, more familiar and well known to those who have dug into the archival records to write about the history of madness, is the bureaucratic legacy of the lunatic asylum. Lunatic asylums generated an enormous amount of documentary evidence, which, partly as the result of the promise of the asylum as a state institution par excellence, found its way into the archives. The second, less familiar bureaucratic system connected to the case of Benjamin Mulford, is what can be conveniently called *lunacy investigation law*. This was a body of law with a much longer file-generating history than that of the asylum, but which has drawn much less attention from those interested in the history of madness. This relative academic neglect can be explained by the fact that the enormous quantity of files that this legal bureaucratic system generated were not stored in a way that preserved them for historians to uncover (Figure 1).

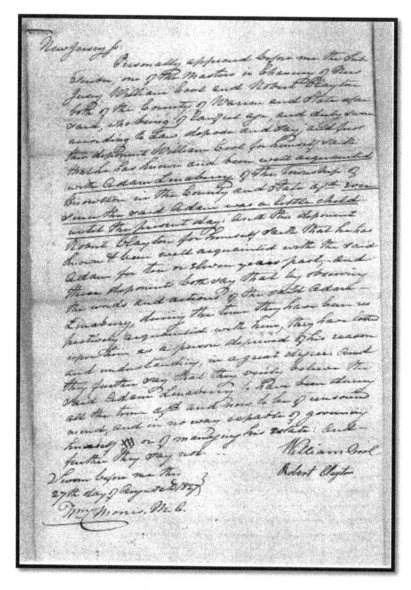

Figure 1. One document relating to a lunacy trial form 1827. There are 15 surviving pages for this trial, and it is one of about 1,800 cases of a similar nature ranging from two pages to over 600 pages in length.

The relative accessibility of these two impressive bureaucracies of madness beg the following questions: How does the existence and accessibility of files influence what is written about the subject to which they are connected? In what ways might the relative availability of well preserved archival files skew the historical importance of the institutions from which they have emerged? How might the discovery, consideration, and use of less accessible archival files about madness challenge the way we produce knowledge about the history of madness? This article will consider these questions through a comparative analysis of the two above-mentioned bureaucratic systems, each of which generated voluminous amounts of paperwork related to madness. As the case of Benjamn Mulford suggests, the files from these two bureaucracies of madness sometimes overlapped and intersected. However, their historical trajectories differed greatly. I will use this comparative analysis to make some preliminary arguments about archival files and knowledge production in the history of madness.

Lunacy law paperwork

The paperwork of lunacy investigation law, a branch of civil law concerned with evaluating the mental capacity of an individual to govern self and property, has not had nearly the same influence on our understanding of the history of madness as asylum paperwork. This has been true despite the fact that this body of law has had an impressive 450-year bureaucratic history that generated mountainous quantities of documents about madness in Europe and in its colonies. Why did the paperwork of lunacy investigation law not exert its full weight in files onto the production of knowledge about madness? There are several reasons. First, this body of law, although producing a plethora of documents pertaining to madness, from legal statutes, to court decisions, to trial testimonials, to trial summaries, was embedded in an even larger corpus of legal files. In England, for example, jurisdiction over lunacy trials was controlled by the court of Wards from 1540–1646 and then by the Court of Chancery until the early twentieth century. Thus, despite the growing use and importance of these files over the course of the eighteenth and nineteenth centuries, they were not generated by a centralized institution dedicated to the treatment and care of the mad, like an asylum. Rather, they formed a part of the much larger production of files by the court system. This made the records of lunacy investigation law less visible to those writing about the history of madness. To give but one concrete example, the case of the madness of Benjamin Mulford mentioned in the introduction to this essay, was one of about 1,800 trial cases of *non compos mentis*, (mental incapacity) in the state of New Jersey from 1790–1890. At some point in the early twentieth century, these cases were pulled out of the larger body of chancery court cases in New Jersey and placed into boxes labeled 'lunacy bundles' which I happened to come across in the New Jersey State Archives in their original manuscript form. This collection represents thousands of pages of trial process and testimony about madness, but had the paperwork not been conveniently pulled together by an office worker for some unknown reason, it would have been nearly impossible to find single trials in the much larger collections of handwritten chancery court records.

The second reason why the files produced by lunacy investigation law generated relatively little traction in the production of knowledge about madness was that they have been more vulnerable to destruction than the files created by the asylum. While it is true that some asylums records fared better than others in this respect, asylums that were state funded and organized were likely to retain their files 'in house' during the life of the asylum, and these collections of files were usually turned over to provincial/state and national archives as deinstitutionalization gained pace in the mid to late twentieth century. Although they tended to 'hide out' in much more extensive documentary collections of civil law, it is increasingly evident that the paperwork of lunacy investigation law was ubiquitous in England, in France and in most colonial and post-colonial contexts in North America and elsewhere. However, despite evidence of this mass documentary production, and of its significance to definitions and responses to madness over multiple jurisdictions and over long periods of time, the paperwork of lunacy investigation law has not proven to be robust.

Two examples are indicative of its relative vulnerability. In England, much of the substance of the lunacy trials, including testimony and judges notes were sacrificed to the massive recycling efforts of World War I and II. During an early investigation at the National Archives in London, an archivist informed me that the substance of most lunacy trial records had been scrapped during World War I. Akihito Suzuki notes that the original manuscripts for the period covered in his study 'were destroyed, unavailable, or scattered' (Suzuki, 26; Thornsheim, 2013). This left the shell of the file intact, leaving behind only basic information about the trial, including the verdict. The historical merits of witnesses' recorded opinions about whether a relative or a friend was mentally capable or not were lost on those who eagerly sought paper to turn into war materials. This has left historians like Akihito Suzuki to resort to more creative ways of understanding the social historical and cultural impact of these sources. In path breaking book, *Madness at Home: The Psychiatrist, the Patient, and the Family in England, 1820–1860*, Suzuki's analysis is based on 196 lunacy trials that were published in the *Times* newspaper (Suzuki 2006). As Suzuki indicates, between the 1640s and 1920 there was considerable paperwork devoted to the business of lunacy investigation in England, but only a fraction of it was reproduced in the newspapers that form the basis of his exploration of lunacy investigation law.

In New Jersey, the approximately 1,800 lunacy trials that have been archived were actually destined for the scrap heap. The boxes in which they were found in the basement of the state courthouse had 'to be destroyed' labels on them. As a PhD student, casting about for an American state in which to compare asylum development with those in the Canadian provinces of Ontario and Quebec, I was offered these boxes as a kind of consolation for the fact that the New Jersey State Lunatic Asylum files had not yet been processed by the state archives. After some deliberation with the state archivists it was decided that they would be preserved at the archives and that I would contribute to their preservation by helping to flat file and catalogue them. This I did for a few visits, after which, convinced of their importance, experts at the New Jersey State Archives took on the work and placed them into their permanent collection where they are publically accessible.

Subsequent research has demonstrated that similar collections of files were generated in much of the British Empire and they continued to be produced as some jurisdictions of empire gained independence. I do not know, however, the extent to which these other file collections have been preserved. Even though more research is needed to determine where pockets of this massive corpus of files on madness have survived, it is clear that it did not enjoy the same shelf life as asylum records. This has serious implications for how we understand madness, past and present.

More recently, as a testimony to the power of the legal profession in England and in North America, reams of legal documents have been digitized primarily for the use of legal experts. Included in this grand digitization effort have been legal files relating to lunacy, which can be found in the *Justis* database, including the English Reports of lunacy trials that were deemed important enough to serve as precedent. In the vast databases of court case reports it is easy enough to search under 'lunacy,' 'madness,' 'non *compos mentis*,' etc. to find English Reports of lunacy trials (Justice database, 2017). This enables the researcher to create a 'second best' archive of files. On the one hand this digitized database research confirms that lunacy investigation law was at work everywhere in Britain, generating documents and influencing the way in which madness was understood and responded to over four centuries. On the other hand, while the researcher is able to ascertain the name and highlights of many individuals who were subjected to these trials, the bulk of the documents connected to these trials is missing. Nevertheless, as Charlotte Macdonald, Rebecca Lenihan and Barbara Brookes have also noted, although in different ways, in their contributions to this special collection, the digitization of lunacy investigation law paperwork in the late twentieth century has breathed new life into the this particular bureaucracy of madness for the historian. At the most basic level, digitization, literally, has brought the bureaucracy of lunacy investigation law, which was hitherto inaccessible to the historian, back into existence. For example, an archive referred to as the *Calendar of State Papers, Colonial: North America and the West Indies 1574–1739*, recently digitized by the National Archives of the United Kingdom, contains a letter from Richard West, dated 11 July 1718, to the Council of Trade and Plantations of North American and the West Indies which outlines the royal prerogative of the King over the estates of those who have been declared to be 'lunatics' (West 1718). This letter was specifically aimed at the New Hampshire colony and it suggests that the process of lunacy investigation law was being outlined to colonial officials early in North American British colonial history. This complements another digitized document pictured below – a draft clause 'to be inserted in the instructions to Governors in America giving them, as Chancellors, the power to issue commissions for the care and custody of idiots and lunatics'. This draft document, addressing the colony of Nova Scotia, but circulated amongst all of England's North American possessions, reiterated the 'Royal Prerogative' in matters of idiocy and lunacy, in England and in 'our Provinces in America', but it also noted that 'great trouble and charges may arise' for colonial officials who 'shall have occasion to resort unto Us for directions'. With this in mind, the colonial Governors were informed that they had 'full Power and Authority without expecting any further special Warrant from Us ... to give Order and Warrant for the preparing of Grants of the Custodies of such Ideots and Lunaticks and their estates as are or shall be found by Inquisitions'. The governors were further encouraged to follow the legal process of lunacy investigation law 'as nearly as may be as hath been heretofore used and accustomed in making the same under the Great Seal of Great Britain'. Given that this clause was circulated to all of England's North American colonies, presumably several or all of them were in the practice of following this kind of procedure in cases of madness where property was involved (Figure 3).

> Draft of a Clause to be inserted in the instructions to Governors in America, giving them as Chancellors the power to issue commissions for the care and custody of idiots and lunatics.
>
> [From P. R. O. B. T. Plantations General, Vol. 42, p. 426.]
>
> WHITEHALL July 29, 1772
>
> To Lord William Campbell, Governor of Nova Scotia
>
> My Lord,
> The King having been pleased, with the Advice of His Privy Council, to signify to Us His Majesty's Pleasure, that We should, in all future draughts of Commissions for Governors in the Plantations, insert a Clause, giving them, as Chancellors, the necessary Powers to issue Commissions for the Care and Custody of Ideots and Lunaticks, agreable to the usage and practice in this Kingdom; inclosed We send you the Draught of such a Clause, as We have prepared for that purpose, desiring to be informed, whether there is any, or, if any, what objection (founded on any provisions, which may have been already made by Law for those Purposes,) to the inserting such Clause in any future Commission for the Governor of Nova Scotia,
>
> We are, My Lords, Your Lordship's
> most obedient hum: Ser^{ts}
> HILLSBOROUGH
> ED: ELIOT.
> BAMBER GASCOYNE.

Figure 3. This draft clause led to the full granting of colonial governors in North America to issue commission in lunacy. Source: 29 July 1772, in Archives of the State of New Jersey, First Series, vol. X, *Documents Relating to the Colonial History of the State of New Jersey*, Frederick Richard and William Nelson (Eds.), vol. X, Administration of Governor William Franklin, 1767–1776 (Newark: Daily Advertiser Printing House, 1886), pp. 382–3. URL
https://books.google.ca/books?id = kbyh32yJvJgC&printsec = frontcover&dq = Documents + Relating+ to+ the+ Colonial+ History+ of+ the+ State+ of+ New +Jersey&hl=en&sa=X&ved=0ahUKEwjywKjc8c3YAhUn2oMKHUJYCzgQ6AEILDAB#v=onepage&q = Documents%20Relating%20to%20the%20Colonial%20History%20of%20the%20State%20of%20New%20Jersey&f = false.

Preliminary searches in other databases including Canada's *Online Globe and Mail Newspaper Archive*, *Early Canadiana Online* and *Colonial Papers Online*, along with the incorporation of some civil law sources by historians writing about the history of madness demonstrates the existence of lunacy investigation law bureaucracies in New Hampshire, New York, New Jersey, South Carolina, Prince Edward Island, New Brunswick, and Upper Canada (later, Ontario) (Jiminez 1987; McCandless 1996; Nootens 2007). Much like in New Jersey, the documentation of cases of *non compos mentis*, including trial procedures, testimony, guardianship, and, occasionally trials of *supercedas*, would have generated prodigious amounts of paperwork throughout the North American colonial landscape. Moreover, the same search engine that allows for quicker access to English Reports of lunacy investigation law in England also reveals a few examples of this bureaucracy of madness operating in Jamaica and Australia.

At a broader level, for this historian at least, digitization has also opened the door to reinterpretation of the significance of civil law in the determination and response to madness, both in England and elsewhere. If we take into account the documentary evidence of lunacy investigation law paperwork now available for examination in the digitized English reports, and if we consider that the fragments of digitized civil legal documents for multiple colonial contexts likely approximated the vast repository of paperwork left intact for the North American colony/state of New Jersey, it is clear that the bureaucracy of madness in civil law needs to be considered more seriously in madness studies. In the Atlantic regions of British and French North America (and probably elsewhere) the bureaucratic colonial inheritance of lunacy investigation law predated the advent of the asylum by well over a century. Moreover, in the absence of a serious asylum movement in North America until the mid-nineteenth century, the paperwork of civil law constituted a colonial and post-colonial inheritance in the understanding and response to madness that predated the asylum by about 150 years.

The bureaucratic structure of lunacy investigation law, producing considerable repositories of files from the early North American colonial period forward, served a major role in the management of madness. As such it could be seen as equally if not more important than asylum paperwork to the consolidation of colonialism and imperial power. What kinds of reinterpretation of the history of madness results from the re/discovery of the bureaucratic legacy of lunacy investigation law? In the case of New Jersey, and, presumably in other colonial contexts, I argue in a forthcoming book on the subject that:

> As the colony developed and evolved through the post-Revolutionary era, it is clear that this law was fundamental to how madness was managed, treated,

and understood. The extensive and detailed surviving New Jersey trial testimonies also reveal the traditions and customs of familial and community management and care of the mad. Finally, the richness of detail from these documents allows for an understanding of how these traditions and customs were tightly woven into the structure of lunacy investigation law. This weave of civil law and custom, established over several generations in New Jersey, was unlikely to be torn apart quickly by reform efforts or by the introduction of the asylum. Instead, the asylum, and its novel set of ideas about madness and what to do about it, was brought into the fabric of civil law and custom at mid century. More dramatic changes to the balance of custom, law and institutionalization were delayed until the latter part of the nineteenth century (Moran forthcoming).

Moreover, there were ways in which legal bureaucracies – of which lunacy investigation law formed a part – helped to consolidate colonial rule at a broader remove. As Christopher Tomlins puts it, 'geography and law' were fundamental elements in the consolidation of colonial power (Tomlins 2001, 28). The bureaucracy of lunacy investigation law helped to uphold the European concepts of property ownership and inheritance in the face of mad colonists and American citizens who had lost their ability to control themselves or their property rationally. At a more abstract level, this bureaucracy of madness also formed part of a larger project of empire building through the imposition of western ideas about settlement, property, ownership and law.

Despite its potential for reinterpretations of the history of madness, the lack of interest by academics in the bureaucracy of lunacy investigation law has not resulted merely from this paperwork being relatively more endangered and hard to locate within larger legal file collections. This bureaucratic legacy also does not fit squarely enough within the 'therapeutic turn' that asylum documents have come to represent. Lunacy investigation law predated the conceptualization of madness as medical, and of mad people as patients, by between three and four centuries depending on when one situates the medicalization process. Moreover, over the course of the eighteenth century, as madness came to be increasingly seen as a medical problem, the lunacy trial process continued to be based upon a standard of mental capacity that was not connected to medical models of madness. Anchored as it was in a legal definition of madness, or incapacity to govern property and self, the files connected to lunacy trials were unlikely to generate much interest in the mainstream of debates about whether the medical response to madness was a medical 'myth' (Szasz 1961), an imposition of the enlightenment (Foucault 1972), the result of bourgeois ascendency in a class-based society (Scull 1979), or a result of scientific progress (Hurd 1916). In the debates about madness and medicalization, the documents that asylums generated have taken pride of place. Whether doggedly defensive of the potential of asylums to improve mental health, fiercely critical of their role as museums of madness, or somewhere in between, the extensive historiographical debates about madness have, by and large pivoted around the asylum and medicalization. This therapeutic turn in madness historiography sits awkwardly beside the focus and purpose of lunacy trial files, further contributing to their place of relative obscurity in the history of madness.

Asylum paperwork

The bureaucratic legacy of the lunatic asylum has had an enormous influence on our overall understanding of the history of madness – one that has distorted our understanding of western responses to madness in the eighteenth and nineteenth centuries. This point is not particularly difficult to establish (nor is it particularly original). The massive scale of production of asylum documents and the sheer quantity of archival files available for consideration has helped to put the asylum center stage in histories of madness. Moreover, the enduring physical presence of asylums – their long lasting appearance in the landscape of countless boroughs, cities, towns and counties in Europe and its colonies – has partly drawn historians to study them. In this sense the asylum was a kind of architectural archival file that drew attention to itself as the central response to madness along with the paper files that it produced. Finally, the roaring historiographical debates about the meaning of the asylum that captivated academic discourse from the 1950s to the 1990s further framed asylums and their archival files as the centerpieces of concern amongst historians. As the asylum became increasingly to symbolize what was wrong with the professional response to mental illness, the focus on mental institutions became more intense. It was as if the intensity of the debate over what asylum archival files revealed about madness, past and present, made it difficult to 'get out of the asylum', as one historian put it (Wright 1997), and, by extension, away from the paperwork that they produced about madness.

In many respects the enormous amount of file generating and organizing prompted by colonial asylums offers a case study par excellence for considering the arguments put forward by Ben Kafka in his recent work, *The Demon of Writing: Powers and Failures of Paperwork* (Kafka 2012). Not only did colonial asylums produce impressive collections of records about patients and institutional management like their counterparts in their respective 'mother' countries, but colonial asylums also created paperwork that connected them to the greater colonial exercise. In the colonial asylum, paperwork was partially about justifying the institution's existence both in the local and the international contexts. Furthermore, Kafka's psychoanalytic approach to the history of paperwork (or bureaucracy) seems ready-made for institutions whose existence was based on the premise that insanity (mental illness) could be cured by establishing regimented, bureaucratized, institutional settings. Having lost their reason, patients were, at the point of asylum committal, reduced to a state of mental infancy. Patients were supposed to be cured of irrational thoughts and behaviors – and brought back into a mental state of civilized adulthood – by well-documented bureaucratized treatment. Carefully kept patient files, diligently drafted rules and regulations, and ward books to regulate the behavior of caregivers were among the most powerful tools of asylum moral therapy. Proof of the asylum's effectiveness was highlighted to the public in the asylum's ultimate piece of propaganda paperwork: the annual report (Fox 1978; Tomes 1984; Warsh 1989; Dwyer 1987; Moran 2000; Piddock 2007; Monk 2008; Coleborne 2015).

Kafka argues that, 'our encounters with paperwork and the people who handle it inevitably reactivate some of our earliest wishes, conflicts and fantasies about familial relations and tensions' (Kafka 2012,15). Although for Kafka these unconscious connections to paperwork are inaccessible to us, close attention to the constant 'chattering of paperwork' at the 'preconscious' level can offer insights into what one might call the bureaucratic turn in modern society.

Although I think that Ben Kafka's work might lead to a reconsideration of the importance of asylum bureaucracy, it deserves mention that historians have been pondering the relationship between bureaucracy and asylum care for many years. The asylum was considered to be a particularly bright star in a constellation of government reform institutions by David Rothman (1971) in his consideration of the United States, by Michael Katz, Michael Doucet and Mark Stern (1982) in their analysis of North America, and by Andrew Scull (1979) and David Garland (1985) in their studies of Britain. These authors represent diverging views in some respects, but they all link institutional and state growth as a response to the development of industrial capitalism, and as a corrective to the perceived social problems of the modern era. The focus of these historians has been state institutions, and all have noted that bureaucracy and paperwork were instrumental to their success.

For example, Susan Houston and Alison Prentice (1988) have considered more directly the bureaucratic aspects of the developing public school system in the colony of Upper Canada (Ontario). In their view: 'Bureaucratic organization was one of the purposes clearly espoused by the architects of mid-nineteenth century educational change … Twenty-one years after the passage of the 1850 school act, thousands of one-time teachers, superintendents, and trustees had been through [Chief Superintendent of Education Egerton] Ryerson's mill. In what ways the process had been educational it is hard to say. But there is no doubt that it had been. Responsible citizens? Or more governable subjects? They all knew, at least, how to fill out a form'

(1988, 155–6). In a manner more in keeping with Kafka's analysis, Bruce Curtis's (1993) more recent publications on educational reform in Ontario and Quebec, and on statistics gathering in colonial British North America, links an emerging quest for statistics with an increasingly rational approach to governance. In his view, the imposition of order and the expression of power in the imperial relationship were partly achieved through the acquisition of empirical knowledge. For example, the 'Blue Books' that the Colonial Office in London made colonial Ontario and Quebec send across the Atlantic from 1822 until the Confederation of Canada in 1867, in some years contained massive document sets relating to various aspects of colonial governance along with an 'analytical report' (Curtis 1993, 535) from the Colonial Governor. The Blue Books were received, reviewed and edited for inclusion in the 'imperial parliamentary papers' (Curtis 1993, 535). In Curtis' view, 'The Blue Books were significant parts of the developing official documentary system implicated both in British imperial government and in the solidification of the basic administrative capacities conditioning the colonial state' (Curtis 1993, 565, Curtis, 2000). In other words the processes whereby paperwork could be gathered, organized, sent across long distances, unpacked, analyzed, repackaged, and reprocessed, helped England to control its colonies.

In some respects the colonial asylum is a perfect fit for the changes outlined above. Asylums that were developed in the shadow of Philip Pinel and William Tuke were institutions that embodied the growing certainty that medical conditions could be treated more successfully through rational empiricism – that is through the testing of therapies by evaluating them against the information gathered and observations made about them. It could be said that the moral therapy that came to dominate asylum care was a system that asylum doctors and reformers were already convinced about. Yet the precise way in which moral therapy was to be organized was subject to myriad observations by medical personnel of the records produced about the institutions and their patients. Asylums also formed part of the larger framework of state regulated institutions that required a sophisticated bureaucratic structure to operate. Finally, colonial asylums were (in theory at least) exemplars of the imperial management and care of those unfortunate enough to go mad (Ernst 1991; el-Khayat 1994; McCulloch 1995; Sadowsky 1999; Mills 2000; Swartz 2007; Parle 2007; Ernst and Mueller, 2010; Sloan and Vaughan 2007; Smith 2014). Patients' care, management and/or recovery in colonial asylums highlighted the triple trajectories of therapeutic empiricism, British imperialism, and colonial governance. This was no different in the United States although the rise of the asylum took place after the American Revolution and was thus, in a literal sense, a postcolonial development (Figure 4).

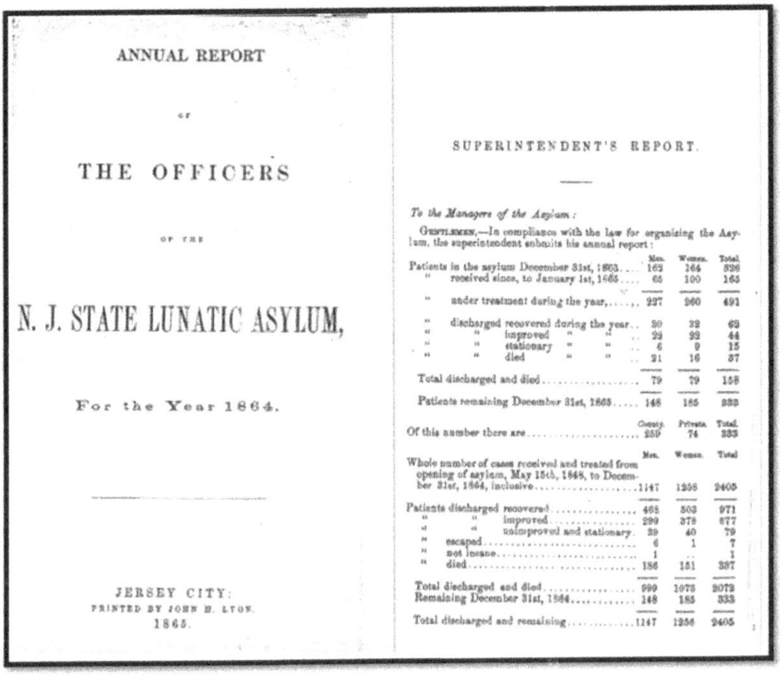

ANNUAL REPORT

OF

THE OFFICERS

OF THE

N. J. STATE LUNATIC ASYLUM,

For the Year 1864.

JERSEY CITY:
PRINTED BY JOHN H. LYON.
1865.

SUPERINTENDENT'S REPORT.

To the Managers of the Asylum:

GENTLEMEN,—In compliance with the law for organizing the Asylum, the superintendent submits his annual report:

	Men.	Women.	Total.
Patients in the asylum December 31st, 1863....	163	164	326
" received since, to January 1st, 1865....	65	100	165
" under treatment during the year,.......	227	260	491
" discharged recovered during the year..	30	32	62
" " improved " " ..	22	22	44
" " stationary " " ..	6	9	15
" " died " " ..	21	16	37
Total discharged and died..................	79	79	158
Patients remaining December 31st, 1865.....	148	185	333

	County.	Private.	Total.
Of this number there are......................	259	74	333

	Men.	Women.	Total
Whole number of cases received and treated from opening of asylum, May 15th, 1848, to December 31st, 1864, inclusive....................	1147	1258	2405
Patients discharged recovered................	468	503	971
" " improved................	299	378	677
" " unimproved and stationary.	39	40	79
" escaped............................	6	1	7
" not insane.........................	1	..	1
" died...............................	186	151	337
Total discharged and died................	999	1073	2072
Remaining December 31st, 1864............	148	185	333
Total discharged and remaining............	1147	1258	2405

Figure 4. Annual Report of the New Jersey State Lunatic Asylum, 1865.

Rethinking bureaucratic legacies of madness

If my arguments about the significance of the colonial legacy of English lunacy investigation law are convincing, they raise curious questions about paperwork, bureaucracy, archival collections, and the response to madness in colonial settings and elsewhere. How important can bureaucratic legacies of madness be if they are not 'discovered' and/or recognized as such by those who write and publish about them? Could the paperwork of lunacy investigation law have made its contribution to the history of madness regardless of how prominently it may have appeared for researchers to document and interpret during and after their production? If lunacy investigation law is any indication, it is likely that there exist other hitherto unexplored bureaucracies of madness generating considerable amounts of paperwork that were of major concern. The paperwork of lunacy investigation law has had an important and underappreciated influence on how lunacy was understood and responded to within a legal framework. Moreover, in its production of a plethora of paper testimonials, this same bureaucracy reveals rich local cultural perspectives on madness, such as those revealed in New Jersey in trials like that of Benjamin Mulford described at the beginning of this article. This paperwork of popular perceptions of madness complements efforts by other historians to understand 'madness at home' and in the community (Suzuki, 2000; Bartlett and Wright 1999; Horden and Smith, 1998; Houston 2000). Although this 'tale of two bureaucracies' is one of overlap between the paperwork of the asylum and of lunacy law, the historical and historiographical therapeutic turn in approaches to madness seems to have contributed to the marginalization of the legal, and to an over privileging of the medical. Ironically, the digitization of paperwork is contributing to the rescue of legal bureaucracies of madness, although it remains to be seen how this will affect our rethinking of the history of madness (Bartlett 2001). If the twentieth century was the period during which asylums seemed to be the most obvious source of paperwork with which to understand madness, including madness in imperial and colonial contexts, perhaps now that we are some decades past the period of deinstitutionalization we are on the road to exploring alternative bureaucratic legacies of madness that will help us to rethink this dynamic field of study.

Acknowledgments

Many thanks to the participants of the Archival Files and Knowledge Production Conference, at the Centre for Research on Colonial Culture at the University of Otago, Dunedin, who provided a stimulating intellectual milieu for early considerations of this article. Thanks also to Professor Brookes and to Dr. James Dunk for their helpful suggestions and crucial support as this article came to completion.

Disclosure statement

No potential conflict of interest was reported by the author.

References

Bartlett, P. 2001. "Legal Madness in the Nineteenth Century." *Social History of Medicine* 14 (1): 107–131.

Bartlett, P., and D. Wright. 1999. *Outside the Walls of the Asylum: The History of Care in the Community, 1750–2000*. London: Athlone Press.

Calendar of State Papers, Colonial: North America and the West Indies 1574–1739 (accessed 1 November 2017) http://www.proquest.com/products-services/Colonial_State_Paper.html

Coleborne, C. 2015. *Insanity, Identity and Empire: Immigrants and Institutional Confinement in Australia and New Zealand, 1873–1910*. Manchester: Manchester University Press.

Curtis, B. 1993. "The Canada 'Blue Books' and the Administrative Capacity of the Canadian State, 1822–67." *Canadian Historical Review* 74 (4): 535–565. doi:10.3138/CHR-074-04-03.

Dickens, C. 1996. *American Notes for General Circulation*. New York: Random House.

Dwyer, E. 1987. *Homes for the Mad: Life inside Two Nineteenth-Century Asylums*. New Brunswick: Rutgers University Press.

el-Khayat, G. 1994. *Une Psychiatrie Modern Pour Le Maghrib*. Paris: Harmattan.

Ernst, W. 1991. *Mad Tales from the Raj: The European Inane in British India, 1800–1858*. New York: Anthem Press.

Foucault, M. 1972. *Histoire De La Folie À L'âGe Classique*. Paris: Gallimard.

Fox, R. 1978. *So Far Disordered in Mind: Insanity in California, 1870–1930*. Berkeley: University of California Press.

Garland, D. 1985. *Punishment and Welfare: A History of Penal Strategies*. Hants: Gower Publishers.

Houston, R. A. 2000. *Madness and Society in Eighteenth-Century Scotland*. Oxford: Clarendon Press.

Houston, S., and A. Prentice. 1988. *Schooling and Scholars in Nineteenth-Century Ontario*. Toronto: University of Toronto Press, 1988.

Hurd, H. 1916. *Institutional Care of the Insane in the United States and Canada*. Vol. 4. Baltimore: Johns Hopkins University Press.

Jiminez, M. A. 1987. *Changing Faces of Madness: Early American Attitudes and Treatment of the Insane*. Hanover: University Press of New England.

Justis (legal documents database: accessed December 15, 2017).

Kafka, B. 2012. *The Demon of Writing: Powers and Failures of Paperwork*. New York: Zone Books.

Katz, M., M. Doucet, and M. Stern. 1982. "The Institutional Legacy." In *The Social Organization of Early Industrial Capitalism*, edited by M. Kat, M. Doucet, and M. Stern. Cambridge: Harvard University Press.

McCandless, P. 1996. *Moonlight, Magnolias and Madness: Insanity in North Carolina from the Colonial Period to the Progressive Era*. Chapel Hill: University of North Carolina Press.

McCulloch, J. 1995. *Colonial Psychiatry and 'The African Mind.'*. Cambridge: Cambridge University Press.

Mills, J. 2000. *Madness, Cannabis, and Colonialism: The 'Native Only' Lunatic Asylums of British India, 1857–1900*. London: Palgrave Macmillan Press.

Monk, L.-A. 2008. *Attending Madness: At Work in the Australian Colonial Asylum*. Amsterdam: Rodopi.

Moran, J. 2000. *Committed to the State Asylum: Insanity and Society in Nineteenth-Century Quebec and Ontario*. Montreal: McGill Queen's University Press.

Moran, J. forthcoming. *Madness on Trial: A Trans Atlantic History of English Civil Law and Lunacy*. Manchester: Manchester University Press.

New Jersey State Archives, Trenton (hereafter *NJSA*), Chancery Court, Lunacy Case Files, Case of Benjamin Mulford, 1865–8.

Nootens, T. 2007. *Fous, Prodigues Et Ivrognes: Familles Et Déviance À Montréal Au XIXe Siècle*. Montreal: McGill Queen's University Press.

Parle, J. 2007. *States of Mind: Searching for Mental Health in Natal and Zululand, 1868–1918*. Scottsville: University of KwaZulu-Natal Press.

Piddock, S. 2007. *A Space of Their Own: The Archaeology of Nineteenth-Century Lunatic Asylums in Britain, South Australia and Tasmania*. New York: Springer.

Richard, F., and W. Nelson, eds. 1886. "Draft of a Clause to Be Inserted in the Instructions to Governors in America, 29 July 1772," Archives of the State of New Jersey, First Series, vol. X, *Documents Relating to the Colonial History of the State of New Jersey*, Frederick Richard and William Nelson (Eds.), vol. X, Administration of Governor William Franklin, 1767–1776 (Newark: Daily Advertiser Printing House, 1886), pp. 382–383. https://books.google.ca/books?id=kbyh32yJvJgC&printsec=front cover&dq=Documents+Relating+to+the+Colonial+History+of+the+State+of+New +Jersey&hl=en&sa=X&ved=0ahUKEwjywKjc8c3YAhUn2oMKHUJYCzgQ6AEIL DAB#v=onepage&q=Documents%20Relating%20to%20the%20Colonial%20History %20of%20the%20State%20of%20New%20Jersey&f=false

Rothman, D. 1971. *The Discovery of the Asylum: Social Order and Disorder in the New Republic*. Boston: Little Brown.

Sadowsky, J. 1999. *Imperial Bedlam: Institutions of Madness in Colonial Southwest Nigeria*. Berkeley: University of California Press.

Scull, A. 1979. *Museums of Madness: The Social Organization of Insanity in Nineteenth-Century England*. New York: St. Martin's Press.

Sloan, M., and M. Vaughan. 2007. *Psychiatry and Empire*. Basingstoke: Palgrave Macmillan.

Smith, L. 2014. *Insanity, Race and Colonialism: Managing Mental Disorder in the Post-Emancipation British Caribbean, 1838–1914*. London: Palgrave Macmillan.

Suzuki, A. 2006. *Madness at Home: The Psychiatrist, the Patient, and the Family in England, 1820–1860*. Berkeley: University of California Press.

Swartz, S. 2007. "Madness and Colonial Spaces: British India, C. 1800–1947." In *Madness, Architecture and the Built Environment: Psychiatric Spaces in Historical Context*, edited by L. Topp, J. Moran, and J. Andrews, 215–238. London: Routledge.

Szasz, T. 1961. *The Myth of Mental Illness: Foundations of a Theory of Personal Conduct*. New York: Harper & Row.

Thorsheim, P. 2013. "Salvage and Descruction: The Recycling of Books and Manuscripts in Great Britain during the Second World War." *Contemporary European History* 22 (3): 431–452. doi:10.1017/S0960777313000222.

Tomes, N. 1984. *A Generous Confidence: Thomas Story Kirkbride and the Art of Asylum Keeping, 1840–1883*. Cambridge: Cambridge University Press.

Tomlins, C. 2001. "Law's Empire: Chartering English Colonies on the American Mainland in the Seventeenth Century." In *Law, History, Colonialism: The Reach of Empire*, edited by D. Kirby and C. Coleborne, 26–43. Manchester: Manchester University Press.

Warsh, C. 1989. *Moments of Unreason: The Practice of Canadian Psychiatry and the Homewood Retreat, 1883–1923*. Montreal: McGill Queen's University Press.

West, R., 1718. "Letter to the Council of Trade and Plantations." Accessed 15 January 2018. http://rlproxy.upei.ca/login?url=https://search.proquest.com/doc view/1845199536?accountid=14670.

Wright, D. 1997. "Getting Out of the Asylum: Understanding the Confinement of the Insane in the Nineteenth-Century." *Social History of Medicine* 10 (1): 137–155.

Index

Note: *Italic* page numbers refer to figures and page numbers followed by 'n' refer to end notes

accountability: asylum repositories 77; colonial doctors 78; emotional elements 78; head attendant's diary 81; individual patient files 77; Jessie's complaint 87; relocation and movement 85; stationers' office 77; systematic overtime 88; transfer operation 79
Act for Regulating Private Madhouses 1774 58
Allen, George 47, 62, 67
Allgemeinen Gerichtsordnung 26
American Revolution 152
Anderson, C. 55, 101
Anderson, Warwick 39, 68
Anzac legend 130
Archer, Andrew 102
archive story 96
Army records 98
Army reforms 98
asylum case records: bits and pieces 10; dirty' or 'faulty' habits 12, 13; dramatic effects 12; newspaper accounts 12; psychiatric training and diagnosis 11; psychiatrist notes 10; psychoanalysis 13–16; therapeutic encounters 9; unifying puzzle 10; warrant enumeration 13
asylum moral therapy 151
asylum paperwork: analytical report 152; annual report 151; architectural archival file 150; moral therapy 152
Atkinson, Alan 128
Aufschreibesystem 24
Australia: bureaucratic context 124; distinct citizenship acts 132; government records in 125; military service files 125; multi-volume official history 128; national archives of 124, 125; national histories 124; *Old Age Pension Act 1908* 136n2; Old Age Pension Acts 128; personnel files 127; self-governing dominions 127
Australian Army Nursing Service 130
Australian Imperial Force (AIF) 123
Australian joint copying project (AJCP) 112
Australian War Memorial 124
Australia's heritage 129

bad characters 26, 101–103, 110
Base Records files 124, 129; Archives New Zealand *134*; director of 134
Bazerman, C. 77
Beckett, Henry 89
Beckett, Johanna 76, 84, 85, 90
Bedlam Point 52
Berlin Lunatic Asylum 25
Between the Acts 10
Black, J. 77
Bland, William 47, 54, 57, 60, 61
Blödsinnigkeitserklärung 25
Blue Books 152
blue pencil: death dates 129; ex-servicepeople 130, *130*; next-of-kin details 129
Bollinger, George 127
Bourke, Richard 50–52, 55
Britain's global expansion 96
British Army: counting and tracking soldiers 99; Horse Guards 97; march routes and returns 98; War Office papers 96

INDEX

British Empire: cultural reach 96; fiscal accountability 99; Liverpool-born Stephen Waterson 99; military's social and cultural reach 96; occupational and epidemiological profiles 96; qualitative or micro-level interest 96; separate archive series 98
British Foreign Office 77
British garrison world 96
British Nationality and Alien Status Act 1914 132
British nursing corps 130
bureaucratic filing system 96
bureaucratic record-keeping 3
bureaucratic systems: archival records 141; comparative analysis 143; history of madness 142; one document relating 142, *142*
Burt, John 82
Burton, A. 96

cameo method 109
Captain Innes' statement 57
Caradus, J. 89
case book 54–56, 60, 81
central registry 37, 38
Charité registry 35, 41n34
Circumlocution Office 98
class coup 53
clerical record 101
click by click path 6
clinical bookkeeping: communicative action 28; confidential disclosures 39; epistemological effects 36; institutional business operations 23; legal judgement 28; long-serving resident doctors 23; lunacy and idiocy 27; material forms 34–35; medical assessment 28; office journal 37; official 'findings report' 26; patient-related documents 23; potential relation 22; psychiatrists love collecting 23
clinical disease patterns 23
Coleborne, Cathy 83
Collegium medicum 26
colonial asylums offers 150
colonial medical community 3
Colonial Papers Online 148
Colquhoun, George James 112
committal papers 79
Coughlan, Daniel 109
court findings report 27
Cowper, Charles 47, 54, 57, 60–63, 65, 67
Crawford, John 127

Crimean war 96, 97
crucial formative role 24
Cumberland Election 65
cumbersome system 37
Curtis, Bruce 152

Dangerous Lunatics Act 56
Dawson, William 49, 50, 53, 56–58, 61, 64, 66, 67
deliberate abuse 27
diagnostic techniques 23
Dickens, Charles 98, 139
Digby, Joseph 51–53, 55–59, 61, 63, 64
Digby's private diary 68
Digby, Susannah 67
digital age 115
digital data teems 1
digitization 5
digitized English reports 148
discharge certificates (WO 64) 111, *111*
disciplinary record 99, 101
documentary identities 2
Dohrmann, Ole 36
Doucet, Michael 151
dream-work: asylum paperwork *vs.* asylum life 16; shadowy/forgotten pieces 17
Dunk, James 3
Durrell, Lawrence: novels 10

Early Canadiana Online 148
early modern kitchen economy 24
ego-document 31
emotional elements 78
Ernst, Wolfgang 6
executive council 79
expert doctors 28

facts indicating Lunacy 85
first world war 6
fiscal accountability 99
FitzRoy, Charles 62, 63
five-page report 50
Flemming, Henry 59
former soldier 112
free clerk 59
Freeman's Journal 65
free society 51
Frost, John 86

Gamble, D. J. 98
Garland, David 151
General Land Law 26, 27
general provincial state poor relief 25

INDEX

Gipps, George 51, 55, 63
Great War: international standards 127; outbreak of 128; social history movement 130

Hadley, Elaine 98
Hall, A.D. 87
Hammill, Joseph 103
Hard Cash 80
Harper, Glyn 129
Harris, Verne 6
Hay, Robert W. 51
Hess, Volker 3, 77, 78, 116
Highland Light Infantry Lahore Division (Indian Expeditionary Force) 135
Hirst, J. 65
historical archive: claims required reference 109; dynamic memory system 114; microfilming project 112; original paper documents 113–114; paybooks and discharge certificates 111; raw archive 114
Honouring military service 110
Horn, Ernst 29
Houston, Susan 151
Howard, John 124
Hull, Matthew 77
human freedom 26
Humanity Robinson 47
Hunter, Kathryn 4

Iatros 63
Ideler, Karl 36
initial assessment 27
institution's staffing plan 33
interpretative act 1

Jenkin, William 80
Johanna's file 90
Johanna's record 85
Johnson, William 101
jurisdictio voluntaria mixta 26

Kafka, B. 2, 66, 77; analysis 152; psychoanalytic approach 150
Kantian theory 36
Katz, Michael 151
kitchen economy 3, 24

Ledebur, S. 116
Lee, Thomas 52, 54, 57, 59
legal bureaucratic system 142
legible people 97

Lenihan, Rebecca 3, 4
letter requesting payment 88
Lieutenant-Colonel Austen 98
Liverpool Hospital legal 71n56
local newspaper 131
looping effects 35
Lowe, Robert 49, 65
Lucifer matches 81
Lunacy Act, 1868 81
lunacy investigation law 142; American colonial landscape 148; colonial and post-colonial contexts 144; court system 143; digitized database 146; documentary evidence of 148; govern self and property 143; handwritten chancery court records 144; New Jersey State Lunatic Asylum files 145; reform efforts 149; therapeutic turn 149
Lunatics Act, 1862 83
Lunatics Act, 1882 84

Macarthur, Hannibal 47, 56, 57, 59
MacDonagh, O. 49
Macdonald, Charlotte 3, 4
madness: complements efforts 153; history 150, 154; management of 148; medical models of 149; rethinking bureaucratic legacies 153–154; therapeutic turn 150
malevolent passions 78
Mann, Alexander 101
Mantel, Hilary 1
McGowan, John 86
McLean, Daniel 54, 55, 60
medical coup 53
Medical Journal recording 81–82
medical model 53
medical officers: 'medical journal' recording 81–82; official visitors 82; private asylums 81–82; public asylums 81–82
medical superintendent's letterbook 87
mental turmoil 18
Mercier, Louis-Sebastien 2
mid-Victorian army 112
military records: commanding officer 102; disciplinary record 99; historical enquiry 100; mid-nineteenth-century 97; non-effective 102; personal archival file 96; scope and methodical arrangement 99
military service files: army service number 126; imperial war graves commission plot *126*, 127; previous military experience 125

Mills, K. 48, 49
mobile workforce 88
modern clinical psychiatry 27
modern memory 110
monthly cash audit 29
Moran, James 4, 77
Morrisey, John 101
Mulford, Benjamin 141
Mulford, Mary Ann 140
mundane acts 83

nation-making: archival and curatorial collection policies 129; national 'character' 124; national welfare provisions 128; rules and codes governing processes 125
Newby, John 101
newspaper accounts 12
New Zealand: bureaucratic context 124; distinct citizenship acts 132; government records in 125; military service files 125; national histories 124; Old Age Pension Acts 128, 136n2; personnel files 127; self-governing dominions 127; steadfast and stubborn 129
New Zealand Army Nursing Service 130
New Zealand Expeditionary Force (NZEF) 123
New Zealand Gazette 101
New Zealand Herald 81
The New Zealand Medal Roll (WO 100/18) *104*
New Zealand Red Cross Record 133
New Zealand's digitization project 125
non compos mentis 143
North American British colonial history 146
North American colonial landscape 148
NZEF *see* New Zealand Expeditionary Force (NZEF)

O'Donnell, Lieutenant 135
office journals 37
Ogden, Thomas 14
Old Age Pension Act 1898 136n2
The Old Age Pension Act 1908 136n2
Old Age Pension Acts 128
Old Lion 134
one-way mirror 10
Online Globe and Mail Newspaper Archive 148
overgrown power 2, 47

paper-based systems 116
paper laws 77
paper soldiers 115
paper technologies: functioning 97; legal file-keeping 29; medical documentation 29
paperwork: birth 4–6; eluded order 91; ends 3–4; error 89; free clerk 59; Henry Beckett liable 85; long medical career 61; lunacy investigation law 143–150; medical recordkeeping 60; original 90; origins 3; pencil-written note 127; public record 58; rebirth 4–6; scraps 132–135; scribbles 132–135; significant body of 124; weight of 124; WWI personnel files 125
Parker, Henry 47
Parramatta Female Factory 71n56
Parris, H. 49
Partikulargesetzgebungen 26
Perry, A. 96
pigeonholes 33
Pinel, Philip 152
post-Crimean War's army 96
Prentice, Alison 151
private anthony toole 107
private asylums: medical officers 81–82
'private' documents 69
Private James Brien record 103
Prussian empire 24
The Prussian General Land Law 26
Prussian legal regulations 31
Prussian reform era 24
psychiatric documentation system 35
psychiatric narration 3, 24
psychiatric reform: lunatic treatment 25; medical assessment and legal judgement 28; official 'findings report 26; therapeutic optimism 25; trustee's nominee 26
psychiatric-scientific system 36
psychic retreat 16
psychoanalysis 13–16
public asylums: medical officers 81–82
public diary 57

Queen of May 86

Raff, Dorothy 130
raw archive 114
record-keeping: church registration 100; methodical process produced offers 115; systems 96
record patient treatment 56
red ink: marginalia and instructions in 130; medal distribution 129; medical care and pensions 129; military and medical abbreviations 131

Rees, W. J. 135
Rolfe, Charles 101
Rothman, David 151
Royal Flying Corps 133
Royal Prerogative 146
Russell, W. H. 97

scrappy records: defence force files 132; ecumenical approach 133; imperial effort 133, *134*
Scull, Andrew 151
Seacliff Asylum Diet 88
self-documenting action 34
self-fashioning 101
sewerage-borne illnesses 13
Sherriff, Royes 133
Silesian institutions 25
simple mania diagnosis 90
social surveys 100
soldiers cost money 103
South African War (1899–1902) 128
Speisekommissär 39n7
The State Lunatic Asylum: colonial and post-colonial contexts 144; digitization effort 145; documentary evidence 141; document relating *142*; odd warps 141; power and authority 146
Stern, Mark 151
Suzuki, Akihito 5, 144
Swartz, Sally 2, 80, 83, 116
Sydney Morning Herald 57

tap by tap path 6
Tarban Creek Lunatic Asylum: bureaucratic modernity 47; colonial legislative process 49; five-page report 50; impressive patronage network 51; irresponsible and unsuitable head 53; paperwork reframes 48; permanent character 51; pre-printed columns 46; professionalising medicine 47; report-writing process 49; therapeutic outlook 52
therapeutic turn 149
Thermic charts 88
Thomson, Alistair 131
Times newspaper 144
Tocqueville's hovering rationalism 67
Tomlins, Christopher 149
Torpey, John 132

transfer operation 79
triangulating reports 12
T-tests 12
Tuke, William 152
Turner, George 57

unifying puzzle 10
United Kingdoms 60

village's pageant 10
violent police 11
violent students 11
Virginia Woolf tracks 10
Vismann, Cornelia 79

War Office 97
wartime/pre-war patient files 23
weaponising paperwork: accountability frameworks 66; anti-Catholic histories 64; fundamental failure 62; history 69; kitchen staff 66; lunacy bill 63; medical witnesses 67; political pragmatism 65; 'private' documents 69; traditional content 66
Weber, Max 78
Wentworth, William 49, 65
West, Richard 146
'white' remembrance 124
William, Thomas 103
Woolf, Virginia 9, 10
World War I (WWI) 113, 124
World War II (WWII) 132
writing illness 31
writing war: bad characters 101; bad – principally drunkenness 103; discharge application 105, *106*; educational measures 102; imprisonment/corporal punishment, 103; own disciplinary record 101; private anthony toole 107; quarterly muster rolls (WO 12) 105, *105*; rational and quantified bureaucratic machinery 98; regimental headquarters 97
WWI *see* World War I (WWI)
WWII *see* World War II (WWII)
WWI-nation nexus 124

Youtube clips 11

Ziino, B. 131